SOURCES OF RENEWAL

Cardinal Karol Wojtyla
(Pope John Paul II)

SOURCES OF RENEWAL

The implementation of the
Second Vatican Council

translated by
P. S. FALLA

1817
HARPER & ROW, PUBLISHERS, San Francisco
Cambridge, Hagerstown, Philadelphia, New York
London, Mexico City, São Paulo, Sydney

Originally published in Polish as *U Podstaw Odnowy* (Pol. Tow. Teol, Cracow, 1972)

Revised edition published in Italian as *Alla Fonti Rinnovamento: Studio sulla Realizazione del Concilio Vaticano II* (Libreria Editrice Vaticana, Vatican City, 1979)

FIRST U.S. EDITION

Library of Congress Cataloging in Publication Data

John Paul II, Pope, 1920–
  Sources of renewal.

  Translation of U podstaw odnowy.
  Includes indexes.
  1. Catholic Church—Doctrinal and controversial works—Catholic authors. 2. Vatican Council, 2d, 1962–1965.
  BX1751.2.J6613   230'.2   79–1780
  ISBN 0–06–064188–6

---

81 82 83 84 10 9 8 7 6 5 4 3 2 1

CONTENTS

PREFACE

by the Reverend Adam Kubiś,
editor of the Polish edition

The present work was published at Cracow by Cardinal Karol
Wojtyla, now Pope John Paul II, at the beginning of October
1972, on the tenth anniversary of the inauguration of the
Second Vatican Council.

The primary object of the Council, it will be recalled, was
to bring the Church up to date and point the way to the union
of Christians. During the Conciliar sessions these objectives
broadened and deepened, as the bishops of the world delibera-
ted on the pastoral implications of many essential elements of
the Christian faith and the reality of the Church. The present
study by Cardinal Wojtyla, which has been translated into
several languages, lies at the very core of these problems.

The title *Sources of Renewal* itself suggests clearly that the
Author regards Vatican II as the cornerstone of the *aggiornamento*. It is his conviction that the Council is a sign of the times
for the Church, relating eternal human problems to the Gospel
in their contemporary forms and clarifying them by its light.
Thus, in the Author's mind, genuine Church reform consists
in nothing else than the implementation of the Council. This
does not mean, however, that in his view Vatican II should be
regarded as the one and only starting-point for the self-
realization of the contemporary Church. The problems of
mankind have existed in all ages, and the unchanging message
of the Gospel endures for ever. The Council's teaching and its
pastoral orientation are set against the background of those
problems and that message: they determine the significance

and direction of reform, but themselves can be understood more deeply against that background.

It should be emphasized that in this 'Study' Cardinal Wojtyla did not address himself directly to the problem of how to implement Vatican II. In Poland as in other countries this problem has been intensively studied: various publications have been issued and pastoral experiments undertaken. At the present time much material might be collected and many suggestions put forward as to how the Council's precepts have been and should be carried out. The Author's intention in this book, however, was to concentrate on defining exactly what was to be put into effect: this appeared to him to be an essential prior question, the elucidation of which would serve as an aid to the implementation of the Council in Poland as elsewhere.

The work falls into three parts, with an Introduction and a Conclusion. Part I makes clear the fundamental significance of the Council's initiative and provides a broad introduction to Parts II and III, which are concerned respectively with the formation of consciousness and the formation of attitudes. The work as a whole is a synthesis of the main points of the teaching of Vatican II, omitting none of the principal problems treated by the Council, and quoting the Council documents in such a way as to maintain a just balance between them. Prominence is given to the two great ecclesiological documents – the Dogmatic Constitution on the Church and the Pastoral Constitution on the Church in the Modern World – while the remaining documents are treated in terms of their relationship to the totality of the Council's teaching.

What precisely is the effect of this synthesis, and what does it teach us about Vatican II? The reader will see that numerous Council texts are quoted, and he is bound to ask himself about the relationship between the synthesis and these texts: are they simply being arranged in systematic order, or is something more intended? This question is of basic importance, as it throws light on a specific feature of Vatican II and on the essential character of the present work.

There is no doubt that at times the book gives the impression of being a synopsis and rearrangement of selected Conciliar texts. Indeed, the Author himself makes this clear when he describes it as a working study or vade-mecum to the Council, summarizing the great wealth of its teaching. But this is not the main point: the question is, on what principle is the summary based and what is its effect from the Author's point of view?

Sources of Renewal is basically a work of research and, at the same time, a reply to questions concerning faith and the whole life of believers: what does it mean to be a Christian, to live in the Church and in the modern world? These are existential questions, as they not only relate to the truth of faith and thus of doctrine in itself, but also situate it in men's minds and call for a determination of the attitudes that arise from being a Catholic and a believer. In other words, they relate to faith not only in the sense of the pure content of revealed truths but in regard to its fullness in the dimension of Christian life. Seeking the answer to these questions has led the Author to re-read and rearrange the Council's message from an existential point of view; at the same time he presents its genuinely pastoral aspect in the light of Christian anthropology, which takes full account of the philosophy of being and the philosophy of the subject.

The teaching of the Council, which is deeply rooted in Scripture and tradition, is at the same time the expression of a deep and full understanding of the deposit of faith, from which it derives a new language, a manner of formulating concepts and apportioning emphasis. The prospects and preoccupations are new; the emphasis is laid on persons and not on the object of faith. This allows men to participate more fully in divine truth; it enriches their faith especially in the subjective, human sense. Thus there has been a profound change in the orientation of the Church, a new mentality, a new consciousness and new attitudes. It is the great merit and achievement of Cardinal Wojtyla's 'Study' that he has brought to light this new orientation and has provided an adequate formulation of it. By making all this available to the Church in Poland and now to a wide range of members of the universal Church, the Author can already be said to have 'repaid a debt towards Vatican II'.

In the light of all that has hitherto been written about the Council, the 'Study' can certainly be regarded as an attempt to present its problems in a comprehensive form. Its importance is enhanced by the Author's personal record: he was not merely a student of the Council's proceedings but took part in them, especially in the Pastoral Constitution on the Church in the Modern World, and today he is the Supreme Pastor and successor of St Peter.

As we know, *Sources of Renewal* was written by Cardinal Wojtyla for the guidance of the Pastoral Synod of the archdiocese of Cracow which was then beginning its work. The object of the Synod was to enrich the religious consciousness of the people of God and to form mature Christian attitudes, by studying the teaching of Vatican II and considering how best to implement it. The committees and study groups set up by the Synod were aided in this work by the 'Study' in which their bishop explained to them from the beginning what it was that had to be put into practice. The Synod's fundamental task was to translate the programme set forth in the 'Study' into the life of the Cracow diocese.

Previous Councils such as Trent and Vatican I were primarily of a dogmatic and apologetic character: defending the Church against perversions of the Catholic faith, they defined the truths that were in peril and condemned erroneous doctrines. By contrast, the aim of Vatican II was primarily pastoral. Avoiding all anathemas, it sought to give a positive presentation of the faith, above all in its relation to modern man and the modern world, and to help mankind by showing the Church to be ready for dialogue, collaboration and solidarity with all men of good will.

Cardinal Wojtyla's study is faithful to that orientation of

the Council. It contains no vestige of polemics, although it was written in a situation of tension and, at times, of contradictory tendencies within the Church. Calmly interpreting the letter and the spirit of Vatican II, it places on record that the Council is still topical and has not grown out of date. The Author of the Study blames and condemns no one, but seeks to open to all the treasure of 'things new and old' (Mt. 13:52). In this way his work clearly presents the authentic Conciliar renewal of the Church. For all these reasons it deserves to be expounded still more deeply by theologians and read by all with particular attention.

INTRODUCTION

A bishop who took part in the Second Vatican Council feels the need to acquit himself of a debt. Apart from other meanings that have been or will be read into the Council, it has a unique and unrepeatable meaning for all who took part, and most particularly for the bishops who were Fathers of the Council. These men took an active part for four years in the proceedings of the Council and in drafting its documents, and at the same time derived great spiritual enrichment from it. The experience of a world-wide community was to each of them a tremendous benefit of historic importance. The history of the Council, which will be written in full one day, was present in 1962–5 as an extraordinary event in the minds of all the bishops concerned: it absorbed all their thoughts and stimulated their sense of responsibility, as an exceptional and deeply felt experience.

That experience is historically a thing of the past but is spiritually still in being, and it is this that gives rise to a sense of indebtedness. When we ask ourselves to whom the debt is owed – after calling to mind all the individuals and statements, different minds, attitudes and approaches, and the whole visible reality of the Conciliar assembly – we realize that we owe it to the Invisible One who without ceasing fulfils the promise made long ago to the Apostles in the upper room, the Holy Spirit who 'will teach you all things, and bring to your remembrance all that I have said to you' (John 14:26).

Through the whole experience of the Council we have

contracted a debt towards the Holy Spirit, the Spirit of Christ which speaks to the churches (cf. Rev. 2:7). During the Council and by way of it, the word of the Spirit became particularly expressive and decisive for the Church. The bishops, members of the College, who inherited from the Apostles the promise made by Christ at the Last Supper, are bound in a special way to be conscious of the debt contracted 'towards the word of the Holy Spirit', since it was they who translated the divine message into human language. The latter, in so far as it is human, may be imperfect and capable of increasingly precise formulation, but at the same time it is authentic because it contains that which the Spirit 'said to the Church' at a particular historical moment. Thus our awareness of the debt derives from faith and from the Gospel, which enable us to express the word of God in the human language of our time, endowing it with the supreme authority of the Church's magisterium.

Christ said: 'Lo, I am with you always, to the close of the age' (Matt. 28:20). During the Council these words took on a new freshness.

Our sense of the debt we owe to the Council is linked with the need for a further response. Such a response is called for by faith, which itself is essentially a reply to the word of God, to the Spirit as it speaks to the Church. When we speak of putting the Council into effect, it is precisely this response that we have in mind.

The perspective to which the problem belongs is that of faith, the vital structure of faith in every Christian. It is at this level, too, that we become aware of the debt we have to pay. If this awareness is strong in every Christian, it must be especially so where bishops are concerned, as it is a question of replying to the word of the Spirit, to the human expression of which every one of the bishops contributed. As a member of the Council, each bishop is a particular witness to the word and is at the same time its debtor. For this reason he feels an authentic responsibility for the integral response of faith, the response of the Church and the world to the word of the Lord, the word of the Spirit. Herein lies the continuity of the witness that once proceeded from the Cenacle.

It would be a mistake not to consider the implementation of Vatican II as the response of faith to the word of God as it proceeded from that Council. It is to be hoped that this implementation will be guided by the idea that the renewal which it set on foot is a historical stage in the self-realization of the Church. Through the Council, the Church has not only shown clearly what it thinks of itself, but also in what way it wishes itself to be realized. The teaching of Vatican II stands revealed as the image, proper to our time, of the Church's self-realization, an image which in various ways should pervade the minds of the whole people of God. If we use from time to time the expression 'Conciliar initiation', we do so in precisely this sense. 'Initiation' may mean either 'introduction' or actual participation in a mystery. The bishop, as a genuine witness of the Council, is he who understands its mystery, and therefore it is he who chiefly bears the responsibility for introduction and initiation into the reality of the Council itself. Since he is an instructor in the faith, it is for him more than others to elicit that response of faith which should be the fruit of the Council and the basis of its implementation.

This book is intended as a study of 'initiation'. It is not a commentary on the Council documents: that is a matter for theologians who, in Poland as elsewhere, are working hard at the task and performing it step by step. This book is rather to be thought of as a vade-mecum introducing the reader to the relevant documents of Vatican II, but always from the point of view of translating them into the life and faith of the Church. Finally it is not to be considered as a scientific study but rather as an extended 'working paper' on the subject of the Church's activity in the world, especially in Poland. For the

Church is seeking in itself and in the world a form adequate to the truth of the Council and to the breath of the Spirit which pervaded it.

I offer and dedicate this book above all to those who, in the Church at Cracow, give me their generous help and co-operate with me as their bishop in giving effect to Vatican II.

PART I

The Basic Significance of Conciliar Initiation

CHAPTER I

The need for
an enrichment of faith

The implementation of Vatican II, or the process of Conciliar renewal, must be based on the principle of the enrichment of faith. This principle is at the same time a postulate, and should first be clarified in this double aspect.

The clarification resides to some extent in the very fact of the Council, its essential purpose. Among the documents of Vatican II it is the Constitution on Divine Revelation – *Dei Verbum* – which throws most light on this theme:

> DV 8 | Thus, as the centuries go by, the Church is always advancing towards the plenitude of divine truth, until eventually the words of God are fulfilled in her.

This advance on the Church's part at the same time indicates the basic direction in which faith develops and enriches itself. The enrichment of faith is nothing else than increasingly full participation in divine truth.

This is the fundamental viewpoint from which we must judge the reality of Vatican II and seek ways of putting it into practice. This is the most adequate criterion and corresponds as well as possible to the reality of the Council, which, as an act of the supreme magisterium, sets out to show our age the way leading to the fulfilment of God's word in the Church (cf. Matt. 27:24–7; Luke 6:46–9). All other formulations seem, by comparison, to present partial and secondary aspects instead of the essential one. Nothing determines more effectively the process of the Church's self-realization than the reality of faith and its gradual enrichment. It is on this that we must concentrate above all, seeking in it the fundamental interpretation of the Council's thought and all the efforts made to put it into practice – many efforts of all kinds, as we know thanks to modern communication facilities, but all directed to a single end which we should pursue as well as we are able.

The call for an enrichment of faith may seem over-bold if we take account of the many voices which speak of a crisis of faith, the weakening of the religious sense and so on – as the documents of Vatican II themselves recognize. We must therefore make clear the sense in which we intend to speak in this book of the enrichment of faith, and in what sense we perceive it as the fundamental requirement for the realization of the Council. For this purpose it is necessary to take precise account not only of the essential purpose of the Council, as already mentioned, but also the purpose which led to the Council's being summoned in the first place which had a particular influence on its development and gave it its distinctive character.

John XXIII, who called the Council, and likewise his Successor and the assembled Fathers, emphasized many times that the Council was above all a 'pastoral' one and that its work should be directed and decisions taken from that point of view. This must be borne in mind when we pass from the work of the Council itself, which already constitutes a complete unity, to that of the Church seeking its self-realization in the Conciliar spirit. Thus it is in the light of the purpose of Vatican II as pre-eminently a pastoral Council that we should consider the postulate of an enrichment of faith as the basis of any realization of the Council and any renewal of the Church.

It may be said that every Council in the Church's history has been a pastoral one, if only because the assembled bishops, under the Pope's guidance, are pastors of the Church. At the same time every Council is an act of the supreme magisterium of the Church. Magisterium signifies teaching based on authority, a teaching which is the mission of the Apostles and their successors: it is part of their function and an essential task. This teaching is concerned essentially with questions of faith and morals: what men and women should believe in and in what manner, and hence how they should live according to their faith. The doctrine of faith and morals (*doctrina fidei et morum*) is the content of the teaching of the pastors of the Church, so that on the one hand doctrinal acts of the magisterium have a pastoral sense, while on the other pastoral acts have a doctrinal significance, deeply rooted as they are in faith and morals. These pastoral acts contain the doctrine that the Church proclaims; they often make it clearer and more precise, striving incessantly to achieve the fulness of the divine truth (cf. John 16:13).

All this has been signally confirmed by Vatican II, which, while preserving its pastoral character and mindful of the purpose for which it was called, profoundly developed the doctrine of faith and thus provided a basis for its enrichment.

While considering this fundamental objective of the Council, which was above all present to the minds of the Pastors assembled at the tomb of St Peter, we must also point out another distinction which will enable us to do justice to the Council's pastoral significance. If we study the Conciliar magisterium as a whole, we find that the Pastors of the Church were not so much concerned to answer questions like 'What should men believe?', 'What is the real meaning of this or that truth of faith?' and so on, but rather to answer the more complex question: 'What does it mean to be a believer, a Catholic and a member of the Church?' They endeavoured to answer this question in the broad context of today's world, as indeed the complexity of the question itself requires.

The question 'What does it mean to be a believing member of the Church?' is indeed difficult and complex, because it not only presupposes the truth of faith and pure doctrine, but also calls for that truth to be situated in the human consciousness and calls for a definition of the attitude, or rather the many attitudes,[1] that go to make the individual a believing member of the Church. This would seem to be the main respect in which the Conciliar magisterium has a pastoral character, corresponding to the pastoral purpose for which it was called. A 'purely' doctrinal Council would have concentrated on defining the precise meaning of the truths of faith, whereas a pastoral Council proclaims, recalls or clarifies truths for the primary purpose of giving Christians a life-style, a way of thinking and acting. In our efforts to put the Council into practice, this is the style we must keep before our minds. In the present study, designed to help towards the realization of Vatican II, we shall concentrate on the consciousness of Christians and the attitudes they should acquire. These attitudes, springing from a well-formed Christian conscience, can in a sense be regarded as true proof of the realization of the Council. This is the direction which should be followed by all pastoral action, the lay apostolate and the whole of the Church's activity.

To sum up, the enrichment of faith[2] which we regard as the fundamental pre-requisite for the realization of Vatican II is to be understood in two ways: as an enrichment of the content of faith in accordance with the Council's teaching, but also, originating from that content, an enrichment of the whole existence of the believing member of the Church. This enrichment of faith in the objective sense, constituting a new stage in the Church's advance towards the 'fulness of divine truth', is at the same time an enrichment in the subjective, human, existential sense, and it is from the latter that realization of the Council is most to be hoped for. The 'pastoral' Council has opened a new chapter of the Church's pastoral activity, interpreting that phrase in its widest sense.

[1] For the exact meaning of the term 'attitude' as used in this book cf. the chapters on the 'Formation of attitudes', pp. 201 ff. (Note by Italian translator.)

[2] When the author speaks of an enrichment of the content of faith he naturally does not mean the discovery of fresh truths not already contained in revelation, but merely the interpretation of revealed truth in relation to new historical exigencies, as a result of which new aspects may come to light that were not previously noticed. (Note by Italian translator.)

CHAPTER II

Faith as God's gift, and also as man's conscious attitude

In speaking of the enrichment of faith and describing it as a fundamental postulate of the Church's activity, we are well aware that we are touching here on supernatural reality, which is in man but does not originate from him. It rises up in him, takes shape and develops as the fruit of a unique encounter, the origin of which is God's revelation of himself. As we read in the Constitution on Divine Revelation:

> DV 2 | It pleased God, in his goodness and wisdom, to reveal himself and to make known the mystery of his will (cf. Eph. 1:9).

This is one of many passages in the extensive Conciliar text which speak of God's initiative in the encounter with mankind. Revelation is, as it were, superimposed on creation, so that the encounter takes on a new supernatural and inter-personal dimension.

> DV 3 | God, who creates and conserves all things by his Word, (cf. Jn. 1:3), provides men with constant evidence of himself in created realities (cf. Rom. 1:19–20). And furthermore, wishing to open up the way to heavenly salvation, he manifested himself to our first parents from the very beginning.

According to the explicit doctrine of Vatican II, faith is a particular response on the part of mankind to God's revelation of himself.

DV 5 | 'The obedience of faith' (Rom. 16:26; cf. Rom. 1:5; 2 Cor. 10:5–6) must be given to God as he reveals himself. By faith man freely commits his entire self to God, making 'the full submission of his intellect and will to God who reveals'.

Faith, as these words show, is not merely the response of the mind to an abstract truth. Even the statement, true though it is, that this response is dependent on the will does not tell us everything about the nature of faith. 'The obedience of faith' is not bound to any particular human faculty but relates to man's whole personal structure and spiritual dynamism.

Man's proper response to God's self-revelation consists in self-abandonment to God. This is the true dimension of faith, in which man does not simply accept a particular set of propositions, but accepts his own vocation and the sense of his existence. This implies, at least in principle and as an existential premiss, that man has the free disposal of himself, since by means of faith he 'abandons himself wholly to God'. This dimension of faith is supernatural in the strict sense of the word.

DV 5 | Before this faith can be exercised, man must have the grace of God to move and assist him; he must have the interior helps of the Holy Spirit, who moves the heart and converts it to God . . . The same Holy Spirit constantly perfects faith by his gifts, so that Revelation may be more and profoundly understood.

It is this fundamental dimension of faith, springing from the supernatural reality in which God is encountered, that must be constantly borne in mind when we speak of the enrichment of faith. It is that which, always and in every aspect, constitutes the essence of the enrichment of faith, whether we develop its substantive or its existential content. In this work it is our intention to do both. The essential enrichment of faith in all its aspects must be achieved in that fundamental dimension which is newly brought into prominence by the Constitution on Divine Revelation.

Man's participation in this enrichment must be considered in due proportion to this. Both parts of the Declaration on Religious Freedom have thrown fresh light on this subject. The first part formulates the general principle of religious freedom based on an analysis of the religious attitude itself, while the second does so in the light of revelation. Both parts agree in affirming the close link between religion and the human person and we may add, the individual in the framework of a community. Our analysis of the communal aspect will, however, be postponed till later; at this stage the personal aspect seems to us primary and fundamental.

| DH 10 | The act of faith is of its very nature a free act. Man . . . cannot give his adherence to God when he reveals himself unless, drawn by the Father, he submits to God with a faith that is reasonable and free. . . |

| DH 11 | God calls men to serve him in spirit and in truth. Consequently they are bound to him in conscience but not coerced. God has regard for the dignity of the human person which he himself created; the human person is to be guided by his own judgment and to enjoy freedom. |

Speaking next of Christ's mode of action in 'completing and perfecting revelation . . . by his death and resurrection and finally by sending the Spirit of truth' (DV 4), the Declaration on Religious Freedom teaches that

| DH 11 | [Christ] bore witness to the truth but refused to use force to impose it on those who spoke out against it . . . |

DH 9 | Revelation . . . shows forth the dignity of the human person in all its fullness. It shows us Christ's respect for the freedom with which man is to fulfil his duty of believing the word of God.

Man's participation in this encounter with God, in which faith consists, is a fully personal one. The Declaration on Religious Freedom points this out, while developing the ideas of the Constitution on Divine Revelation concerning the subject of faith, i.e. man as the subject of an encounter with God who reveals himself. These ideas point to the human depth which distinguishes man as a person and which is implied by faith; they thus concern the dimension of the human person which, in conscious faith, is manifested in all its fulness. It is from this point of view of the personal subject that the possibility and need for an enrichment of faith must also be considered, especially as the teaching of Vatican II provides a solid foundation for the purpose. Thus the implementation of this teaching must be considered a fundamental task of Conciliar renewal. It is not a completely new task: it has always been expressed in the endeavour to foster what is called 'conscious Catholicism'; but the Conciliar teaching enables us to confront it with greater courage and also greater responsibility. This is clear from the Declaration on Religious Freedom, which gives a penetrating analysis of the religious act; and this analysis shows up in all its fulness the personal significance of the answer given, in faith, to God's revelation of himself.

DH 2 | It is in accordance with their dignity that all men, because they are persons, that is, beings endowed with reason and free will and therefore bearing personal responsibility, are both impelled by their nature and bound by a moral obligation to seek the truth, especially religious truth. They are also bound to adhere to the truth once they come to know it and direct their whole lives in accordance with the demands of truth.

Religion may be generically defined as man's relationship with God. As far as man is concerned this relationship is based on the free, rational nature which properly belongs to the individual. Religion is thus something personal. Man brings his freedom into religion and engages himself on the basis of coherence between truth and reality: a principle according to which faith comes about as a response to the word of God, who in turn reveals himself in it. This response, as we have seen, is essentially supernatural, and at the same time strictly personal. Man brings his own freedom into religion and commits himself, accepting as truth the word of God and the self-revelation of God which it contains.

In this way man's personal nature is expressed in the act of faith, an act springing from the depths of man's humanity which must be defined as personal. Faith is a problem of conscience:

> DH 3 | Everybody has the duty and consequently the right to seek the truth in religious matters so that, through the use of appropriate means, he may prudently form judgments of conscience which are sincere and true.

The postulate of conscious faith and conscious Catholicism is fully supported by the Council's standpoint in defence of the right of religious freedom in the social and public dimension. If the right to religious freedom appears from the text of the Declaration to present itself *ad extra*, in relation to secular public order, at the same time the postulate of conscious faith becomes clear on reading the Declaration *ad intra*, i.e. in relation to believers and to the Church seeking its own self-realization. This postulate must above all be understood as a postulate of the enrichment of faith on the part of the subject: an enrichment corresponding to the subject's nature, which is personal, and which must also contribute to the development of the Christian's entire personality. The consciousness of faith has not only psychological but ethical significance; it involves a profound sense of responsibility as regards the response to God's self-revelation. Awareness of faith is not identical with knowledge, even with a complete knowledge of the content of revelation; rather it is based on the existential factor, since it is faith that gives meaning to human existence. The believer's whole existence constitutes his response to the gift of God which is revelation. The postulate of conscious faith should be understood accordingly.

The postulate of conscious faith, as a postulate of the enrichment of faith on the subject's part, is nothing but a constant concern on man's part to respond to the God who reveals himself. This response presupposes the grace of faith and springs not only from the fact of revelation but above all from God's action within the human soul, while at the same time it is also a conscious act of the man himself. This is a response given personally:

> DH 3 | The reason is because the practice of religion of its very nature consists primarily of those voluntary and free internal acts by which a man directs himself to God.

But it is also a response given in association with others:

> DH 3 | His own social nature requires that man give external expression to these internal acts of religion, that he communicate with others on religious matters, and profess his religion in community.

In accordance with the ideas of Vatican II, the enrichment of the subject's faith should be conceived of and understood as the development of the religious attitude, conscious of both its inner content and transcendent significance, as well as its exterior and social character.

DH 3 | Furthermore, the private and public acts of religion by which men direct themselves to God according to their convictions transcend of their very nature the earthly and temporal order of things.

CHAPTER III

Faith and dialogue

DH 3 | The search for truth . . . must be carried out in a manner that is appropriate to the dignity of the human person and his social nature, namely, by free inquiry with the help of teaching or instruction, communication and dialogue. It is by these means that men share with each other the truth they have discovered, or think they have discovered, in such a way that they help one another in the search for truth. Moreover, it is by personal assent that men must adhere to the truth they have discovered.

In our thoughts on the implementation of the Council we propose to explore various ways of enriching faith which have been pointed out by the Council itself. True to its pastoral orientation, Vatican II gives an answer to the question: What does it mean to be a believer, a member of the Church? In so doing it takes into account the integral truth concerning man as a being who lives in the world and is conditioned in various ways by other human beings and human society. This is the truth we must keep before our minds as the starting-point of our reflection on the relationship between faith and dialogue. The concept of dialogue appeared in the Church's pronouncements during the Council, and Paul VI gave it particular significance in his encyclical *Ecclesiam Suam* (AAS, 56 (1964). 609–59); in that encyclical, too, it takes on various meanings according to the different contexts to which it applies. It seems to us essential, however, to define clearly the relationship between dialogue and faith, not only in order to explain the concept of dialogue itself, but also the direction this indicates for the Church and Christian life.

This becomes especially clear when faith is conceived in a somewhat existential sense, as a state of consciousness and an attitude on the part of individual believers. This point of view seems indeed to correspond with the Council's orientation. Faith, thus conceived, is an act and also a permanent disposition (*habitus*) from which particular acts derive. Faith is therefore man's conscious response to the God who reveals himself – the response to a purely supernatural gift. This response is also a gift of God, but at the same time, as we pointed out in the previous chapter, it has a personal character: it represents a mature religious attitude on man's part and a mature relationship with truth. Faith is 'assent', as we read in paragraph 3 of the Declaration on Religious Liberty – that is, it signifies being convinced of the truth of revelation. It is thus no longer a search for truth in the strict sense of the term, but it opens up the possibility of research on the basis and within the scope of the truth already known. This in fact is the ordinary way leading towards the enrichment of faith, of which we have already spoken.

Thus dialogue, as well as coexisting with faith, can also contribute to enriching it. Here, in accordance with the Declaration on Religious Liberty, we use the term 'dialogue' in its most general and simple sense of an exchange of ideas:

> DH 3 | Men share with each other the truth they have discovered, or think they have discovered, in such a way that they help one another in the search for truth.

If faith signifies on the one hand assent, i.e. conviction concerning the truth taught by Revelation, and on the other a conscious religious attitude seeking to enrich itself, it is thus linked with dialogue and accepts it. Vatican II accepts dialogue as a means of enriching faith. In answer to the question 'What does it mean to be a believing member of the Church?', the Council states that it means being convinced of the truth of revelation and at the same time capable of maintaining a dialogue. The dialogue in question is with those who are not convinced or who have a different conviction concerning the revealed truth; and it is concerned not only with many topics common to all mankind irrespective of their attitude towards revelation or God himself, but also with the truth of revelation and the Christian's conviction of that truth.

It is easy to see that dialogue thus conceived makes explicit demands on faith and on the conscious religious attitude, and that these demands can and should have the effect of enriching faith. However it is not a matter of purely intellectual enrichment. In this case dialogue has not a purely theological significance, and still less an 'apologetic' one. It would seem that the Council's orientation touches a still deeper reality, namely the reply to the existential question as to what it means to be a believing member of the Church. The man who believes and is a member of the Church professes as regards faith not only his God, as a reply to his revelation, but as regards mankind as well. The Council in fact teaches, in the Constitution on the Church, that 'All men are called to belong to the new People of God' (LG 13), while at the same time this and other documents recognize the existence of separated Christians, followers of non-Christian religions, unbelievers and atheists. This means that in every believer and every member of the Church, faith – when it is truly a mature and personal conviction of the truth of revelation – can and must be linked with the principle of dialogue.

> GS 92 | In virtue of its mission to enlighten the whole world with the message of the Gospel and gather together in one Spirit all men of every nation, race and culture, the Church shows itself as a sign of the spirits of brotherhood which renders possible sincere dialogue and strengthens it.

Dialogue in the present sense signifies an exchange of ideas, a question and answer, or rather a series of questions and answers; but in addition we must consider dialogue in the potential sense, that is to say readiness to engage in it. This readiness becames a reality in the believer when, in the community of the Church, he gives his answer to the divine revelation: it exists precisely because there are men who do not give that answer, or do not appear to give it, or give it differently. This does not apply only to individuals but to large sections of contemporary humanity, 'circles of dialogue' as Paul VI put it in his encyclical *Ecclesiam Suam*. It would be possible to separate ourselves from these men and these circles by giving our own personal answer to God through faith in the Church, but the Council has adopted a different position. If in the past there was a tendency to use the method of separation to preserve the purity of the faith, Vatican II has indicated a different way of enriching it.

This new way corresponds more closely to the global situation of the present-day believer who, enlightened by faith, puts a question to himself which affects believers and unbelievers in a different manner. It is a question which should not lead him into some kind of indifferentism but should induce him to pay attention to every circle outside the church and each individual in those circles, with full respect for his human personality and conscience. This respect goes hand in hand with a sense of responsibility to the truth and with the duty of every man to seek it sincerely, as we read in the Declaration on Religious Freedom. Those who adopt an indifferentist attitude consider themselves and others exempt from this duty, whereas the method of dialogue presupposes and in a sense imposes it:

> DH 1 | All men are bound to seek the truth, especially in what concerns God and his Church, and to embrace it and hold on to it as they come to know it.

The sacred Council likewise proclaims that these obligations bind man's conscience. Truth can impose itself on the mind of man only in virtue of its own truth, which wins over the mind with both gentleness and power.

Having present in our minds the Council's teaching on the human person and conscience, we can better understand the meaning of dialogue with all circles and groups 'outside the Church'. When the Council urges us to engage in dialogue and suggests methods and possibilities, it always conceives this exhortation from the standpoint of faith. It suffices to consider the following texts:

NA 2 | The Church, therefore, urges her sons to enter with prudence and charity into discussion and collaboration with members of other religions. Let Christians, while witnessing to their own faith and way of life, acknowledge, preserve and encourage the spiritual and moral truths found among non-Christians, also their social life and culture.

The Declaration on the Church's relations with non-Christian religions was also careful to emphasize, concisely but with much eloquence, the virtues and values that are to be found in those religions.

NA 2 | The Catholic Church rejects nothing of what is true and holy in these religions. She has a high regard for the manner of life and conduct, the precepts and doctrines which, although differing in many ways from her own teaching, nevertheless often reflect a ray of that truth which enlightens all men. Yet she proclaims and is in duty bound to proclaim without fail, Christ who is the way, the truth and the life (Jn. 1:6). In him, in whom God reconciled all things to himself (2 Cor. 5:18–19), men find the fullness of their religious life.

Similar but more numerous formulations on the relationship between faith and dialogue can be found in the Decree on Ecumenism, which is almost wholly devoted to this subject and to which we reserve a special chapter; we should, however, draw attention at once to some highly significant formulae:

UR 4 | . . . Catholics must gladly acknowledge and esteem the truly Christian endowments for our common heritage which are to be found among our separated brethren. It is right and salutary to recognize the riches of Christ and virtuous works in the lives of others who are bearing witness to Christ, sometimes even to the shedding of their blood.

Elsewhere we read:

UR 11 | The manner and order in which Catholic belief is expressed should in no way become an obstacle to dialogue with our brethren. It is, of course, essential that the doctrine be clearly presented in its entirety. Nothing is so foreign to the spirit of ecumenism as a false irenicism which harms the purity of Catholic doctrine and obscures its genuine and certain meaning.

At the same time, Catholic belief must be explained more profoundly and precisely, in such a way and in such terms that our separated brethren can also really understand it.

A glance at the above texts will illuminate the central point of our argument. It is clear that dialogue, even if considered only in its potential reference to men of 'different faiths', requires the individual not only to show respect for persons and consciences but to display a consciously religious attitude. The

Council documents give us clearly to understand that this is an attitude based on a relationship to truth. It is an attitude, as we saw in the previous chapter, that, far from avoiding the 'test' of dialogue, manifests in dialogue its own spiritual maturity. We have to do here not only with an examination on the truths of faith and our minds' assent to them, but an examination concerning our love towards men and especially those of different beliefs and convictions – an examination that we undergo on the basis of faith, and not an easy one. Faith without dialogue would certainly be less exacting, but the Council cannot exempt us from it, concerned as it is to answer the question as to what it means to be a believing member of the Church.

How difficult this examination of a mature faith can be is clearly shown by the pages of the Conciliar documents which deal with relations with unbelief and atheism:

GS 19 | Without doubt those who wilfully try to drive God from their heart and to avoid all questions about religion, not following the biddings of their conscience, are not free from blame. But believers themselves often share some responsibility for this situation. For atheism, taken as a whole, is not present in the mind of man from the start (*Atheismus, integre consideratus, non est quid originarium*). It springs from various causes, among which must be included a critical reaction against religions and, in some places, against the Christian religion in particular. Believers can thus have more than a little to do with the rise of atheism. To the extent that they are careless about their instruction in the faith, or present its teaching falsely, or even fail in their religious, moral, or social life, they must be said to conceal rather than to reveal the true nature of God and of religion.

Here, perhaps even more than in the two preceding 'circles of dialogue', it is shown what a 'dialogue' can and should mean as a way of enriching faith. It creates a mature faith which keeps extreme contrasts before its eyes and requires of itself the fullest consistency. In fact, and especially where unbelievers and atheists are concerned, the most difficult examination is that which tests our love for men and for mankind in the context of faith. Such an examination is a judgement, and the Council does not refrain from judging the motives of atheists themselves:

GS 21 | [The Church] tries nevertheless to seek out the secret motives which lead the atheistic mind to deny God. Well knowing how important are the problems raised by atheism, and urged by her love for all men, she considers that these motives deserve an earnest and more thorough scrutiny.

This judgement, however, is at the same time directed towards the faith of believing Christians and members of the Church, and makes grave demands upon them as regards the maturity and coherence of their faith:

GS 21 | Atheism must be countered both by presenting true teaching in a fitting manner and by the full and complete life of the Church and of her members ... This is brought about chiefly by the witness of a living and mature faith, one namely that is so well formed that it can see difficulties clearly and overcome them. Many martyrs have borne, and continue to bear, a splendid witness to this faith. This faith should show its fruitfulness by penetrating the whole life, even the worldly activities, of those who believe, and by urging them to be loving and just especially towards those in need.

The Council teaches that dialogue is the way to enrich faith not only because it increases the maturity of conviction but also, and above all, because thanks to it faith becomes particularly strong, vivified as it is by love.

GS 3 | The Council, as witness and guide to the faith of the whole people of God, gathered together by Christ, can find no more eloquent expression of its solidarity and respectful affection for the whole human family, to which it belongs, than to enter into dialogue with it about all these different problems. The Council will clarify these problems in the light of the Gospel and will furnish mankind with the saving resources which the Church has received from its founder under the promptings of the Holy Spirit.

GS 92 | For our part, our eagerness for such dialogue, conducted with appropriate discretion and leading to truth by way of love alone, excludes nobody; we would like to include those who respect outstanding human values without realizing who the author of those values is, as well as those who oppose the Church and persecute it in various ways. Since God the Father is the beginning and the end of all things, we are all called to be brothers; we ought to work together without violence and without deceit to build up the world in a spirit of genuine peace.

As will be seen, the idea of dialogue is deeply rooted in the content of faith – that content which Vatican II emphasized and illuminated with its own teaching – and at the same time involves profound moral values, which condition the existence and development of the human family in the world.

CHAPTER IV

The consciousness of the Church as the main foundation of Conciliar initiation

The way towards the enrichment of faith rediscovered by Vatican II passes through the mind and consciousness of the Church. Paul VI formulated it similarly in the first encyclical of his pontificate, published in the same year as *Lumen gentium*, the Council's Dogmatic Constitution on the Church. This Constitution is in a sense the key to the whole of the Council's thought. In it we find once more the complex variety of ways towards the enrichment of faith, leading from Vatican II into the future. This variety inspires nearly all the Council's documents, albeit in different degrees. The dogmatic Constitution is best complemented by the pastoral Constitution on the Church in the modern world, known by the title *Gaudium et spes*.

For this reason it was important to begin by clarifying the relationship between faith and dialogue, as it is closely linked with the consciousness of the Church. The Church is itself a truth of faith and is the subject of an article in the Creed: 'I believe in one holy, catholic and apostolic Church.' If the Council's approach had been 'purely doctrinal', its teaching concerning the truth of faith as regards the Church might have taken a different form; but on this very point it had to be pastoral first and foremost. It was impossible to treat the Church merely as an 'object': it had to be a 'subject' also. This was certainly the intention behind the Council's first question:

Ecclesia, quid dicis de te ipsa? Church, what do you say of yourself? This direct question to the Church as a subject was also addressed to all the individuals of whom the Church is composed. The entity known as the Church is in fact a community unique in its kind. It is undoubtedly a community of faith, a community returning a continuous answer to the Word of God, a community of men and women united and bound together by that answer. The community formed by that answer, by the dialogue with God, in a certain sense determines the vertical dimension of the Church and is at the same time open to all men. Faith together with dialogue constitutes the Church's horizontal dimension, which is not solely a 'humanistic' one. The horizontal dimension derives from the vertical one and corresponds to the reality of revelation, from which we know that 'God desires all men to be saved and to come to the knowledge of the truth' (I Tim. 2:4). The mind of the Church must not be restricted, but must correspond to the universality of the divine plan of salvation and the work of redemption. For its part, the horizontal dimension penetrates the vertical one. The Council rightly discerns the foundation of this latter in every human being:

> GS 76   The Church, by reason of her role and competence, is not identified with any political community . . . It is at once the sign and the safeguard of the transcendental dimension of the human person.

The transcendent character of the person, together with man's responsibility to the truth, not only constitutes the basis of the dialogue but also defines the subjective range of the Church's consciousness, in which the Church in a sense discovers itself.

This range is wider than that defined by membership of any religion, inasmuch as the spiritual link and the possibility of dialogue are instituted by a ray of that 'light which enlightens every man', to use the words quoted in the Declaration on relations with non-Christian religions. The Council here voices the conviction that 'The private and public acts of religion by which men direct themselves to God according to their convictions transcend of their very nature the earthly and temporal order of things' (DH 3). The conviction concerning the transcendent character of religion and the religious act is closely linked with the conviction of the transcendency of the human person, which is indeed the proper characteristic of a human being. If the Church, as we read in the Pastoral Constitution, is the sign and safeguard of the transcendent character of the human person, this means that the mind of the Church is open not merely to every man but, even more, that it cannot be rightly formed except in relation to man and in union with him.

Hence the enrichment of faith, which is to spring from the Church's consciousness in the ways indicated by Vatican II, involves, as the expression of faith, both profession of one's faith and dialogue. Dialogue is not a departure from the vertical dimension of the Church, as it is sometimes thought to be: it is an effort which accompanies the profession and witness of the whole Church and every Catholic, in order to discover and define the right place for every man in the response of faith addressed to God. This definition is important for the mind of the Church, whose horizontal dimension follows the vertical one and not vice versa. Only on the basis of this principle can dialogue enrich faith. Pope Paul VI opportunely recalled that only the dialogue of salvation can correspond to the mind of the Church. The concept of 'dialogue of salvation' is not so much concerned with the purposes and effects of that dialogue, but rather with its presuppositions and the meaning that should attach to it in the mind of the Church and of every believer.

The fact that the ways of enriching faith, which radiate from Vatican II into the future, must pass through the consciousness of the Church has another important meaning for us in the present context, from the practical and organizational point of view. Pursuing the pastoral aim of the Council, we wish to reply in more detail to the question: what does it mean to be a believing member of the Church? In reply to this question we would like, as it were, to 'organize' the Catholic consciousness in conformity with the Council's thought, and we would like to see corresponding to it the spiritual attitudes proposed by Vatican II. We desire all this, animated by the belief that the Council was the 'word of the Spirit' (cf. Apoc. 2:7, 11, 17, 29), and must be gradually but thoroughly implemented in the life of the Church and hence of every Christian. From the consciousness of the Church as a subject uniting us all in the community and sustaining our relationship with everyone else, we turn to the Church as an object of faith. This does not mean that there are two poles between which our thoughts oscillate, but merely two aspects of a single reality. We ourselves are the Church, and at the same time we believe in it; it is the object of our faith, and it is ourselves. The whole movement instituted by the Council must be a reflection of this reality.

The truth concerning the Church comes near the end of the Christian Creed. The Church as an object of faith, as objective revealed reality, presupposes the reality of God and the Holy Trinity, of creation, revelation and redemption. The Church derives from these realities in which it finds its explanation, and therefore it is mentioned after them in the Creed. This too is the order of reality which should be expressed in the Church's mind. We shall try presently to show how Vatican II helps us to organize and form our consciousness on these lines. The truth concerning the Church is not simply added to the other truths in our Creed but is closely and organically connected with them: the truths of faith are not only interrelated but interpenetrate one another. It is impossible to conceive the reality of the Church without considering all the truths that surround it in the Creed. This is the way in which Vatican II presents that reality, and it is in the living and organic context of the Creed that it calls on the Church to answer the question:

What do you say of yourself?

As we embark, therefore, on the ways of enriching faith which pass through the consciousness of the Church, we must always bear in mind the principle of integration. First and foremost, all that Vatican II has said must be subjected to the principle of the integration of faith. The Council did not concern itself with the whole content of our faith, and did not formulate a Creed comprising all its truths. This was done only after the Council, on 30 June 1968, by Paul VI in the *Credo Populi Dei* (AAS, 60 (1968) 443–5), with explicit reference to the Council's magisterium. This *Credo* clearly indicates that the teaching of Vatican II, which centres above all on the reality of the Church, must be organically inserted into the whole deposit of faith, so as to be integrated with the teaching of all preceding Councils and pontiffs. If the truth concerning the Church is enunciated near the end of our Creed, in logical sequence to the other truths of faith, it is right to point out that this also corresponds to the historical sequence. Vatican II – an ecclesiological Council, which was concerned especially with the truth concerning the Church – took place in the twentieth century and was the successor to many other Councils which dealt particularly with the truths that we profess in earlier parts of the Creed, before professing our faith in the Church.

Although this point should not be insisted on too exclusively or 'disjunctively', precisely because the faith is a single whole and all its parts are interdependent, both as we profess them and live them, nevertheless we cannot disregard the analogy between the internal logic of the faith as we profess it in the Creed and the history of its gradual enrichment. Against this background it is easier to see in what the principle of integration consists and why it works both ways, in the reciprocal relationship between the deposit of revelation and the Conciliar mind of the Church. This is important both for the Church's whole activity and self-realization and also for the thoughts and actions of every Catholic, his consciousness and general attitude. It is important to theology and also from the point of view of universal teaching, catechesis and homiletics – fields of action which now lie open to us and which all more or less consciously await this kind of reciprocal integration.

It must be seen therefore that the post-Conciliar integration of faith is not a mechanical addition, by the magisterium of the Council, to all that was hitherto comprised in the Church's teaching; nor is it what would be called in strict scholastic language a *juxtaposition*, since the incorporation of the thought of Vatican II in all the Church's previous formulations has already taken place on the basis of the historical succession of documents. Integration means something more: an organic cohesion expressing itself simultaneously in the thought and action of the Church as a community of believers. It expresses itself, that is, in such a way that on the one hand we can rediscover and, as it were, re-read the magisterium of the last Council in the whole previous magisterium of the Church, while on the other we can rediscover and re-read the whole preceding magisterium in that of the last Council. It would seem that the principle of integration, thus conceived and applied, is indirectly the principle of the Church's identity, dating back to its first beginnings in Christ and the Apostles. This principle of identity operated in the Council and must continue to do so, integrating the whole patrimony of faith with and in the consciousness of the Church.

In what follows we shall constantly endeavour to apply this principle, which is indispensable for the Church's progress along the road of self-realization. In judgements passed on the work necessary for Council and on the Church's activity in the post-Conciliar period, undue emphasis was laid on divisions and differences between so-called integralists and progressives, while too little was said about the fact that both groups, in their responsibility towards the Church, must be unswervingly guided by the principle and demands of its identity, and that they must both therefore respect the principle of integration which is a precondition of the Church's identity. We do not intend to go into that aspect of the matter here, but rather wish to base ourselves on the Conciliar 'word of the Spirit' in its fundamental, organic simplicity. The whole Creed is mirrored in the mind of the Church, and the mind of the Church embraces the whole Creed, finding in all the truths of faith a basis on which to form itself and increase in depth. The documents of Vatican II are an eloquent proof of this.

In what follows we shall try to outline this fact even if it is not possible to present it in a complete and exhaustive manner. This will help to make it even clearer that the way of the enrichment of faith is through the consciousness of the Church, and we shall give at least some idea of the course of these various ways. The mind of the Church is not only a historical moment in the course and development of our faith, but is also one of the terms by which we can define our faith in all its multiple richness.

PART II

The Formation of
Consciousness

CHAPTER I

The consciousness of creation

In the teaching of Vatican II, the Church's consciousness of itself is fundamentally united with the consciousness of creation, and it is to this that our attention must first be directed. When we speak of the consciousness of creation we have in mind first and foremost our faith in God, the almighty Father and creator – to recall the opening words of the Creed. This is the truth of faith which comes first and permeates all the others. Thus it also permeates the truth concerning the Church, and forms the Church's consciousness from its very foundations. That consciousness is in organic union with the consciousness of the existence of God as creator of the world, to which corresponds the consciousness of the work of creation.

In what way does Vatican II enrich our faith in this respect? First of all, it takes over our faith and proclaims it in all the richness and essential force with which it has been transmitted by all the generations of the People of God on earth.

LG 2 | The eternal Father, in accordance with the utterly gratuitous and mysterious design of his wisdom and goodness, created the whole universe.

AGD 2 | As the principle without principle . . . God in his great and merciful kindness freely creates us and moreover, graciously calls us to share in his life and glory. He generously pours out, and never ceases to pour out, his divine goodness, so that he who is creator of all things might at last become 'all in all' (1 Cor. 15:28).

Here the main emphasis is on God as Creator. We shall speak presently of the work of creation, which is linked with the progression of knowledge from the creation to the creator and is thus part and parcel of faith, as the Constitution *Dei Verbum* recalls:

> DV 3 | God, who creates and conserves all things by his Word, (cf. Jn. 1: 3), provides men with constant evidence of himself in created realities (cf. Rom. 1:19–20).

This is the way by which human reason can by its own powers arrive at the knowledge of God, as the first Vatican Council taught in detail and as Vatican II recalled:

> DV 6 | The sacred Synod professes that 'God, the first principle and last end of all things, can be known with certainty from the created world, by the natural light of human reason' (cf. Rom. 1:20).

Such is the knowledge that derives from created things: it remains an open question whether this knowledge constitutes essential knowledge of God and the work of creation. The concept of the Creator and the work of creation involves in some measure the fatherhood of God and his 'hidden design', the plan which is full of wisdom and is the fruit of the Creator's goodness and benevolence. The work of creation was prompted by love. Human reason is capable of knowing God, the principle of all that exists, by the 'natural light', but it is clear that knowledge of the Creator and the work of creation already involves God's revelation of himself: without this the human mind could not fathom the 'hidden design', i.e. the eternal plan of creation, or comprehend its motives.

The mind of the Church is here confronted by the primal, basic truth that formed it from the beginning. We may say that this is also the first step towards faith and the first word of man's response to God as he reveals himself. The Council teaches explicitly that God 'provides men with constant evidence of himself in created realities' (DV 3). The term 'evidence' is particularly significant because it indicates the element of revelation in creation itself, which is, as it were, the first and fundamental expression of God, by which he speaks to us and calls for the response of faith. Vatican II seeks to guide the response of faith in this, its essential foundation. Although it may not seem to elaborate much on this theme, but rather to emphasize the need for integration with the previous content of faith, in this field too it brings an enrichment of its own.

This enrichment proceeds from the reality of the world. The way in which this point of view came to the fore during the Council is significant. Originally it was much less clearly defined. It was John XXIII who introduced it by pointing out to the Council the need to compose a document on the presence of the Church in the contemporary world. Such a document was indeed drafted, and aroused considerable interest; but more important is the fact that it gave an opportunity to point out the relationship between the consciousness of the Church and that of creation. At the beginning of the Constitution on the Church in the Modern World the Council makes clear in what sense it speaks of the 'world'; and before coming to describe the 'modern world' it uses the formula that we shall quote in a moment, as if to show that the modern world is simply one aspect of the totality of creation and its multiple development in relation to the Creator:

> GS 2 | Therefore, the world which the Council has in mind is the whole human family seen in the context of everything which envelops it: it is the world as the theatre of human history . . . the world, which in the Christian vision has been created and is sustained by the love of its maker, which has been freed from the slavery of sin by Christ . . . so that it might be fashioned anew according to God's design and brought to its fulfilment.

Thus the concept of the 'world' has several meanings in the Conciliar document, but its basic and proper significance is that which corresponds to the reality of creation, 'created by the love of its Creator'; by maintaining it in existence he creates it ever anew. It is noteworthy that the Council, which set out to concentrate on the reality of the Church, at once encountered in its path – apparently only indirectly – the reality of creation. If the Pastoral Constitution on the Church in the Modern World is generally regarded as complementary to the Dogmatic Constitution on the Church, I presume that this came about not only because of the problems of the modern age as such but perhaps even more on account of the problem of the 'world' and of a fuller and more detailed connection between the consciousness of the Church and that of creation than that found in the Dogmatic Constitution on the Church. We shall see later what the 'world' signifies for the enrichment of faith in the consciousness of the Church, but for the present we are concerned with the consciousness of creation.

The whole of *Gaudium et spes*, and particularly Chapter III of its first part, which is devoted to analyzing human activity in the world, throws especial light on this question. The Council significantly declares that 'the Church . . . is eager to associate the light of revelation with the experience of mankind in trying to clarify the course on which mankind has just entered' (GS 33). This is the way which the Creator prescribed to mankind from the beginning:

GS 34 | Man was created in God's image and was commanded to conquer the earth with all it contains and to rule the world in justice and holiness: he was to acknowledge God as maker of all things and relate himself and the totality of creation to him.

We may say that this sentence formulates the very essence of the consciousness of creation, the objects of which are both the 'world' and 'mankind'. Thus in regard to the works of creation man is either outside himself as conscious of the world, or inside himself as conscious of himself. The Council is aware of the conviction, which is becoming ever stronger at the present day, 'of mankind's ability and duty to strengthen its mastery over nature' (GS 9); and it sets out to illuminate in depth this conviction and this dynamic process, by proclaiming the truth concerning creation.

This is expressed perhaps most clearly in the well-known paragraph on the problem of the autonomy of created things:

> GS 36 | If by the autonomy of earthly affairs is meant the gradual discovery, exploitation, and ordering of the laws and values of matter and society, then the demand for autonomy is perfectly in order: it is at once the claim of modern man and the desire of the creator.

and here we find a passage which is of crucial importance in defining the way in which modern man can enrich his faith:

> GS 36 | By the very nature of creation, material being is endowed with its own stability, truth and excellence, its own order and laws. These man must respect as he recognizes the methods proper to every science and technique. Consequently, methodical research in all branches of knowledge, provided it is carried out in a truly scientific manner and does not override moral laws, can never conflict with the faith, because the things of the world and the things of faith derive from the same God. The humble and persevering investigator of the secrets of nature is being led, as it were, by the hand of God in spite of himself, for it is God, the conserver of all things, who made them what they are.

The autonomy of created things is not only man's right but is in the first place his duty as the lord of creation who has been given authority to subject them to himself. The way to this goal leads through a specific subordination of human knowledge and activity to that reality which lies in every created being. This knowledge and activity, even if not accompanied by awareness of creation and a conscious relationship with the Creator, already constitutes a certain encounter with him – an encounter in the work of creation and within its purview. This encounter is indeed the portion of all those who respect the rightful autonomy of created things. It may be said that this autonomy indirectly indicates the necessity of 'ordering' (or rather subordinating) 'all things in truth', a necessity which applies to man and all his activity in relation to the world. As the Council teaches, at this point there is always an encounter with the Creator.

The continuation of the above passage, in which the Council opposes the erroneous interpretation of the 'autonomy of earthly affairs', tells us more on the subject of the consciousness of creation.

GS 36 | However, if by the term 'the autonomy of earthly affairs' is meant that material being does not depend on God and that man can use it as if it had no relation to its creator, then the falsity of such a claim will be obvious to anyone who believes in God. Without a creator there can be no creature. In any case, believers, no matter what their religion, have always recognized the voice and the revelation of God in the language of creatures. Besides, once God is forgotten, the creature is lost sight of as well.

This passage is of a figurative character and is in a sense elliptical, but we nevertheless feel clearly that we have reached the inmost heart of the dogma of creation and are able to draw the fullest sustenance from it. The Council affirms first of all that the truth concerning creation and the Creator is common to almost all religions – hence the religious eloquence of created things. The idea that 'material being does not depend on God' is basically at variance with this truth and with the message of creation, as if one were to say that 'created things are not created'. Nor is this merely a contradiction of a conceptual kind. The dogma of creation defines reality itself in the profoundest way. Not only does the concept of 'creation' make no sense without that of a Creator, but the reality which we thus define cannot exist without Him who gave it its life and continuously keeps it in being. Created being presupposes a Creator, and without him it disappears. Hence the 'autonomy of earthly affairs', if conceived as a negation of God the Creator, is at the same time a negation of creatures and a denial of their ontological character: 'once God is forgotten, the creature is lost sight of as well' – and this leads to a fundamental disorientation of man's cognitive and active powers.

This line of thought appears negative on the surface, but from it there emerges indirectly the affirmation of the work of creation which is at the root of the Church's consciousness. The Church is always 'in the world' and derives its conscious-ness from the mystery of creation to which the 'world' corre-sponds; and the whole development of the world, brought about by man, is nothing but a progressive manifestation and revelation of God's work of creation.

> GS 34 | Far from considering the conquests of man's genius and courage as opposed to God's power, as if he set himself up as a rival to the creator, Christians ought to be convinced that the achievements of the human race are a sign of God's greatness and the fulfilment of his mysterious design.

> GS 34 | This holds good also for our daily work. When men and women provide for themselves and their families in such a way as to be of service to the community as well, they can rightly look upon their work as a prolongation of the work of the creator.

The truth concerning creation is that truth of faith which man encounters first and foremost in the world. It seems to respond to the fundamental questions concerning the existence of the world and man's existence in the world. It enables us to impose a basic order on our whole scheme of values and to realize, for instance, that 'it is what a man is, rather than what he has, that counts' – as *Gaudium et spes* puts it, following the thought of Paul VI, and continuing with the words: 'Technical progress may supply the material for human advance, but it is powerless to actualize it' (GS 35).

When we ascertain that awareness of the fact of creation is the basis of awareness of the Church, we can discover the ways of enriching faith which are marked out by the Council when it points to the work of creation in order to proclaim the Creator. The truth that God creates the world and maintains it in being reveals to us his transcendence and his basic presence in the world, as man encounters it without ceasing. The Church proclaims this truth at the beginning of its Creed, and the Council helps us not merely to see it as a reality 'outside' the Church's consciousness, but to bring it within that consciousness. For the present we have taken only a first step in this direction, but this first step conditions others. On account of the work of creation, the consciousness of the Church is in a sense also consciousness of the world, and conversely awareness of the world, being permeated by the truth concerning creation and the Creator, becomes awareness of the Church at its very foundation, on which we shall continue to build.

It seems, indeed, that the enrichment of faith that is the gift of Vatican II does not so much proceed from awareness of the creation to the truths subsequently proclaimed in the Creed, but rather begins with those truths and proceeds to awareness of the creation, which it thus provides with a richer context of faith.

CHAPTER II

Revelation of the Trinity, and awareness of salvation

DV 3 | God, who creates and conserves all things by his
Word, (cf. Jn. 1:3), provides men with constant
evidence of himself in created realities (cf. Rom.
1:19–20). And furthermore, wishing to open up
the way to heavenly salvation, he manifested
himself to our first parents from the very
beginning.

Faith is derived from revelation: it is the acceptance of
revelation and the response to it. The Second Vatican Council
confirms once again the way that leads to God through the
evidence of created things. Indirect though this may be, it is of
great importance for man's encounter with God: but he must
himself prepare for this encounter and bring his intellect to
bear on it.

The Council also gave prominence to the way of revelation
which leads from God to man. From the beginning, God
revealed himself to our first forefathers. The purpose of that
revelation was man's salvation, and from the beginning man
was made aware of its supernatural meaning and character.
It would seem that the Council, confronting the great problem
of the Church's self-knowledge, expressly connected the image
of God's interior life as presented by revelation with man's
awareness of salvation, which lies in participation in that life.
For this reason the response to revelation is not simply a
matter of intellectually accepting its content but, as we read in

the Constitution *Dei Verbum*, is an attitude in which man 'freely commits his entire self to God' (DV 5).

DV 2 | It pleased God, in his goodness and wisdom, to reveal himself and to make known the mystery of his will (cf. Eph. 1:9). His will was that men should have access to the Father, through Christ, the Word made flesh, in the Holy Spirit, and thus become sharers in the divine nature (cf. Eph. 2:18; 2 Pet. 1:4). By this revelation, then, the invisible God (cf. Col. 1:15; 1 Tim. 1:17), from the fullness of his love, addresses men as his friends (cf. Ex. 33:11; Jn. 15:14–15), and moves among them (cf. Bar. 3:38), in order to invite and receive them into his own company.

DV 6 | By divine Revelation God wished to manifest and communicate both himself and the eternal decrees of his will concerning the salvation of mankind. He wished, in other words, 'to share with us divine benefits which entirely surpass the powers of the human mind to understand'.

It will be seen that God's revelation of himself and his will that man should be saved constitute a single act on his part, to which mankind – the human family in the Church – responds with knowledge of God in the mystery of his inner being and also knowledge of salvation. This is brought about by knowledge of God's 'mysterious design', revealed to man at the same time as his revelation of himself. God revealed himself not only in order that all men should know him as Father, Son and Holy Spirit in the unity of the Godhead, but also in order that through the Son – the Word of God made flesh – they might, in the Holy Spirit, have access to the Father and become sharers in the divine nature, that is in the Godhead itself. The work of salvation signifies a particular union with God, or rather a communion which is mysterious and at the same time profoundly real. This is the realism of grace in which God, in his superabundant love, adopts man as his son and lives with him as a friend. Thus revelation is not only the manifestation of the mystery of God, but is also an invitation, by accepting which man participates in the work of salvation.

The consciousness of the Church is closely bound up with consciousness of salvation. The Church confesses the truth of a God who saves, and this truth complements that of God as the Creator. Awareness of salvation is, as it were, super-imposed on awareness of creation, which it penetrates through and through, and it is the true response to the mystery of the most holy Trinity. This truth of faith which enables man to perceive thoroughly the transcendent reality of the divine being constitutes, we may say, the acme of the Church's consciousness. Vatican II expressed itself very clearly on this point. Through the truth of faith concerning the Holy Trinity the Church not only comes close to the most intimate mystery of God but also to its own mystery. This is confirmed by the very title of Chapter I of the Constitution *Lumen Gentium*, viz. 'The Mystery of the Church'. This consciousness on the Church's part results, we may say, from the manner in which God has revealed himself, as a unity and yet a community of persons. In accepting this revelation men are not only con-fronted with a reality which is God in himself, but at the same time find that they have been led into the depths of this mysterious, supernatural reality and thus that their vocation is to be united with God.

Perhaps at this point it would be best simply to quote the first paragraphs of *Lumen Gentium* concerning the divine unity of the Father, the Son and the Holy Spirit not only in the transcendence of divinity but also in the fullness of revelation which constitutes the mystery of the Church:

LG 2 | The eternal Father, in accordance with the utterly gratuitous and mysterious design of his wisdom and goodness, created the whole universe, and chose to raise up men to share in his own divine life; and when they had fallen in Adam, he did not abandon them, but at all times held out to them the means of salvation, bestowed in consideration of Christ, the Redeemer 'who is the image of the invisible God, the firstborn of every creature' (Col. 1:15) and predestined before time began 'to become conformed to the image of his Son, that he should be firstborn among many brethren' (Rom. 8:29). He determined to call together in a holy Church those who should believe in Christ.

LG 3   The Son, accordingly, came, sent by the Father who, before the foundation of the world, chose us and predestined us in him for adoptive sonship. For it is in him that it pleased the Father to restore all things (cf. Eph. 1:4–5 and 10). To carry out the will of the Father Christ inaugurated the kingdom of heaven on earth and revealed to us his mystery; by his obedience he brought about our redemption. The Church – that is, the kingdom of Christ – already present in mystery, grows visibly through the power of God in the world.

LG 4   When the work which the Father gave the Son to do on earth (cf. Jn. 17:4) was accomplished, the Holy Spirit was sent on the day of Pentecost in order that he might continually sanctify the Church, and that, consequently, those who believe might have access through Christ in one Spirit to the Father (cf. Eph. 2:18). He is the Spirit of life, the fountain of water springing up to eternal life (cf. Jn. 4:47; 7:38–9). To men, dead in sin, the Father gives life through him, until the day when, in Christ, he raises to life their mortal bodies (cf. Rom. 8:10–11). The Spirit dwells in the Church and in the hearts of the faithful, as in a temple (cf. 1 Cor. 3:16; 6:19). In them he prays and bears witness to their adoptive sonship (cf. Gal. 4:6; Rom. 8:15–16 and 26). Guiding the Church in the way of all truth (cf. Jn. 16:13) and unifying her in communion and in the works of ministry, he bestows upon her varied hierarchic and charismatic gifts, and in this way directs her; and he adorns her with his fruits (cf. Eph. 4:11–12; 1 Cor. 12:4; Gal. 5:22). By the power of the Gospel he permits the Church to keep the freshness of youth. Constantly he renews her and leads her to perfect union with her Spouse. For the Spirit and the Bride both say to Jesus, the Lord: 'Come!' (cf. Apoc. 22:17).

This is what Vatican II has to say of the mystery of the divine Trinity and at the same time that of the Church. Here we should refer once again to the principle of integration in order to perceive the direction in which our faith is to be enriched. The revelation of the Father, Son and Holy Spirit has from the beginning oriented the faith of the Church, its teaching and theology, towards the mystery of God. This is eloquently shown by the testimony of the first Councils and by the Creed as it is to this day recited in the Mass. God having revealed himself and unveiled to man the mystery of his own being and the inner life of three Persons in a single divinity, it follows that the basic act of faith, man's fundamental response to God's self-revelation, is the profession of the truth of God 'in himself'. Vatican II endorses this expression of faith, which corresponds to the absolute transcendence of divinity.

But the revelation of the Trinity also gives our faith another expression, which the Council placed at the very outset of its chief document and which it consistently developed throughout its teaching – namely the expression of vocation. God not only revealed himself to man, but at the same time singled him out and called him. This expression of faith thus has its foundation in the very manner in which the divine Trinity revealed itself: a revelation closely linked to the Father's plan for our salvation, and essential to its fulfilment.[1] This may be briefly expressed by saying that God wishes to save man by means of himself, offering him a share in his own divine being. The revelation of this is not merely a verbal declaration but a particular action on God's part in the trinity of Persons, the object of which is to enable man to share in the divine nature and the divine life. In the above passages from *Lumen Gentium* we find expressed in a concise and authentic manner this revelation by the Father, the Son and the Holy Spirit. It constitutes the supernatural order of grace and the mystery of the Church: this is why insight into the mystery of the Trinity is relevant to the consciousness of the Church.

The God who saves is the Father who desires to save man; he is the Son sent by the Father in order to bring about, through his incarnation and human nature, the renewal of all things and above all the adoption of men as sons of God; and finally he is the Holy Spirit who was sent after the Son had accomplished the work entrusted to him by the Father, 'in order that he might continually sanctify the Church ... The Spirit dwells in the Church and in the hearts of the faithful, as in a temple (cf. 1 Cor. 3:16, 6:19). In them he prays and bears witness to their adoptive sonship (cf. Gal. 4:6; Rom. 8:15–16 and 26)' (LG 4). The mystery of the Godhead, the most holy Trinity, lies open to the consciousness of the Church not only as the supreme and complete truth concerning God 'in himself' as it is professed by the Church, but also as the truth concern-

---

[1] When the author uses the term 'faith of profession' he refers to man's response to God's self-revelation, to the truth of God in Himself. 'Faith of vocation' refers to the aspect of faith by which man believes that God has not only revealed himself to man but also chosen and called him. (Italian translator's note.)

ing salvation, to which man is called and invited by God. It is likewise the truth concerning the Father who from eternity begets the Son who is the Word, and who with the Son is the eternal source of the Spirit who is Love. Again, it is the truth concerning the Father who works in human history through the visible incarnation of the Son and the descent of the Holy Spirit, to whom the Council refers as an 'effusion' because he exists in a continuous and invisible manner.

The enrichment of faith in the Holy Trinity, expressed in the teaching of Vatican II, is linked to the reality of the mission of the divine Persons. This mission, addressed to man, constitutes the divine reality of the Church; thanks to it the Church bears in itself the consciousness of salvation and seeks to impart it to every human being, to the whole human family. This consciousness is expressed in one of the first sentences of *Lumen Gentium*:

> LG 1 . . . the Church, in Christ, is in the nature of a sacrament – a sign and instrument, that is, of communion with God and of unity among all men.

It can also be said that this self-knowledge on the Church's part, as expressed by the Council, is the starting-point of the principal road towards the enrichment of the faith which unites the divine reality of the Trinity with the reality of mankind. The reality of mankind is both personal and communal, though in a different way from divine reality. Thus the mission of the Holy Trinity encounters familiar ground, as it were: God comes to save the creature whom he has made like to himself thus preparing the ground for him to accept the divine mission.

Perhaps the most concise expression of the truth concerning the mission of the divine Persons is found in the Decree on the Church's Missionary Activity:

AGD 2 | The Church on earth . . . according to the plan of the Father, has its origin in the mission of the Son and the Holy Spirit. This plan flows from 'fountain-like love,' the love of God the Father. As the principle without principle from whom the Son is generated and from whom the Holy Spirit proceeds through the Son, God in his great and merciful kindness freely creates us and moreover, graciously calls us to share in his life and glory. He generously pours out, and never ceases to pour out, his divine goodness, so that he who is creator of all things might at last become 'all in all' (1 Cor. 15:28), thus simultaneously assuring his own glory and our happiness.

We shall not add any particular exegesis to this text, just as we have not done in previous cases. We are only concerned to outline the principal directions leading to the enrichment of faith as presented in the Council's teaching. The passage quoted from the Decree on Missions is an excellent confirmation of the close union, to which we have already referred, between the 'faith of profession' and the 'faith of vocation'. As regards the faith of vocation, the Council discreetly raised the question of the reason for man's calling. Why is he summoned towards the ultimate reality which is God – the Father, Son and Holy Spirit? Why are the *missiones Divinarum Personarum* addressed to him, and why do these in particular constitute the profoundest divine mystery of the Church? The Church discovers in its own mission the consciousness of salvation through the fundamental comparison of the revealed truth concerning God and that concerning man, a truth which constitutes the perennial deposit of its doctrine and teaching; but the emphasis is new, as was necessary.

Here is a significant statement:

GS 24 | Furthermore, the Lord Jesus, when praying to the Father 'that they may all be one . . . even as we are one' (Jn. 17:21–2), has opened up new horizons closed to human reason by implying that there is a certain parallel between the union existing among the divine persons and the union of the sons of God in truth and love. It follows, then, that if man is the only creature on earth that God has wanted for its own sake, man can fully discover his true self only in a sincere giving of himself.

Man's resemblance to God finds its basis, as it were, in the mystery of the most holy Trinity. Man resembles God not only because of the spiritual nature of his immortal soul but also by reason of his social nature, if by this we understand the fact that he 'cannot fully realize himself except in an act of pure self-giving'. In this way 'union in truth and charity' is the ultimate expression of the community of individuals. This union merits the name of communion (*communio*), which signifies more than community (*communitas*). The Latin word *communio* denotes a relationship between persons that is proper to them alone; and it indicates the good that they do to one another, giving and receiving within that mutual relationship.

The Council did not carry out an analysis of the work of salvation from the point of view of diectly enriching the doctrine of grace by its own magisterium: it left open a wide field for theological and kerygmatic integration. Nevertheless, on the basis of the oldest tradition, it did in a sense rediscover the very poles of the mystery of salvation between which the supernatural operation of grace takes place as an interior event, while at the same time the history of salvation unrolls itself as a succession of what I would call exterior events culminating in the visible Church. This conception and position of Vatican II not only admits the possibility of integration but demands it. None the less, very ancient themes here take on a genuinely new aspect, as appears from the text last quoted. Christ himself suggests to us this resemblance, or metaphysical analogy as we may call it, between God as person and community (i.e., the communion of Persons in the unity of the Godhead) on the one hand and, on the other, man as a person and his vocation towards the community 'in truth and charity' – a community founded on his right to realize himself through self-giving. How eloquent is the statement in *Gaudium et spes* that 'man is the only creature on earth that God has wanted for its own sake', as an end and not a means! The design and work of salvation correspond to this fundamental reality in man. Salvation is both personal and communal, and is realized in and through the community of the Church.

Thus the Council sets us upon the track of the Father's eternal design, a plan inspired by love. The plan is in God and from God, but its traces can be discovered in man's nature and the order of creation itself. It is as if the Council wished to show that by following this track man is capable of discovering his own relationship to the divine and supernatural order, not only after the manner of a likeness seeking its prototype but also on the basis of that encounter in which the consciousness of salvation emerges and is made manifest. God indeed reveals himself to man so as to bring this consciousness to light. Consciousness of salvation is also the fundamental element of the response of faith. The Church considers it an essential part of its mission to mankind, and therefore the Council proclaims in *Gaudium et Spes*: 'It is man himself who must be saved: it is mankind that must be renewed' (GS 3). Awareness of salvation as something once accomplished yet continuously effected by God is the leitmotiv of the Council's teaching. Through this awareness the Church attains eschatological dimensions, looking towards the final encounter with God who calls her and at the same time introduces her into the ever-changing modern world.

Consciousness of salvation means that the Church feels herself closely linked to all that is most intimate and perhaps also most secret in man.

GS 21 | For the Church knows full well that her message is in harmony with the most secret desires of the human heart, since it champions the dignity of man's calling, giving hope once more to those who already despair of their higher destiny. Her message, far from impairing man, helps him to develop himself by bestowing light, life, and freedom. Apart from this message nothing is able to satisfy the heart of man: 'Thou hast made us for thyself, O Lord, and our heart is restless until it rest in thee.'

GS 41 | The Church knows well that God alone, whom it serves, can satisfy the deepest cravings of the human heart, for the world and what it has to offer can never fully content it. It also realizes that man is continually being aroused by the Spirit of God and that he will never be utterly indifferent to religion – a fact confirmed by the experience of ages past and plentiful evidence at the present day. For man will ever be anxious to know, if only in a vague way, what is the meaning of his life, his activity, and his death. The very presence of the Church recalls these problems to his mind. The most perfect answer to these questionings is to be found in God alone, who created man in his own image and redeemed him from sin.

Vatican II sees in revelation the reply to man's eternal questioning. Consciousness of salvation springs from the faith with which we accept God's answer and ourselves reply to him and his self-revelation. This reply of ours is a profession of faith and, as we have already seen, an acceptance of the call which, in the relevation of the most holy Trinity, brings to light that which pervades the hearts and souls of men, including followers of non-Christian religions.

NA 2 | Throughout history even to the present day, there is found among different peoples a certain awareness of a hidden power, which lies behind the course of nature and the events of human life. At times there is present even a recognition of a supreme being, or still more of a Father. This awareness and recognition results in a way of life that is imbued with a deep religious sense. The religions which are found in more advanced civilizations endeavour by way of well-defined concepts and exact language to answer these questions.

The Decree on Missions expresses itself in even more detail on this point:

AGD 3 | This universal plan of God for the salvation of mankind is not carried out solely in a secret manner, as it were, in the minds of men, nor by the efforts, even religious, through which they in many ways seek God in an attempt to touch him and find him, although God is not far from any of us (cf. Acts 17:27); their efforts need to be enlightened and corrected, although in the loving providence of God they may lead one to the true God and be a preparation for the Gospel.

Against this broad background we may perhaps more easily grasp the meaning of the sentence in which Vatican II summed up its view of the vital link between the Church and the Trinity: 'The Church is a people brought into unity from the unity of the Father, the Son and the Holy Spirit' (LG 4). This thought was expressed by fathers of the Church such as St

Cyprian, St Augustine, and St John Damascene, and is now endorsed and corroborated by the Council. In the light of our analysis we can see more clearly how to understand the 'unification' of the People of God through the trinitarian unity of God himself. We know, too, that in the Council's teaching the trinitarian consciousness of the Church is united to the consciousness of salvation.

CHAPTER III

Christ and the consciousness of redemption

The enrichment of our faith to which Vatican II shows the way on the basis of awareness of the Church finds its pivotal point in Jesus Christ; or we should say 'way' rather than 'pivot' since we are concerned with ways of enriching our faith. Thus Christ is the way whereby we are to enrich this faith. Following the Council's teaching, therefore, we propose to analyse the consciousness of redemption which, in the structure of our faith, corresponds to Christ's person and sums up his life, death and resurrection. Redemption is the work of Christ, the Son of God made man; it is the essence of the mission of the second Person of the Trinity whereby God entered visibly into human history and made it a history of salvation. The work of redemption is, as Christ himself said (cf. John 16:7), the explicit condition of the 'mission' of the Holy Spirit, his descent on the day of Pentecost and his continual visitation of the souls of men and the Church. All this is recalled in the 'trinitarian' texts of Vatican II that we have already quoted.

The Conciliar texts treat of redemption itself in a concise manner, recalling merely what is the subject-matter of our faith:

LG 3 | Christ . . . by his obedience brought about our redemption.

LG 2 | The eternal Father . . . created the whole universe, and chose to raise up men to share in his own divine life; and when they had fallen in

> Adam, he did not abandon them, but at all times
> held out to them the means of salvation, bestowed
> in consideration of Christ, the Redeemer.

The work of redemption is always closely linked with the
plan and work of salvation and is in fact its basis, especially
since Adam's fall. That basis is found in God himself, but is
realized in human nature and history.

LG 7 | In the human nature united to himself, the son
of God, by overcoming death through his own
death and resurrection, redeemed man and
changed him into a new creation (cf. Gal. 6:15;
2 Cor. 5:17).

LG 5 | The wonderful works of God among the people
of the Old Testament were but a prelude to the
work of Christ our Lord in redeeming mankind
and giving perfect glory to God. He achieved his
task principally by the paschal mystery of his
blessed passion, resurrection from the dead, and
glorious ascension.

The work of redemption is the work of the Mediator: it is
the concrete form of mediation between God and man, linked
with the mission of Jesus Christ.

AGD 3 | Jesus Christ was sent into the world as the true
Mediator between God and men.

As Mediator, Christ is the redeemer of the world, that
world 'which in the Christian vision has been created and is
sustained by the love of its maker, which has been freed from
the slavery of sin by Christ, who was crucified and rose again
in order to break the stranglehold of the evil one, so that it
might be fashioned anew according to God's design and
brought to its fulfilment' (GS 2). This text has already been
quoted in the chapter on the consciousness of creation; we
repeat it here because from the viewpoint of Vatican II the

consciousness of creation is closely linked with the consciousness of redemption.

> GS 41 | . . . it is the same God who is at once saviour and
> creator, Lord of human history and of the
> history of salvation.

It is significant that this same Constitution offers us a wider
vision of the work of redemption, just as it did concerning the
work of creation. A deeper analysis reveals, so to speak, the
common origin of both the dogmatic Constitution and its
pastoral counterpart. The world, which is the object of the
work of creation, is also that of redemption; but the redemption of the world was accomplished in the world as *Gaudium
et Spes* describes it: 'the whole human family . . . the theatre of
human history' (GS 2). The world was redeemed by God
made man, and it was redeemed in man. The redemption of
the world is essentially the redemption of man.

> SC 5 | God who 'wills that all men be saved and come
> to the knowledge of the truth' (1 Tim. 2:4) . . .
> when the fullness of time had come sent his Son,
> the Word made flesh, anointed by the Holy
> Spirit, to preach the Gospel to the poor, to heal
> the contrite of heart, to be a bodily and spiritual
> medicine: the Mediator between God and man.
> For his humanity united with the Person of the
> Word was the instrument of our salvation.

The consciousness of redemption runs like a broad stream
through the magisterium of Vatican II, and is addressed to
all those who seek from it an enrichment of their faith. We
shall analyse this consciousness in its two complementary
aspects, as it is delineated in the two principal documents of
Vatican II.

The redemption of the world continues in the Church.
However, in the light of the Conciliar texts we shall consider
it first as a reality that is constantly presented to the world

and to man in the world: and here the Constitution *Gaudium et Spes* will be our chief guide. Afterwards we shall consider in what way the reality of redemption continues in the Church, and our chief guide will then be the Constitution *Lumen Gentium*. In both aspects the reality of redemption is closely linked with Jesus Christ: the Council expresses anew the faith of the whole Church in Christ, and on the basis of this profession it enriches our consciousness of redemption.

1. *Redemption as a reality constantly directed towards man in the world*

It may seem surprising that we turn our attention first towards the world which appears to be outside the Church, taking as our guide the pastoral dogmatic Constitution *Gaudium et Spes*; but on reflection it will be seen that this document completes the Constitution *Lumen Gentium* on the Church not only by being directed to what is 'outside' but also because it reveals what the Church essentially is, and displays the dynamism of the Church's mystery with greater fullness. The redemptive work of Jesus Christ which determines the inmost nature of the Church is in fact the work of the redemption of the world. Without the Constitution *Gaudium et Spes*, which speaks of the Church in the modern world, we should lack that dimension of our faith in redemption and in the Church, and that orientation of its enrichment.

The pastoral Constitution not only teaches us in a new way the truth concerning the redemption of the world and of man in the world (as it likewise teaches the truth about creation), but also enables us to see this truth in the wide context of modern life. In a sense it 'actualizes' the truth of redemption by bringing it close to the experience of modern man. In this the Council follows the example of St Paul, who likewise related the truth of redemption to the experience of men of his day, making use of his observation of their lives and also sometimes of introspection; and in that case the consciousness of redemption was united with the inner experience of the Apostle himself. The Conciliar document cannot go so far, since it belongs to a different literary genre, but the direction in which the consciousness of redemption is formed is very similar.

From this point of view we should re-read the full expository introduction to *Gaudium et Spes*:

GS 4 | At all times the Church carries the responsibility of reading the signs of the time and of interpreting them in the light of the Gospel, if it is to carry out its task. In language intelligible to every generation, she should be able to answer the ever recurring questions which men ask about the meaning of this present life and of the life to come, and how one is related to the other. We must be aware of and understand the aspirations, the yearnings, and the often dramatic features of the world in which we live.

It is impossible to quote here the whole of that introduction, which is more than a simple description of 'the situation of man in the world today', as the sub-title has it. It is both an analysis and a synthesis illustrating facts already known from other sources, as commonplaces of present-day information and understanding of man and the world. These facts have been studied with the utmost thoroughness. As we also read:

GS 9 | These claims are but the sign of a deeper and more widespread aspiration. Man as an individual and as a member of society craves a life that is full, autonomous, and worthy of his nature as a human being; he longs to harness for his own welfare the immense resources of the

> modern world. Among nations there is a growing movement to set up a worldwide community.
>
> In the light of the foregoing factors there appears the dichotomy of a world that is at once powerful and weak, capable of doing what is noble and what is base, disposed to freedom and slavery, progress and decline, brotherhood and hatred. Man is growing conscious that the forces he has unleashed are in his own hands and that it is up to him to control them or be enslaved by them. Here lies the modern dilemma.

The text quoted is only a kind of summary, and it is worth looking at earlier paragraphs of the document which present particular elements of the analysis more clearly. We shall not do so here, but will follow the document as it treats of the profoundest questions concerning mankind: those perennial questions, which confirm the essential continuity of man's condition in the world, despite the mutability of the external factors of his existence. The essential point is the profundity of these questions, like a probe inserted into depths of the reality of man and man's existence in the world. It is vital to reach the fundamental depths to which *Gaudium et Spes* leads us; and it can be stated that these depths are comparatively easy to reach by an ordinary exertion of any man's powers of thought.

GS 10 | The dichotomy affecting the modern world is, in fact, a symptom of the deeper dichotomy that is in man himself. He is the meeting point of many conflicting forces. In his condition as a created being he is subject to a thousand shortcomings, but feels untrammelled in his inclinations and destined for a higher form of life. Torn by a welter of anxieties he is compelled to choose

> between them and repudiate some among them.
> Worse still, feeble and sinful as he is, he often
> does the very thing he hates and does not do
> what he wants. And so he feels himself divided,
> and the result is a host of discords in social life.

This is not only a description of man's condition in the modern world, and nor were these found in St Paul's letters, especially the Epistle of the Romans which is also mentioned here. The descriptive method is useful at the outset but is no longer sufficient in a further analysis; it may even give rise to a certain alienation, if by this one understands talking about essentially human phenomena without referring them to their cause which is man himself. Hence the necessity of a deeper analysis of man as the cause of these phenomena. *Gadium et Spes* performs this analysis twice: first in the introduction, and secondly in the first chapter of Part 1. Here we shall have to refer to both, bearing in mind that the analysis in the first chapter is more of a systematic summary, while the introduction is more narrative and existential in its approach. Each analysis in its own way serves to present the person of Jesus Christ and to re-examine the mystery of redemption.

The redemption of the world by God in Jesus Christ corresponds, so to speak, to the twofold human reality in which man's dignity and his vocation to all that enhances that dignity is cut across by human weakness and sin.

GS 12 | But what is man? He has put forward, and
> continues to put forward, many views about
> himself, views that are divergent and even
> contradictory. Often he either sets himself up
> as the absolute measure of all things, or debases
> himself to the point of despair. Hence his doubt
> and his anguish. The Church is keenly sensitive
> to these difficulties. Enlightened by divine revela-
> tion she can offer a solution to them by which the
> true state of man may be outlined, his weakness

> explained, in such a way that at the same time
> his dignity and his vocation may be perceived
> in their true light.

At the centre of this response on the Church's part is the mystery of redemption: the work of Jesus Christ that is continually being effected in the Church and, through the Church, in mankind and the world. The Council is aware that many men, for various reasons, refuse to accept this response. For some the reason lies in practical materialism and the consumer-oriented mentality; for others it lies in extreme poverty. There are some 'whose hopes are set on a genuine and total emancipation of mankind through human effort alone and who look forward to some future earthly paradise where all the desires of their hearts will be fulfilled' (GS 10). Finally there are those who see no meaning in human existence. It is clear how different are the answers that man offer to other men, and it is clear that some of them are no answers at all.

GS 21 | Meanwhile, every man remains a question to
       | himself, one that is dimly perceived and left
       | unanswered. For there are times, especially in
       | the major events of life, when no man can
       | altogether escape from such self-questioning.
       | God alone, who calls man to deeper thought and
       | to more humble probing, can fully and with
       | complete certainty supply an answer to this
       | questioning.

The answer that God offers to men in Jesus Christ takes account of the profoundest questions to which men must continually revert.

GS 10 | What is man? What is the meaning of suf-
       | fering, evil, death, which have not been eli-
       | minated by all this progress? What is the
       | purpose of these achievements, purchased at so

> high a price? What can man contribute to
> society? What can he expect from it? What
> happens after this earthly life is ended?

Taking up once again these fundamental questions, 'the Council . . . proposes to speak to all men in order to unfold the mystery that is man' (GS 10) in the light of Christ.

> GS 10 | The Church believes that Christ, who died and
> was raised for the sake of all, can show man the
> way and strengthen him through the Spirit in
> order to be worthy of his destiny: nor is there
> any other name under heaven given among men
> by which they can be saved. The Church likewise
> believes that the key, the centre and the purpose
> of the whole of man's history is to be found in
> its Lord and Master. She also maintains that
> beneath all that changes there is much that is
> unchanging, much that has its ultimate founda-
> tion in Christ, who is the same yesterday, and
> today, and forever.

We have quoted this text in full so as not to divide the profession of faith in Christ that it contains. We shall return in due course to the second part of that profession, but here we must emphasize the consciousness of redemption that is clearly expressed in it. Redemption is the answer to man's perennial questioning, but not only in the sense that it explains 'the mystery of man'. Redemption at the same time offers man a source of enlightenment and strength to respond to his own supreme vocation. Christ, who died for all and rose from the dead, can give every man this light and strength by means of his Spirit – such is the Church's belief. The work of redemp-tion is identified with the paschal mystery of the Redeemer, followed not only by the descent of the Holy Spirit on the historic day of Pentecost but also by his descent throughout time. It is he who endows men directly with supernatural light and strength, and his work is universal in its scope.

GS 10 | ... the Council ... proposes to speak to all men in order to unfold the mystery that is man.

The mystery of redemption, closely linked with Jesus Christ, his life, death and resurrection, is the central reality of our faith. Here Vatican II offers a great contribution to the enrichment of faith from the point of view of consciousness of redemption. This central Christian reality is presented to man in such a way that, following the expression of *Gaudium et Spes*, we can perceive a specific kind of anthropocentrism emerging through the Christocentrism which the Constitution reflects so clearly.

GS 22 | In reality it is only in the mystery of the Word made flesh that the mystery of man truly becomes clear. For Adam, the first man, was a type of him who was to come, Christ the Lord. Christ the new Adam, in the very revelation of the mystery of the Father and of his love, fully reveals man to himself and brings to light his most high calling.

We seem here to have reached a key point in the Council's thought. The revelation of the mystery of the Father and his love in Jesus Christ reveals man to man, and gives the ultimate answer to the question, 'What is man?' This answer cannot be separated from the problem of man's vocation: man confirms his identity by accepting that vocation and making it a reality.

Through Jesus Christ and through the mystery of redemption there runs continuously towards man the intensive current of that faith of vocation in which he must recognize himself and his central position in God's eternal plan, the plan of love that has opened itself upon the world. The consciousness of redemption relates to the whole man, to his inward reality as much as his situation in the external world.

GS 14 | Man is not deceived when he regards himself as superior to bodily things and as more than just a speck of nature or a nameless unit in the city of man. For by his power to know himself in the depths of his being he rises above the whole universe of mere objects. When he is drawn to think about his real self he turns to those deep recesses of his being where God who probes the heart awaits him, and where he himself decides his own destiny in the sight of God. So when he recognizes in himself a spiritual and immortal soul, he is not being led astray by false imaginings that are due to merely physical or social causes. On the contrary, he grasps what is profoundly true in this matter.

This orientation towards man's inner being enables us to discover, as is made clear in *Gaudium et Spes*, the fundamental elements of man's spiritual nature which constitute the dignity of the human person: knowledge, conscience and freedom. By way of this analysis man discovers his own vocation, which is not only confirmed by God through revelation but is also continually being renewed. 'The ferment of the Gospel has aroused and continues to arouse in the hearts of men an unquenchable thirst for human dignity' (GS 26).

This strong statement in a sense sums up the whole reflection of faith on man's situation in the modern world. The consciousness of redemption is close to everything in which man's dignity is reflected in spite of his weakness. Thanks to redemption, man can and must strive towards his own dignity even along the tortuous and difficult paths that lead through his own heart.

GS 13 | For when man looks into his own heart he finds that he is drawn towards what is wrong and sunk in many evils which cannot come from his good creator. Often refusing to acknowledge

> God as his source, man has also upset the relationship which should link him to his last end; and at the same time he has broken the right order that should reign within himself as well as between himself and other men and all creatures.
>
> Man therefore is divided in himself. As a result, the whole life of men, both individual and social, shows itself to be a struggle, and a dramatic one, between good and evil, between light and darkness. Man finds that he is unable of himself to overcome the assaults of evil successfully, so that everyone feels as though bound by chains. But the Lord himself came to free and strengthen man, renewing him inwardly and casting out the 'prince of this world' (Jn. 12:31), who held him in the bondage of sin. For sin brought man to a lower state, forcing him away from the completeness that is his to attain.

Thus redemption, the work of Christ which gives a Christo-centric dimension to the life of mankind in the Church, is, in this same dimension, profoundly anthropocentric- in every man and in humanity as a whole it stands between good and evil, sin and salvation. Redemption is from sin which degrades man, and in this redemption – in its essence and effects – we find the fundamental and inexhaustible means by which man is restored to his proper value.

The consciousness of this restoration of man's value by Christ is an integral element of faith, linked to the very mystery of the incarnation of God made man.

GS 22 | He who is the 'image of the invisible God' (Col. 1:15), is himself the perfect man who has restored in the children of Adam that likeness to God which had been disfigured ever since the first sin. Human nature, by the very fact that it was assumed, not absorbed, in him, has been raised in us also to a dignity beyond compare. For, by his incarnation, he, the son of God, has in a certain way united himself with each man. He worked with human hands, he thought with a human mind. He acted with a human will, and with a human heart he loved. Born of the Virgin Mary, he has truly been made one of us, like to us in all things except sin.

AGD 3   Since he is God, all the fullness of the divine nature dwells in him bodily (Col. 2:9); as man he is the new Adam, full of grace and truth (Jn. 1:14), who has been constituted head of a restored humanity. So the Son of God entered the world by means of a true incarnation that he might make men sharers in the divine nature; though rich, he was made poor for our sake, that by his poverty we might become rich (2 Cor. 8:9). The Son of man did not come to be served, but to serve and to give his life as a ransom for many, that is for all (cf. Mk. 10:45). The fathers of the Church constantly proclaim that what was not assumed by Christ was not healed. Now Christ took a complete human nature just as it is found in us poor unfortunates, but one that was without sin (cf. Heb. 4:15; 9:28).

The incarnation of the Son of God was the beginning of redemption, which in due time fulfilled the essential purpose of the incarnation. Accordingly the restoration of man's value, the elevation of the human nature of each one of us to supernatural dignity is accomplished through participation in redemption.

GS 22 | Conformed to the image of the Son who is the firstborn of many brothers, the Christian man receives the 'first fruits of the Spirit' (Rom. 8:23) by which he is able to fulfil the new law of love. By this Spirit, who is the 'pledge of our inheritance' (Eph. 1:14), the whole man is inwardly renewed, right up to the 'redemption of the body' (Rom. 8:23). 'If the Spirit of him who raised Jesus from the dead dwells in you, he who raised Christ Jesus from the dead will give life to your mortal bodies also through his Spirit who dwells in you' (Rom. 8:11).

The pouring forth of the Holy Spirit is a fruit of the Paschal mystery of Jesus Christ: a fruit which lasts for ever, the everlasting fulfilment of the work of redemption. The Christian is aware of this through faith, and this awareness determines his attitude towards the 'dramatic struggle between good and evil' and the 'enigma of his human condition', which is 'most shrouded in doubt' by the mystery of death (GS 18). Thus we read:

GS 22 | The Christian is certainly bound both by need and by duty to struggle with evil through many afflictions and to suffer death; but, as one who has been made a partner in the paschal mystery, and as one who has been configured to the death of Christ, he will go forward, strengthened by hope, to the resurrection.

The work of redemption is universal: it extends and fructifies more widely than men realize. All of us are involved in the paschal mystery of Jesus Christ.

GS 22 | All this holds true not for Christians only but also for all men of good will in whose hearts grace is active invisibly. For since Christ died for all, and since all men are in fact called to one and the same destiny, which is divine, we must hold that the Holy Spirit offers to all the possibility of being made partners, in a way known to God, in the paschal mystery.

The universality of redemption throws into still greater prominence the intrinsic anthropological content, the 'mystery of man' which, through the mystery of Jesus Christ, constitutes one of the principle directions of the enrichment of faith that springs from the Council's teachings.

GS 22 | Such is the nature and the greatness of the mystery of man as illuminated for the faithful by the Christian revelation. It is therefore through Christ, and in Christ, that light is thrown on the riddle of suffering and death which, apart from his Gospel, overwhelms us. Christ has risen again, destroying death by his death, and has given life abundantly to us so that, becoming sons in the Son, we may cry out in the Spirit: Abba, Father!

Following step by step the magisterium of the Council which dwelt on this subject especially in *Gaudium et Spes*, we arrive at a profound consciousness of redemption as a reality presented to man. The sins of mankind, both personal and social, the whole *mysterium iniquitatis* and all the sinfulness and weakness of human nature constitute the object of redemption. It is, however, clear from the texts quoted that redemption is not confined to this multiform negative aspect but that it also emphasizes human values and human dignity. In Jesus Christ, God enters human history to reveal himself to man and at the same time to reveal the inmost depths of human nature. In the light of the Council's teaching redemption is seen to be a real though mysterious thing, a soil in which values – above all human values – may grow and flourish. We must likewise refer this indirectly to other values, taking into account that they too are subjectively linked with man.

> GS 11 | ... the Council intends first of all to assess those values which are most highly prized today and to relate them to their divine source. For such values, in so far as they stem from the natural talents given to man by God, are exceedingly good. Not seldom, however, owing to corruption of the human heart, they are distorted through lack of due order, so that they need to be set right.

For this reason 'it remains each man's duty to safeguard the notion of the human person as a totality in which predominate values of intellect, will, conscience and brotherhood, since these values were established by the Creator and wondrously restored and elevated by Christ' (GS 61).

Gaudium et Spes teaches in particular how the redemption of man by Christ brings out the value of the human community and of the multiform activities of man in the world. The Constitution is also heedful of the values of marriage and family life, culture, socio-economic life, politics, and international relations, which are in harmony with the work of Jesus Christ. A correct and thoroughgoing study of these chapters of the pastoral Constitution, which perhaps throw into greater prominence the ethical aspect of the problems of which it treats, also presupposes the whole world of values that the Christian perceives in the light of faith permeated by the mystery of redemption, or, as we may say, in the light of the paschal faith.

So as not to multiply quotations, we shall concentrate only on passages from Chapter III of Part I.

> GS 37 | The whole of man's history has been the story of dour combat with the powers of evil, stretching, so our Lord tells us, from the very dawn of

history until the last day. Finding himself in the midst of the battlefield man has to struggle to do what is right, and it is at great cost to himself, and aided by God's grace, that he succeeds in achieving his own inner integrity . . . To the question of how this unhappy situation can be overcome, Christians reply that all these human activities, which are daily endangered by pride and inordinate self-love, must be purified and perfected by the cross and resurrection of Christ. Redeemed by Christ and made a new creature by the Holy Spirit, man can, indeed he must, love the things of God's creation: it is from God that he has received them, and it is as flowing from God's hand that he looks upon them and reveres them. Man thanks his divine benefactor for all these things, he uses them and enjoys them in a spirit of poverty and freedom: thus he is brought to a true possession of the world, as having nothing yet possessing everything: 'All [things] are yours; and you are Christ's; and Christ is God's' (1 Cor. 2:22–3).

GS 38   Constituted Lord by his resurrection and given all authority in heaven and on earth, Christ is now at work in the hearts of men by the power of his Spirit; not only does he arouse in them a desire for the world to come but he quickens, purifies, and strengthens the generous aspirations of mankind to make life more humane and conquer the earth for this purpose.

AGD 8   . . . all have need of Christ who is the model, master, liberator, saviour, and giver of life.

AGD 7   And thus, finally, the intention of the creator in creating man in his own image and likeness will be truly realized, when all who possess human nature, and have been regenerated in Christ through the Holy Spirit, gazing together on the glory of God, will be able to say 'Our Father'.

Many other passages could be quoted from the Council's magisterium, but in the light of those quoted here it is clear that the implementation of Vatican II must take the form of deepening awareness of redemption as a reality profoundly and universally open to mankind and to the world – profoundly, because it penetrates the most intimate secrets of the human soul, and universally, because it permeates every scale of values by which man is linked to the world. For this very reason the redemption accomplished by Jesus Christ is the redemption of the world. And it is this aspect of faith that has been especially enriched by the Council's teaching. This enrichment might be described as 'paschal' in view of the texts quoted and of many others, including the basic theme of the Constitution on the Sacred Liturgy that through the liturgy, especially in the divine sacrifice of the Eucharist, 'the work of our redemption is accomplished' (SC 2).

The 'paschal' enrichment of faith consists in accepting the mystery of Christ as it was announced from the beginning, and in so applying it to man in every dimension of his being as to reveal his deepest truth and value. The paschal mystery, as the mystery of the Cross, has full power to judge and convert human hearts (*scrutatio cordium*), and at the same time the Council shows how much room there is in that mystery for man's authentic value and all the values connected with him. It is almost a reflection of the Resurrection, which always and in every way shines through the Sacrifice – thus instilling hope into the minds of Christians, not only in the eschatological sense but also in the temporal dimension in every one of its aspects.

2. *Redemption as a reality permanently at work in the Church*

LG 5 | When Jesus, having died on the cross for men, rose again from the dead, he was seen to be constituted as Lòrd, the Christ, and as Priest for ever (cf. Acts 2:36; Heb. 5:6; 7:17–21), and he poured out on his disciples the Spirit promised by the Father (cf. Acts 2:23). Henceforward the Church, endowed with the gifts of her founder and faithfully observing his precepts of charity, humility and self-denial, receives the mission of proclaiming and establishing among all peoples the kingdom of Christ and of God, and she is, on earth, the seed and the beginning of that kingdom. While she slowly grows to maturity, the Church longs for the completed kingdom and, with all her strength, hopes and desires to be united in glory with her king.

Redemption as a reality which is always open to man and to the world, and always offered to man as if for the first time – such is the redemption which abides in the Church. It is the meeting-place of the two dimensions clearly described by Vatican II – the vertical dimension constantly extends into the horizontal and transforms it again into the vertical. The concept of the People of God has entered the mind of the Church in a dominant fashion. A close analysis of the Council's teaching will show how this concept operates as regards the consciousness of redemption, that is to say how, against the background of that consciousness, the whole realism of faith (which is in accordance with Conciliar auto-determination of the Church) is manifested. Indeed 'That messianic people has as its head Christ, "who was delivered up for our sins and rose again for our justification" (Rom. 4:25)' (LG 9). Christ as the head of the Church influences the whole complex mechanism of its body; by his redemption of us he penetrates the Church and unceasingly fills its mystic body with life. According to this ancient Pauline analogy we can understand how the reality of redemption abides permanently in the Church. 'The Son of God, . . . communicating his Spirit, mystically constitutes as his body those brothers of his who are called together from every nation'.

LG 7 | In that body the life of Christ is communicated to those who believe and who, through the sacraments, are united in a hidden and real way to Christ in his passion and glorification. Through baptism we are formed in the likeness of Christ: 'For in one Spirit we were all baptized into one body' (1 Cor. 12:13) . . . The head of this body is Christ. He is the image of the invisible God and in him all things came into being. He is before all creatures and in him all things hold together. He is the head of the body which is the Church. He is the beginning, the firstborn from the dead, that in all things he might hold the primacy (cf. Col. 1:15–18). By the greatness of his power he rules heaven and earth, and with his all-surpassing perfection and activity he fills the whole body with the riches of his glory (cf. Eph. 1:18–23).

All the members must be formed in his likeness, until Christ be formed in them (cf. Gal. 4:19). For this reason we, who have been made like to him, who have died with him and risen with him, are taken up into the mysteries of his life,

until we reign together with him (cf. Phil. 3:21;
2 Tim. 2:11; Eph. 2:6; Col. 2:12, etc.). On
earth, still as pilgrims in a strange land, following in trial and in oppression the paths he trod,
we are associated with his sufferings as the body
with its head, suffering with him, that with him
we may be glorified (cf. Rom. 8:17).

The work of redemption continues 'in us', that is in the
Church; which can also be expressed by saying that the Church
is a permanent redemption, and that the form which redemption took in Christ must almost flow back 'from us' into the
Church. The Church is here understood not merely as an
institution but, far more widely and deeply, in a mystical
sense. In this sense it was founded and is maintained in being
by Christ and by the reality of redemption, which abides and
constantly renews itself in the Church. Thus the consciousness
of redemption move is intimately and directly bound up with
the consciousness of the Church.

This consciousness is expressed in the doctrine of the
Mystical Body of Christ, which Vatican II again recalls and
to which it gives new life. As we read:

LG 7 | From him 'the whole body, supplied and built up
by joints and ligaments, attains a growth that
is of God' (Col. 2:19). He continually provides
in his body, that is, in the Church, for gifts of
ministries through which, by his power, we
serve each other unto salvation so that, carrying
out the truth in love, we may through all things
grow unto him who is our head (cf. Eph. 4:11–16,
Gk.).

In order that we might be unceasingly renewed in him (cf. Eph. 4:23), he has shared
with us his Spirit who, being one and the same in
head and members, gives life to, unifies and

> moves the whole body. Consequently, his work
> could be compared by the Fathers to the function
> that the principle of life, the soul, fulfils in the
> human body.

'Carrying out the truth in love' – that is the aspect of human
activity in which the redemption of Christ bears fruit. This
fruit of redemption has in man an interior and spiritual
dimension in which we must on each occasion discern the
influence of the Holy Spirit as the continuation of that Descent
which completed the paschal mystery of the Redeemer. As
we have already seen, the reality of redemption is constantly
presented to man and always manifests itself in what is good
and valuable, in conquering evil and sin. This widely ramified
process, penetrating the minds and consciences of individuals,
springs from the reality of redemption itself; at the same time
it re-presents and completes it, striking root not only in individuals but also in the community of the Mystical Body which is
thus built up and unceasingly developed. To define the way in
which the reality of redemption abides in the Church we must
first touch on the invisible dimension suggested to us by the
analogy with the Mystical Body. If the matter is thought
through, we may say that the reality of redemption abides
in the Church above all because its effects are realized in man
and in the world. There is a close link between the two aspects
of redemption which we are studying here in accordance
with the principal statements of Vatican II.

The redemption of the world subsists continuously in the
Church, above all thanks to the will of Christ the Redeemer.

AGD 5
> . . . after he had fulfilled in himself the mysteries
> of our salvation and the renewal of all things
> by his death and resurrection, the Lord, who had
> received all power in heaven and on earth (cf.
> Mt. 28:18), founded his Church as the sacrament
> of salvation . . .

Elsewhere we read:

LG 7 | Christ loves the Church as his bride, having been established as the model of a man loving his wife as his own body (cf. Eph. 5:25–8); the Church, in her turn, is subject to her head (Eph. 5:23–4). 'Because in him dwells all the fullness of the Godhead bodily' (Col. 2:9), he fills the Church, which is his body and his fullness, with his divine gifts (cf. Eph. 1:22–3) so that it may increase and attain to all the fullness of God (cf. Eph. 3:19).

To express the manner and degree of Christ's union with the Church, and so to emphasize that Christ's redemption lives on in the Church, Vatican II refers to the basic analogies in which St Paul expounded this truth of faith, comparing it with the unity of the head and members of the human body and with that of husband and wife in marriage. The two analogies complement each other and are in a sense intertwined. They both indicate the supreme degree of union between Christ and the Church – obviously without compromising their particular attributes – which at the same time determines the profound and efficacious indwelling of the reality of redemption in the Church.

The union of Christ with the Church derives from the Redeemer's will. The Church for its part tries to do all it can to live in that union and preserve the gift of redemption with which Christ endowed it from the beginning.

LG 8 | Just as Christ carried out the work of redemption in poverty and oppression, so the Church is called to follow the same path if she is to communicate the fruits of salvation to men. Christ Jesus, 'though he was by nature God . . . emptied himself, taking the nature of a slave' (Phil. 2:6, 7), and 'being rich, became poor' (2 Cor. 8:9) for our sake. Likewise, the Church, although she needs human resources to carry out her mission, is not set up to seek earthly glory, but to proclaim, and this by her own example, humility and self-denial. Christ was sent by the Father 'to bring good news to the poor . . . to heal the contrite of heart' (Lk. 4:18), 'to seek and to save what was lost' (Lk. 19:10). Similarly, the Church encompasses with her love all those who are afflicted by human misery and she recognizes in those who are poor and who suffer, the image of her poor and suffering founder. She does all in her power to relieve their need and in them she strives to serve Christ. Christ, 'holy, innocent and undefiled' (Heb. 7:26) knew nothing of sin (2 Cor. 5:21), but came only to expiate the sins of the people (cf. Heb. 2:17). The Church, however, clasping sinners to her bosom, at once holy and always in need of purification, follows constantly the path of penance and renewal.

These words not only bear witness that the Church, while deeply feeling its own human weakness, endeavours to imitate Christ; they also show that the Church feels itself to be permeated and fashioned by the mystery of redemption, and considers that mystery as a reality endowing the Church with inner strength and vitality. The mind of the Church is deeply impregnated with the consciousness of redemption, and the Church cannot for an instant separate itself either from its aspect of 'passion' or from that of 'resurrection'.

LG 8 | The Church, 'like a stranger in a foreign land, presses forward amid the persecutions of the world and the consolations of God,' announcing the cross and death of the Lord until he comes (cf. Cor. 11:26). But by the power of the risen

Lord she is given strength to overcome, in
patience and in love, her sorrows and her
difficulties, both those that are from within
and those that are from without, so that she
may reveal in the world, faithfully, however
darkly, the mystery of her Lord until, in the
consummation, it shall be manifested in full
light.

The Decree on Missions has this to say concerning the
Church's principal task:

AGD 5 | Since this mission continues and, in the course
of history, unfolds the mission of Christ, who
was sent to evangelize the poor, the Church,
urged on by the Spirit of Christ, must walk the
road Christ himself walked, a way of poverty
and obedience, of service and self-sacrifice
even to death, a death from which he emerged
victorious by his resurrection. So it was that the
apostles walked in hope and by much trouble
and suffering filled up what was lacking in the
sufferings of Christ for his body, which is the
Church. Often, too, the seed was the blood of
Christians.

Meditating in the spirit of Vatican II on redemption as a
reality continuously present in the Church and maintaining
it in being, we must also have in mind the link between the
Mystical Body of Christ and the People of God. The Church
is at the same time both one and the other. In *Lumen Gentium*
the picture of the Church as the People of God is perhaps the
more prominent. But in the Council's teaching as a whole we
find sufficient reason to affirm that the People of God is also
the Mystical Body of Christ, and to throw light on this
theological identity. It is the reality of redemption that helps
us to do so. The consciousness of redemption is logically

prior to the consciousness of the People of God: this will appear more clearly when we come to talk of the latter. But the consciousness of redemption had to be analysed first, in accordance with the logic of faith and, in turn, as a condition of the enrichment of faith. That logic requires that, in order to profit from the conciliar magisterium, we should first address our minds to the reality of redemption; following that magisterium, we should first explore fully the consciousness of redemption and only afterwards consider the reality of the People of God. If we did not do this, or if we proceeded too rapidly from the theme of redemption to that of the People of God, the latter would not appear to us in the fullness of its significance. In this case one might speak here of a unilateral 'sociologization' of the concept, which itself is laden with enormous theological potential. One might also speak of the vertical dimension being overshadowed by the horizontal. Certainly it is a great merit of Vatican II to have revealed that horizontal dimension and to have given the concept of the People of God so central a place in its teaching, provided we keep in mind the theological richness which is proper to it, and which derives from the fact that the People of God is contained in the Mystical Body of Christ and vice versa.

Redemption is an ever-present reality in the Church also because the latter is the permanent heir to the Redeemer's threefold mission.

LG 13 | It was for this purpose that God sent his Son, whom he appointed heir of all things (cf. Heb. 1:2), that he might be teacher, king and priest of all, the head of the new and universal People of God's sons.

Thus Christ is head of the Mystical Body and head of the people of the sons of God as their master, king and priest. The threefold mission and triple office of the Redeemer is closely linked with the work of redemption and abides in the Church because the People of God shares continuously in the prophetic, priestly and kingly office of Christ. This participation is what ensures the continuity of the work of redemption in the People of God; it is of tremendous importance for the consciousness of redemption itself and the enrichment of faith in this respect. The threefold mission of Christ, in which the People of God come to share, enables us to define that People more precisely as a messianic one, linked closely with the Messiah's work of redemption.

> SC 6   Just as Christ was sent by the Father so also he sent the apostles, filled with the Holy Spirit. This he did so that they might preach the Gospel to every creature and proclaim that the Son of God by his death and resurrection had freed us from the power of Satan and from death, and brought us into the Kingdom of his Father. But he also willed that the work of salvation which they preached should be set in train through the sacrifice and sacraments, around which the entire liturgical life revolves. Thus by Baptism men are grafted into the paschal mystery of Christ; they die with him, are buried with him, and rise with him. They receive the spirit of adoption as sons 'in which we cry, Abba, Father' (Rom. 8:15) and thus become true adorers such as the Father seeks. In like manner, as often as they eat the Supper of the Lord they proclaim the death of the Lord until he comes.

A special analogy would be needed in order to show how the mission of prophet, priest and king is rooted in the work of redemption accomplished by Jesus Christ, and in what way it gives it its character. The Council's teaching helps us to see this above all from the point of view of the participation of the People of God, and thus not so much in Christ as in the Church. Christ and the reality of redemption abide in the Church thanks to the participation of the People of God in the triple office of Christ. It can be said that the reality of redemption which continues in the Church in a mystic manner as the permanent fruit of the Bridegroom's love for his Bride, and as a mystery of the unity of the Head with its Body, finds expression in the consciousness and attitude of the Church as a People, which inherits the mission of Christ the Redeemer. We shall speak separately of this expression as an integral part of the consciousness of redemption, and we shall revert to it when analysing the attitudes which, in the formation of the Christian life, should, according to Vatican II, correspond to the prophetic, kingly and priestly function of Christ the Lord.

LG 12 | The holy People of God shares also in Christ's prophetic office: it spreads about a living witness to him, especially by a life of faith and love and by offering to God a sacrifice of praise, the fruit of lips praising his name (cf. Heb. 13:15). The whole body of the faithful who have an anointing that comes from the holy one (cf. 1 Jn. 2:20 and 27) cannot err in matters of belief. This characteristic is shown in the supernatural appreciation of the faith (*sensus fidei*) of the whole people, when, 'from the bishops to the last of the faithful' they manifest a universal consent in matters of faith and morals. By this appreciation of the faith, aroused and sustained by the Spirit of truth, the People of God, guided by the sacred teaching authority (*magisterium*), and obeying it, receives not the mere word of men, but truly the word of God (cf. 1 Th. 2:13), the faith once for all delivered to the saints (cf. Jude 3). The People unfailingly adheres to this faith, penetrates it more deeply with right judgment, and applies it more fully in daily life.

And elsewhere:

LG 35 | Christ is the great prophet who proclaimed the kingdom of the Father both by the testimony of his life and by the power of his word. Until the full manifestation of his glory, he fulfils this prophetic office, not only by the hierarchy who teach in his name and by his power, but also by the laity. He accordingly both establishes them as witnesses and provides them with the appreciation of the faith (*sensus fidei*) and the grace of the word (cf. Acts 2:17–18; Apoc. 19:10) so that the power of the Gospel may shine out in daily family and social life.

The sharing of the People of God in the mission of Christ, which is in the first place a prophetic one, goes to show that the reality of redemption continues in the Church. Christ is the Teacher who transmits the word of God to man and, by the power of that word, constructs the community of the People of God in the Church. That community, as we know, is constructed on the basis of the vital participation of all who believe in the prophetic mission of Christ. The word of God, transmitted in and by Christ, becomes the participation of men, whom it binds together and unites. All mankind, as the community of the Church, spread the word of the Gospel and bear witness to it not only by professing the same truth but also by realizing it in their lives. Teaching, which is the function of the hierarchy, joins with the supernatural sense of faith in which the community of believers shares, thus constituting the participation of all God's people in the prophetic mission of Christ. As will be seen, that participation consists both of teaching and of profession, two currents which complement and support each other. The magisterium exercises a directive function in this process, in strict accordance with the Church's hierarchical constitution. But the teaching and profession of faith are united on a single common foundation which is the prophetic mission of Christ and participation therein.

This aspect of the Council's teaching must be emphasized as particularly important for the enrichment of faith, not only as regards its content but as regards its subjective meaning. Faith – its profession and teaching, increased knowledge of it and its fuller realization in life – determines a particular union of each believer with the mission of Christ; not only a passive acceptation, but also a creative continuation of that prophetic mission.

The Council refers several times to the Redeemer's priestly mission and the sharing in it of the People of God in the Church. The teaching of Vatican II enables us to learn more about the truth of the fact that the reality of redemption, accomplished in particular by the sacerdotal act of Christ, continues in a particular manner in the Church through the continuation of Christ's priestly office.

LG 10 | Christ the Lord, high priest taken from among men (cf. Heb. 5:1–5), made the new people 'a kingdom of priests to God, his Father' (Apoc. 1:6; cf. 5:9–10). The baptized, by regeneration and the anointing of the Holy Spirit, are consecrated to be a spiritual edifice and a holy priesthood, that through all works of Christian men they may offer spiritual sacrifices and proclaim the perfection of him who has called them out of darkness into his marvellous light (cf. 1 Pet. 2:4–10). Therefore all the disciples of Christ, persevering in prayer and praising God (cf. Acts 2:42–7), should present themselves as a sacrifice, living, holy and pleasing to God (cf. Rom. 12:1). They should everywhere on earth bear witness to Christ and give an answer to everyone who asks a reason for the hope of an eternal life which is theirs (cf. 1 Pet. 3:15).

Lumen Gentium speaks next of the relationship between the

common priesthood of the faithful and the priesthood of ministers or the hierarchy. We shall revert to this elsewhere, but here we are concerned with what is significant for the whole people of God as regards its participation in Christ's sacerdotal mission.

> LG 11 | The sacred nature and organic structure of the priestly community is brought into operation through the sacraments and the exercise of virtues.

Both *Lumen Gentium* and the Constitution on the Liturgy emphasize the special link between Christ's redemption and the Christian's sacramental life.

> SC 2 | For it is the liturgy through which, especially in the divine sacrifice of the Eucharist, 'the work of our redemption is accomplished,' and it is through the liturgy, especially, that the faithful are enabled to express in their lives and manifest to others the mystery of Christ and the real nature of the true Church.

> SC 7 | The liturgy, then, is rightly seen as an exercise of the priestly office of Jesus Christ. It involves the presentation of man's sanctification under the guise of signs perceptible by the senses and its accomplishment in ways appropriate to each of these signs. In it full public worship is performed by the Mystical Body of Jesus Christ, that is, by the Head and his members.

We do not intend to enter here into the details of this subject, to which we shall return, but only to trace its main feature: the reality of redemption always present in the Church through participation in the priesthood of Christ, the sacramental life of the Church and the liturgy. Within the framework of the whole logic of faith professed and lived, this represents a kind of descending course along which we are to seek the ways of enriching faith that Vatican II has laid down for the future. When we analyse the 'liturgical attitude' which was so carefully elaborated during the Council's proceedings, we must recall that the basis and motivation of this spiritual attitude is awareness of redemption as a reality continually present in the priesthood of Christ, in which the whole People of God has come to share by means of the sacraments of the Church: 'The sacred nature and organic structure of the priestly community is brought into operation through the sacraments and the exercise of virtues' (LG 11).

Thus it is brought into operation by virtues also. Redemption as a permanent reality in the Church manifests itself not only in the sacramental life of Christians but also in their moral life, in Christian morality. Here we are, so to speak, at the point where the divine and human elements merge closely together on the basis of participation in the threefold mission of Christ: for it may be said that morality represents man's contribution in the first instance. It is easy to see that participation in the priesthood of Christ by means of the sacraments is also participation in his prophetic mission, since sacramental life is at the same time the profession and the proclamation of faith. Both contain in themselves the elements of a lively, genuine Christian morality, indissolubly united with sacramental life, as a necessary component and condition of man's sanctification. It seems that this aspect of redemption as a reality ever-present in the Church displays itself above all in the form of participation in the kingly mission of Christ. Thus we read:

LG 36 | Christ, made obedient unto death and because of this exalted by the Father (cf. Ph. 2:8–9), has entered into the glory of his kingdom. All things are subjected to him until he subjects himself and all created things to the Father, so that God

> may be all in all (cf. 1 Cor. 15:27–8). He com-
> municated this power to the disciples that they
> be constituted in royal liberty and, by the self-
> abnegation of a holy life, overcome the reign
> of sin in themselves (cf. Rom. 6:12) – that indeed
> by serving Christ in others they may in humility
> and patience bring their brethren to that king,
> to serve whom is to reign.

The continuation of the above text refers directly to lay
Catholics, in accordance with the title of Chapter IV of *Lumen
Gentium*. The Council teaches that:

LG 36
> The Lord also desires that his kingdom be
> spread by the lay faithful: the kingdom of truth
> and life, the kingdom of holiness and grace, the
> kingdom of justice, love and peace. In this king-
> dom creation itself will be delivered from the
> slavery of corruption into the freedom of the
> glory of the sons of God (cf. Rom. 8:21).

After this comes the precept that the laity should 'impregnate
culture and human works with a moral value' and that 'in
every temporal affair they are to be guided by a Christian
conscience' (LG 36).

Thus participation in the Redeemer's kingly mission is
explicitly presented in the Council's teaching as the source of a
true, living Christian morality. Man bears in his nature, as it
were, a twofold pledge or earnest of that 'kingship' which
Jesus Christ revealed and to which every man is called in Christ,
a kingship consisting in mastery over himself and the world.
Vatican II enables us to look at human and Christian morality
from this point of view, discerning in it the characteristic of
man's 'kingship'. The latter determines man's participation
in the fullness of the reality of redemption and also expresses
the kingly mission of the Redeemer in addition to his prophetic
and priestly mission – a kingly mission which is assumed and

continued, ever anew, in the whole people of God. A more detailed analysis of this subject must wait till later; suffice it here to recall that the Church, in which the reality of redemption abides by the will of Christ himself, is in its deepest nature not only a 'priestly community' but combines the element of sacrifice, proper to a priesthood, with the kingly element of victory, of man's dominion over himself and the world of nature. These two elements are comprised in human and Christian morality: both of them constitute the very root of that morality. Therefore the reality of redemption which abides in the Church through participation in the priestly and kingly mission of the Redeemer finds expression in Christian morality understood in all its fullness and in every aspect: personal and social morality, that of marriage, the family and professional life, the morality of economics and politics – in short, morality in the deepest and fullest sense of the term.

This in fact is one of the ways towards the enrichment of faith as pointed out by the Council, and one of particular importance from the point of view of actual Christian life. The key problem of life as actually lived by Christians is that of the link between faith and morals. The process of the enrichment of faith must also be considered from the point of view of its relation to morality. This is a matter of Christian morality manifesting itself not only in the field of behaviour and its governing norms, but still more in the field of motivation and the influence of *logos* on *ethos*. In this respect it appears that the Council's teaching points a way to which we must return in due course for a deeper analysis of attitudes: for the enrichment of faith also implies the formation of attitudes and of conscience.

In any case the Council has brought out clearly the link between the reality of redemption and morality, in such a way as to give a new impulse to moral theology and Christian pedagogy and, finally, to the practical life of Christians aware of their own faith. In this field too there seems to be an enormous wealth of tradition, in a broad sense of the term, which the Council simply upholds and revivifies by its light. Redemption is the reality which abides constantly in the Church.

LG 3 | As often as the sacrifice of the cross by which 'Christ our Pasch is sacrificed' (1 Cor. 5:7) is celebrated on the altar, the work of our redemption is carried out. Likewise, in the sacrament of the eucharistic bread, the unity of believers, who form one body in Christ (cf. 1 Cor. 10:17), is both expressed and brought about. All men are called to this union with Christ, who is the light of the world, from whom we go forth, through whom we live, and towards whom our whole life is directed.

LG 7 | In that body the life of Christ is communicated to those who believe and who, through the sacraments, are united in a hidden and real way to Christ in his passion and glorification.

3. Mary in the mystery of Christ and the Church

Our thoughts concerning Christ and redemption must be completed by the teaching of Vatican II concerning Christ's Mother. Chapter VIII of *Lumen Gentium* is devoted to 'the blessed Virgin Mary, mother of God, in the mystery of Christ and the Church'. This is an important text for theologians, dealing as it does with relations between ecclesiology and Mariology. In our present study, which is concerned with the enrichment of faith in the ways pointed out by Vatican II, we must first underline the solution chosen by the Council with its decision not to promulgate a separate document concerning Our Lady but to include what would have been the content of such a document in the Dogmatic Constitution on the Church. This in a sense confirms that the mind of the Church is permeated in a special way by the mystery of the Mother of God, which is fully present in the mystery of Christ the Incarnate Word and hence in that of the Mystical Body of Christ. A reading of Chapter VIII of *Lumen Gentium* will show that these mysteries are linked together by the redemptive work that Christ performed not only as the Son of God but as the Son of Mary. Hence, according to the Council's teaching, our thoughts on redemption are the right context in which to contemplate the mystery of the Mother of God.

From its very first words Chapter VIII is imbued with the particular veneration which the Church feels towards Our Lady. Here is a passage from the Introduction:

> **LG 52** Wishing in his supreme goodness and wisdom to effect the redemption of the world, 'when the fullness of time came, God sent his Son, born of a woman . . . that we might receive the adoption of sons' (Gal. 4:4). 'He for us men, and for our salvation, came down from heaven, and was incarnated by the Holy Spirit from the Virgin Mary.' This divine mystery of salvation is revealed to us and continued in the Church, which the Lord established as his body. Joined to Christ the head and in communion with all his saints, the faithful must in the first place reverence the memory 'of the glorious ever Virgin Mary, Mother of God and of our Lord Jesus Christ'.

The central part of the chapter is devoted to the unique participation of the Blessed Virgin in the economy of salvation. This is linked with the historical and eschatological aspect of the Church's consciousness, with which we shall deal later: at that point it will certainly be proper to speak again of the part played by the Mother of God in the development of the story of our salvation. Since the historical and the eschatological aspects meet and merge in the fullness of the economy of salvation, especially as far as Our Lady's share in it is concerned, we shall refer here to a passage which really belongs to a later Chapter (Part II, Chapter V).

LG 55 | The sacred writings of the Old and New Testaments, as well as venerable tradition, show the role of the Mother of the Saviour in the plan of salvation in an ever clearer light and call our attention to it. The books of the Old Testament describe the history of salvation, by which the coming of Christ into the world was slowly prepared. The earliest documents, as they are read in the Church and are understood in the light of a further and full revelation, bring the figure of a woman, Mother of the Redeemer, into a gradually clearer light. Considered in this light, she is already prophetically foreshadowed in the promise of victory over the serpent which was given to our first parents after their fall into sin (cf. Gen. 3:15). Likewise she is the virgin who shall conceive and bear a son, whose name shall be called Emmanuel (cf. Is. 8:14; Mic. 5:2–3; Mt. 1:22–3). She stands out among the poor and humble of the Lord, who confidently hope for and receive salvation from him. After a long period of waiting the times are fulfilled in her, the exalted Daughter of Sion, and the new plan of salvation is established, when the Son of God has taken human nature from her, that he might in the mysteries of his flesh free man from sin.

The figure of the Mother of God is delineated against the background of the history of salvation above all as that of the one who most perfectly sums up in herself the longing of mankind for salvation which can come only from God. The Constitution underlines the primacy of Mary among 'the humble and poor in spirit'; to this primacy of humility and poverty of spirit corresponds a primacy of hope and expectation. The spiritual figure of the Virgin is here described forcefully though in few words. It is she who, more than any other creature, put her trust in God's work as an undeserved gift to mankind, and who was to play a unique part in that work and in the economy of man's salvation.

> LG 56 | The Father of mercies willed that the Incarnation should be preceded by assent on the part of the predestined mother, so that just as a woman had a share in bringing about death, so also a woman should contribute to life. This is pre-eminently true of the Mother of Jesus, who gave to the world the Life that renews all things . . .

This passage underlines the aspect of 'contribution', the fact that Mary not only contributed to life but first of all gave her assent to doing so. In this way the Mother of Christ belongs to the content of our faith and is connected in a special way with the consciousness of redemption. The Conciliar document analyses still more deeply this central theme of Mariology, the mystery of the Incarnation and redemption:

> LG 56 | [The Mother of Christ] was enriched by God with gifts appropriate to such a role. It is no wonder then that it was customary for the Fathers to refer to the Mother of God as all-holy and free from every stain of sin, as though fashioned by the Holy Spirit and formed as a new creature. Enriched from the first instant of her conception with the splendour of an entirely unique holiness, the virgin of Nazareth is hailed by the heralding angel, by divine command, as 'full of grace' (cf. Lk. 1:28), and to the heavenly messenger she replies: 'Behold the handmaid of

the Lord, be it done unto me according to thy word' (Lk. 1:38). Thus Mary, the daughter of Adam, consenting to the word of God, became the Mother of Jesus. Committing herself whole-heartedly and impeded by no sin to God's saving will, she devoted herself totally, as a handmaid of the Lord, to the person and work of her Son, under and with him, serving the mystery of redemption, by the grace of Almighty God.

The way in which Mary was brought by God into the reality of the Incarnation and in which she herself entered into that reality constitutes the first beginning of her participation in the work of redemption. The Conciliar document dwells once again on the words uttered by the Virgin of Nazareth at the Annunciation – we say 'once again' because they have often been meditated upon in the tradition of the Church – and notes that these words bore fruit in the incarnation and Mary's divine motherhood. At the same time these words point to the work of redemption itself, as they express Mary's complete and mature readiness to devote herself to the Person and work of her Son.

LG 56 | Rightly, therefore, the Fathers see Mary not merely as passively engaged by God, but as freely cooperating in the work of man's salvation through faith and obedience. For, as St Irenaeus says, she 'being obedient, became the cause of salvation for herself and for the whole human race'. Hence not a few of the early Fathers gladly assert with him in their preaching: 'the knot of Eve's disobedience was united by Mary's obedience: what the virgin Eve bound through her disbelief, Mary loosened by her faith.' Comparing Mary with Eve, they call her 'Mother of the living,' and frequently claim: 'death through Eve, life through Mary'.

As will be seen, the whole attitude of the ancient and modern Church to the Mother of God is based not only on the exceptional honour due to her divine maternity but also on her awareness of the redemption and her own participation in the work of Christ: she 'cooperated in the work of man's salvation', as the Constitution says. This active cooperation on Mary's part is expressed above all in her obedience. By being thus obedient she did not merely submit passively to the salvific action of the Most Holy Trinity, but with all her life and behaviour embraced it and shared in it: so that our consciousness of redemption must always see the 'maternal act' as united to not only the 'act of Christ' but also 'under and with him', as the Council declares in the passage just quoted.

'This union of the Mother with the Son in the work of salvation is made manifest from the time of Christ's virginal conception up to his death' (LG 57). The Council's teaching illustrates this union by following the incidents of the life of Christ and Our Lady as we find them in Scripture. All-important is the moment of Calvary, which is intimately linked with that of the Annunciation and corresponds fully to Mary's response at that time.

LG 58 | Thus the Blessed Virgin advanced in her pilgrimage of faith, and faithfully persevered in her union with her Son unto the cross, where she stood, in keeping with the divine plan, endured with her only begotten Son the intensity of his suffering, associated herself with his sacrifice in her mother's heart, and lovingly consented to the immolation of this victim which was born of her.

These words definitively explain the faith of the Church expressed in the phrase 'cooperated in the work of man's salvation'. They also clarify to the uttermost the 'maternal act' involved in that obedience which, whether at the Annunciation or at the foot of the Cross, manifested her complete acceptance of the divine plan. The acceptance of the divine economy at the moment when the 'victim born of her' was sacrificed on the Cross is identified with the complete sacrifice of Mary's heart.

With this maternal act – which is linked, as the Council shows us, with the reality of redemption – Mary enters the history of the salvation of mankind as Mother of us all. This was expressed by Christ's own words on the Cross, when 'she was given by the same Christ Jesus . . . as a mother to his disciple, with these words: "Woman, behold thy son" (John 19:26–7)' (LG 58). Again, we find Mary present and participating at the birth of the Church:

> LG 59 | But since it had pleased God not to manifest solemnly the mystery of the salvation of the human race before he would pour forth the Spirit promised by Christ, we see the apostles before the day of Pentecost 'persevering with one mind in prayer with the women and Mary the Mother of Jesus, and with his brethren' (Acts 1:14), and we also see Mary by her prayers imploring the gift of the Spirit, who had already overshadowed her in the Annunciation.

The birth of the Church on the day of Pentecost is, as it were, the continuation of the mystery of the Incarnation which took place in Mary by the operation of the Holy Spirit. Since Vatican II we have also called her Mother of the Church.

> LG 61 | The predestination of the Blessed Virgin as Mother of God was associated with the incarnation of the divine word: in the designs of divine Providence she was the gracious mother of the divine Redeemer here on earth, and above all others and in a singular way the generous

associate and humble handmaid of the Lord. She conceived, brought forth, and nourished Christ, she presented him to the Father in the temple, shared her Son's sufferings as he died on the cross. Thus, in a wholly singular way she cooperated by her obedience, faith, hope and burning charity in the work of the Saviour in restoring supernatural life to souls. For this reason she is a mother to us in the order of grace.

LG 62 | This motherhood of Mary in the order of grace continues uninterruptedly from the consent which she loyally gave at the Annunciation and which she sustained without wavering beneath the cross, until the eternal fulfilment of all the elect. Taken up to heaven she did not lay aside this saving office but by her manifold intercession continues to bring us the gifts of eternal salvation. By her maternal charity, she cares for the brethren of her Son, who still journey on earth surrounded by dangers and difficulties, until they are led into their blessed home. Therefore the Blessed Virgin is invoked in the Church under the titles of Advocate, Helper, Benefactress, and Mediatrix. This, however, is so understood that it neither takes away anything from nor adds anything to the dignity and efficacy of Christ the one Mediator.

Mary's divine maternity is a unique fact in the history of our salvation, closely linked with the incarnation of the Word to which it belongs. But her spiritual maternity in the order of grace goes far beyond that fact, extending as widely as her Son's work of redemption 'until the eternal fulfilment of all the elect' (LG 62). The Mother of God fulfils her universal maternity as a mediatrix in the economy of grace. The

Church professes its faith in that maternal mediation of divine grace, while clearly distinguishing it from the mediation of the Redeemer himself.

LG 62 | No creature could ever be counted along with the Incarnate Word and Redeemer; but just as the priesthood of Christ is shared in various ways both by his ministers and the faithful, and as the one goodness of God is radiated in different ways among his creatures, so also the unique mediation of the Redeemer does not exclude but rather gives rise to a manifold cooperation which is but a sharing in his one source.

The Church does not hesitate to profess this subordinate role of Mary, which it constantly experiences and recommends to the heartfelt attention of the faithful, so that encouraged by this maternal help they may the more closely adhere to the Mediator and Redeemer.

Thus the mediation of the Mother of God is subordinate to the unique mediation of Christ, which alone constitutes the foundation and source of the supernatural economy of grace and salvation. Nevertheless Mary's mediation, as an expression of her spiritual maternity in the order of grace, is universal in its range and is specially efficacious.

The truth concerning the Mother of God and men, which the Church professes and by which it lives, is, it will be seen, most intimately connected with the consciousness of redemption: it is comprised in it, derives from it and leads to it.

LG 60 | In the words of the apostle there is but one mediator: 'for there is but one God and one mediator of God and men, the man Christ Jesus, who gave himself a redemption for all' (1 Tim. 2 : 5–6). But Mary's function as mother of men in no way obscures or diminishes this unique mediation of Christ, but rather shows its power. But the Blessed Virgin's salutary influence on men originates not in any inner necessity but in the disposition of God. It flows forth from the superabundance of the merits of Christ, rests on his mediation, depends entirely on it and draws all its power from it. It does not hinder in any way the immediate union of the faithful with Christ but on the contrary fosters it.

The same can be said regarding the worship that the Church pays to the Mother of God:

LG 66 | This cult, as it has always existed in the Church, for all its uniqueness, differs essentially from the cult of adoration, which is offered equally to the Incarnate Word and to the Father and the Holy Spirit, and it is most favourable to it. The various forms of piety towards the Mother of God, which the Church has approved within the limits of sound and orthodox doctrine, according to the dispositions and understanding of the faithful, ensure that while the mother is honoured, the Son through whom all things have their being (cf. Col. 1:15–16) and in whom it has pleased the Father that all fullness should dwell (cf. Col. 1:19) is rightly known, loved and glorified and his commandments are observed.

From this fullness of God the Son, his Mother has abundantly drawn the 'fullness of grace' that the Church proclaims and praises in her who, having begun her earthly existence as the Immaculate Conception, completed it when she was assumed into heaven.

LG 59 | The Immaculate Virgin, preserved free from all stains of original sin, was taken up body and soul into heavenly glory when her earthly life was over, and exalted by the Lord as Queen over all things, that she might be the more fully conformed to her Son, the Lord of lords (cf. Apoc. 19:16) and conqueror of sin and death.

When describing the ways towards the enrichment of faith which the Council's teaching links with the consciousness of redemption, we used the term 'paschal enrichment'. The same feature may be discovered in the Council's teaching concerning the Mother of God, when it speaks of her maternal participation in the work of Christ and the mission of the Church. Redemption is a reality constantly addressed to mankind and the world, and constantly present in the Church. This reality of redemption brings to light the profoundest truth and most authentic value of man and his life and activity in all its forms. The cross of Christ does not prevent all this but in fact fosters it. Mary shares in a special way in the paschal mystery of Christ came to perfect fulfillment in her, as witness all the mysteries of her life and her vocation; she also shares fully in the work of redemption, which is always directed towards man in the world and also abides constantly in the Church.

This explains the unique position that the Mother of God occupies in the Church's mind. As Vatican II eloquently expresses it:

LG 65 | The Church, therefore, in her apostolic work too, rightly looks to her who gave birth to Christ, who was thus conceived of the Holy Spirit and born of a virgin, in order that through the Church he could be born and increase in the hearts of the faithful. In her life the Virgin has been a model of that motherly love with which all who join in the Church's apostolic mission for the regeneration of mankind should be animated.

The Church of Vatican II sees in the Mother of God a model for itself. We shall return later to this theme of the Council's magisterium.

CHAPTER IV

The consciousness of the Church as the People of God

Thanks to Vatican II, the ancient biblical concept of the People of God has become one of the main elements in the historic process of the enrichment of faith that is associated with the Council. However, the self-awareness of the Church as the People of God presupposes all that has been the object of our study up to this point. Thus the reality of the People of God is rooted first of all in the reality revealed by God, who in a free act of love turns to mankind, to man in the world. The consciousness of the Church as the People of God presupposes awareness of creation, salvation and redemption, and is based on such awareness. Thus the Council propounds the truth concerning the People of God, and it is on this doctrine that the mature faith of the modern Church must be founded. The essential point is that the whole reality of the People of God has its permanent source and origin in God 'who reveals himself'; while, in turn, man's faith and that of humanity determines the reality of the People of God, since it constitutes a reply to God expressed in men's minds and lives.

'Hence the universal Church is seen to be "a people brought into unity from the unity of the Father, the Son and the Holy Spirit" ' (LG 4): we repeat once again this classic quotation, derived from Fathers of the Church, which forms the keystone of the whole construction of *Lumen Gentium*. This mystical union with the unity of the Trinity finds its counterpart in God's historical covenant with men, not only as individuals but as a people.

LG 9 | At all times and in every race, anyone who fears God and does what is right has been acceptable to him (cf. Acts 10:35). He has, however, willed to make men holy and save them, not as individuals without any bond or link between them, but rather to make them into a people who might acknowledge him and serve him in holiness. He therefore chose the Israelite race to be his own people and established a covenant with it . . . All these things, however, happened as a preparation and figure of that new and perfect covenant which was to be ratified in Christ, and of the fuller revelation which was to be given through the Word of God made flesh. Christ instituted this new covenant, namely the new covenant in his blood (cf. 1 Cor. 11:25); he called a race made up of Jews and Gentiles which would be one, not according to the flesh, but in the Spirit, and this race would be the new People of God. For those who believe in Christ, who are reborn, not from a corruptible seed, but from an incorruptible one through the word of the living God (cf. 1 Pet. 1:23), not from flesh, but from water and the Holy Spirit (cf. Jn. 3:5–6), are finally established as 'a chosen race, a royal priesthood, a holy nation . . . who in times past were not a people, but now are the People of God' (1 Pet. 2:9–10).

The reality of Christ's redemption continues in the Church, that is to say in men who 'grow together' into a single people thanks to the effective inner working of the Holy Spirit. The union which forms this people is a union of men in spiritual community, but the content and principle of that community are of God: it proceeds from the divine choice, from Christ's redeeming act and the sanctification of the Spirit, as we may see in the First Epistle of St Peter, quoted by the Council. In the formation of the consciousness of the Church as the People of God we must have the skill to combine theology with sociology, bearing in mind the 'great things of God' as well as the rights of human existence which is both personal and social, but above all personal and communal.

In fact, 'All those who in fatih look towards Jesus, the author of salvation and the principle of unity and peace, God has gathered together and established as the Church, that it may be for each and everyone the visible sacrament of this saving unity' (LG 9). In forming the consciousness of the Church as the People of God we must constantly maintain the 'vertical' orientation required by the transcendent reality of God, and the reality of creation, salvation and redemption; while at the same time we must also extend our minds horizontally towards man in the world, in whose nature the personal and the communal element are profoundly intertwined and complete each other. In the teaching of Vatican II we must therefore perceive the clear connection between the reality of the People of God and man's vocation as a person, which is at the same time a vocation to communal life. For 'man, the only creature on earth that God wanted for its own sake, cannot fully find himself except in sincere self-giving' (GS 24). This statement indicates the nature of man's person and the uniqueness of his relationship to God.

1. *The individual's vocation in the community*

The Constitution *Gaudium et Spes* strongly emphasizes this point, and thus appears not for the first time as a complement to *Lumen Gentium*. Man's vocation as a person in a community constitutes the basis of the reality of the People of God, and if we direct our attention to the base we shall have a clearer idea of that reality, in which reason and faith complement and confirm each other.

GS 11 | For faith throws a new light on all things and makes known the full ideal which God has set for man, thus guiding the mind towards solutions that are fully human.

The Council presents this solution, teaching us that man is called to realize the dignity of his own person and that the basis of this vocation must be sought in his very nature, that is to say in the work of creation.

'Sacred Scripture teaches that man was created "in the image of God", as able to know and love his creator, and as set by him over all earthly creatures, that he might rule them and make use of them while glorifying God' (GS 12). From the very beginning, however, man as an individual was created and called on to live in a state of community. 'God did not create man a solitary being: . . . "male and female he created them" (**Gen.** 1:27). This partnership of man and woman constitutes the first form of communion between persons. For by his innermost nature man is a social being, and if he does not enter into relations with others he can neither live nor develop his gifts' (GS 12).

Man as a person 'transcends the universe' and rightly considers himself 'superior to bodily things . . . recognizing in himself a spiritual and immortal soul' (GS 14). It is the soul which constitutes the depth of the human person, where man 'himself decides his own destiny in the sight of God' (ibid.). Man's nature is intellectual, and as such 'finds at last its perfection, as it should, in wisdom, which gently draws the human mind to look for and to love what is true and good. Filled with wisdom man is led through visible realities to those which cannot be seen' (GS 15). Freedom is a characteristic property of the human person, and it is also his duty.

GS 17 | Man's dignity requires him to act out of con-
scious and free choice, as moved and drawn in a
personal way from within, and not by blind
impulses in himself or by mere external con-
straint. Man gains such dignity when, ridding
himself of all slavery of the passions, he presses
forward towards his goal by freely choosing
what is good, and, by his diligence and skill,
effectively secures for himself the means suited
to this end.

The intellectual nature of the person and, united with it,
the self-determining faculty of free will find expression in
conscience, which enables man to 'search for the right solution
to so many moral problems which arise both in the lives of
individuals and from social relationships. Hence, the more a
correct conscience prevails, the more do persons and groups
turn aside from blind choice and try to be guided by the
objective standards of moral conduct' (GS 16).

Such, in summary, is the basic framework of man's vocation
to human dignity as proclaimed by Vatican II. The reality of
grace corresponds fully to that vocation: 'the dignity of man
rests above all on the fact that he is called to communion
with God' (GS 19). Since the Pastoral Constitution also speaks
of the problem of atheism, it emphasizes in a special way the
truth concerning man's supernatural vocation. For example:

GS 21 | The Church holds that to acknowledge God is
in no way to oppose the dignity of man, since
such dignity is grounded and brought to perfection in God. Man has in fact been placed in
society by God, who created him as an intelligent
and free being; but over and above this he is
called as a son to intimacy with God and to share
in his happiness. She further teaches that hope
in a life to come does not take away from the
importance of the duties of this life on earth but

rather adds to it by giving new motives for ful-
filling those duties. When, on the other hand,
man is left without this divine support and
without hope of eternal life his dignity is deeply
wounded, as may so often be seen today. The
problems of life and death, of guilt and of
suffering, remain unsolved, so that men are not
rarely cast into despair.

As will be seen, the Council's teaching includes the doctrine
and vindication of man's vocation to communion with God
and supernatural participation in the life of God. As we saw
in the previous Chapter, this evangelical teaching is permeated
by the consciousness of redemption, which it in turn permeates. As the Council observes in this context:

GS 17 | Since human freedom has been weakened by
sin it is only by the help of God's grace that man
can give his actions their full and proper relationship to God. Before the judgment seat of
God an account of his own life will be rendered
to each one according as he has done either
good or evil.

The vocation of the individual to communion with God is
closely linked with his vocation to human dignity, and is
furthermore, in the most authentic manner, given him by
reason of his own inner nature.

This intimately personal vocation of man, which is the main
theme of the Gospel, must, however, be realized in communion
with other men, and therefore it is also a vocation to communal
life.

GS 23 | Christian revelation greatly fosters the establish-
ment of such fellowship and at the same time
promotes deeper understanding of the laws of
social living with which the creator has endowed
man's spiritual and moral nature.

This communion 'calls for mutual respect for the full spiritual dignity of men as persons' (GS 23). The Pastoral Constitution *Gaudium et Spes* is concerned particularly with the communal character of man's vocation within the divine plan, and with the ethical aspect of that vocation.

> GS 25 | The social nature of man shows that there is an interdependence between personal betterment and the improvement of society. Insofar as man by his very nature stands completely in need of life in society, he is and he ought to be the beginning, the subject and the object of every social organization. Life in society is not something accessory to man himself: through his dealings with others, through mutual service, and through fraternal dialogue, man develops all his talents and becomes able to rise to his destiny.

The ethical aspect of human communities and their life is a frequent theme of the Pastoral Constitution. It recurs not only in Chapter II of Part 1, which is expressly devoted to the human community, but also in the Chapters of Part 2, which deal with the most urgent problems of the Church in the modern world such as marriage and the family, culture and economic life, politics and international relations. In all these fields, man's vocation as a member of society expresses itself in diverse ways, and to all of them must be applied the evangelical principle which Vatican II recalls, adapting them to the needs of our time:

> GS 26 | The order of things must be subordinate to the order of persons and not the other way around, as the Lord suggested when he said that the Sabbath was made for man and not man for the Sabbath. The social order requires constant improvement: it must be found in truth, built on justice, and animated by love: it should grow

> in freedom towards a more humane equili-
> brium. If these objectives are to be attained there
> will first have to be a renewal of attitudes and
> far-reaching social changes.
> The Spirit of God, who, with wondrous provi-
> dence, directs the course of time and renews the
> face of the earth, assists at this development. The
> ferment of the Gospel has aroused and continues
> to arouse in the hearts of men an unquenchable
> thirst for human dignity.

We do not propose here to concern ourselves in detail with the ethical aspect of the problem. The sole purpose of our considerations concerning man's vocation as a person in society is to prepare the ground for an analysis of the conscious- ness of the Church as the People of God. The human com- munity and the 'community character' were 'perfected and fulfilled in the work of Jesus Christ, for the Word made flesh willed to share in human fellowship' (GS 32). Here the Conciliar document recalls how Christ by his actions 'sanctified those human ties, above all family ties, which are the basis of social structures', and in his preaching 'clearly commanded the sons of God to treat each other as brothers . . . He delivered himself freely unto death for the sake of all . . . His command to the Apostles was to preach the Gospel to all peoples in order that the human race should become the family of God, in which love would be the fullness of the law' (GS 32). And finally:

GS 32 | As the firstborn of many brethren, and by the
> gift of his Spirit, he established, after his death
> and resurrection, a new brotherly communion
> among all who received him in faith and love;
> this is the communion of his own body, the
> Church, in which everyone as members one of
> the other would render mutual service in the
> measure of the different gifts bestowed on each.
> This solidarity must be constantly increased

> until that day when it will be brought to fulfil-
> ment; on that day mankind, saved by grace, will
> offer perfect glory to God as the family beloved of
> God and of Christ their brother.

The reality of redemption thus continues in the Church, as
we tried to show in the previous Chapter. This reality unites
individuals in a community in such a way that 'members
render one another mutual service in the measure of the
different gifts bestowed on each' (GS 32). These words express
the truth of the Mystical Body of Christ, and this revealed
truth enables us to see in the Church more than can be discerned through the categories of the 'sociology of communities'
that applies to all other human associations. Therefore, in the
text just quoted, Vatican II teaches, among other things, that
the Church is more than a community (*communitas*) – it
possesses the nature of a communion (*communio*) in which,
by means of mutual services, in different ways and in various
relationships, 'that sincere giving of himself' takes place in
which man can fully discover his true self' (GS 24). Thus
conceived, the *communio* constitutes their common and
reciprocal membership of the Mystical Body of Christ, in
which all are members one of another (GS 32).

Thus the consciousness of the Church as People of God is
profoundly permeated by the consciousness of personal
vocation and of that communion of persons which realizes
itself in the Church as the People of God because it is at the
same time the Mystical Body of Christ. The reality of the
Mystical Body indicates and announces to all men, each of
whom is called to his own proper dignity, the discovery and
fulfilment of themselves by means of sincere self-giving to
other. Since this gift is made to a multitude, it imparts a
character of 'communion' to it. *Communio* in fact means the
actualization of a community in which the individual not only
preserves his own nature but realizes himself definitively.

The enrichment of faith which springs from Vatican II is

thus profoundly linked to the concept of the People of God. As we shall see, this concept throws additional light on the truth concerning the fatherhood of God and the universal scope of redemption.

The faith of profession coincides here with the faith of vocation. On the basis of the work of creation and redemption, men are called to communal life. This fundamental call is involved in the concept of the Church as People of God, and at the same time the full consciousness of the vocation of the person endows this fundamental call with the prospect of communion. Consciousness of the Church as People of God can never cease to pursue the prospect thus opened up. As faith advances, it will always have in view, as its ultimate reality and model, the *communio personarum* of God himself in the Trinity of Persons. As *Gaudium et Spes* suggests, it is Jesus who has shown us that there is 'a certain parallel between the union existing among the divine persons and the union of the sons of God in truth and love' (GS 24).

In this way, even at the very beginning of our thoughts – the purpose of which is to form the awareness of the Church as People of God in the post-Conciliar enrichment of faith – we point out the main trends of the inner forces which underlie and determine the reality of the People of God. In the Council's teaching these trends are profoundly linked with man's vocation as an individual to share in the divine life which must be realized in the community. Thus the concept of the People of God manifests itself to us, even at first glance, in its revealed and theological content. This essential content is the proper basis for further considerations which will show more clearly how Vatican II contributes to the enrichment of faith, giving new vitality to the ancient biblical concept of the People of God and applying it to the consciousness of the Church in the modern world.

2.   *The consciousness of the Church as People of God* ad intra *and* ad extra

The distinction between *ad intra* and *ad extra* was applied by the Council from its first session in 1962 and proved very useful in its work. It would seem that, in particular, the theology of the People of God makes possible the introduction of this distinction and its precise application to the conscious-ness of the Church. Taking into account the complex reality of humanity, the Council takes note that large sections of humanity are – in a theologically differentiated manner – outside the Church; at the same time the Council declares with full conviction that all men are included in God's fatherly plan, that all are redeemed by Christ and that the Holy Spirit exercises its sanctifying influence on the souls of all. All this belongs to the concept of the People of God. In that concept, and in the reality to which it corresponds, the determining and constituent element is that which comes to mankind from God, thus creating the first basis for speaking of 'God's People'. Man-made distinctions and differentiations of all kinds are seen to take second place. Thus the concept of 'God's People' serves above all to reaffirm the reality of creation, redemption and salvation, which as it were situates the consciousness of the Church in the concrete historical dimensions of humanity, and not vice versa. The Church as the People of God recognizes itself not only *ad intra* (from the internal point of view) but also *ad extra* (from the external). This is how the mind of the Church was formed by Vatican II, and this is the direction in which the deepening and enrichment of faith should take place. Clearly there is at the root of this process a salutary new insight into the reality of revelation and redemption, which is why we have devoted so much attention to these in the foregoing pages.

In this sense we may read the following passage from *Lumen Gentium*:

LG 13 | All men are called to belong to the new People of God. This People therefore, whilst remaining one and only one, is to be spread throughout the whole world and to all ages in order that the design of God's will may be fulfilled: he made human nature one in the beginning and has decreed that all his children who were scattered should be finally gathered together as one (cf. John 11:52). It was for this purpose that God sent his Son, whom he appointed heir of all things (cf. Heb. 1:2), that he might be teacher, king and priest of all, the head of the new and universal People of God's sons. This, too, is why God sent the Spirit of his Son, the Lord and Giver of Life. The Spirit is, for the Church and for each and every believer, the principle of their union and unity in the teaching of the apostles and fellowship, in the breaking of bread and prayer (cf. Acts 2:42 Gk.).

And again:

LG 9 | That messianic people has as its head Christ, 'who was delivered up for our sins and rose again for our justification' (Rom. 4:25), and now, having acquired the name which is above all names, reigns gloriously in heaven. The state of this people is that of the dignity and freedom of the sons of God, in whose hearts the Holy Spirit dwells as in a temple. Its law is the new commandment to love as Christ loved us (cf. Jn. 13:34). Its destiny is the kingdom of God which has been begun by God himself on earth and which must be further extended until it is brought to perfection by him at the end of time when Christ our life (cf. Col. 3:4), will appear and 'creation itself also will be delivered from its slavery to corruption into the freedom of the glory of the sons of God' (Rom. 8:21). Hence that messianic people, although it does not actually include all men, and at times may appear as a small flock, is, however, a most sure seed of unity, hope and salvation for the whole human race. Established by Christ as a communion of life, love and truth, it is taken up by him also as the instrument for the salvation of all; as the light of the world and the salt of the earth (cf. Mt. 5:13–16) it is sent forth into the whole world.

It is clear in what sense the reality of the People of God is the fundamental dimension of the Church. The Church is identified above all with this concept. This identity bears witness that the Church follows first and foremost God's fatherly plan, the plan of salvation. It also confirms that the Church always remains faithful to the divine missions of the Son and the Holy Spirit, that these are addressed to all men and that they are not limited by the visible structure of the Church. The visible structure remains always turned towards the mystery of the Church, towards that 'invisible structure' which ensures that the whole 'People' is really 'of God'.

The fact that the Church sees in the reality of the People of God its own fundamental dimension, with which it is identified first and foremost, provides a theological justification for the categories *ad intra* and *ad extra*. This also enables us to understand the whole series of formulations which we encounter both in *Lumen Gentium* and in the whole of the Council's teaching. We read there, for instance:

LG 13 | All men are called to this Catholic unity which prefigures and promotes universal peace. And in different ways to it belong, or are related: the Catholic faithful, others who believe in Christ, and finally all mankind, called by God's grace to salvation.

From the fundamental dimension, the almost invisible structure of the People of God which constitutes the essential element of the mystery of the Church, we pass gradually to the visible structure:

LG 8 | This Church, constituted and organized as a society in the present world, subsists in the Catholic Church, which is governed by the successor of Peter and by the bishops in communion with him. Nevertheless, many elements of sanctification and of truth are found outside its visible confines. Since these are gifts belonging to the Church of Christ, they are forces impelling towards Catholic unity.

This is quoted from the first chapter of *Lumen Gentium*, entitled 'The Mystery of the Church'. We see how under the influence of this mystery, with which is closely linked the idea that all men are called to be saved, Vatican II weighs every word it utters, speaking not only of 'belonging to the Catholic unity of the People of God' but also of being 'associated with it'. This careful choice of words derives from the special sense of responsibility which goes with the belief that 'the pilgrim Church is necessary to salvation'. The Council professes and teaches that belief 'on the basis of Holy Scripture and tradition':

LG 14 | . . . the one Christ is mediator and the way of salvation; he is present to us in his body which is the Church. He himself explicitly asserted the necessity of faith and baptism (cf. Mk. 16:16;

Jn. 3:5), and thereby affirmed at the same time the necessity of the Church which men enter through baptism as through a door. Hence they could not be saved who, knowing that the Catholic Church was founded as necessary by God through Christ, would refuse either to enter it, or to remain in it.

'Those who, knowing . . ., would refuse . . .' – with these words we enter the internal sphere of every man, the sphere of his intellect, will and conscience. At this point the teaching of *Lumen Gentium* comes closest to the Declaration on Religious Freedom, as we have shown previously. The dimension of the People of God – that fundamental dimension with which the Church identifies above all – is at the same time the authentic dimension of persons. The truth concerning the objective necessity of the Church for salvation is presented by the Conciliar teaching also from the point of view of each man's consciousness and choice. From this viewpoint, too, the Council is at pains not to prejudge anything: it manifestly endeavours not to judge the subjective order from the point of view of the objective, or vice versa.

This explains what we read on the subject of membership of the Church by Catholics themselves:

LG 14 | Fully incorporated into the Church are those who, possessing the Spirit of Christ, accept all means of salvation given to the Church together with her entire organization, and who – by the bonds constituted by the profession of faith, the sacraments, ecclesiastical government, and communion – are joined in the visible structure of the Church of Christ, who rules her through the Supreme Pontiff and the bishops. Even though incorporated into the Church, however, one who

> does not persevere in charity is not saved. He
> remains indeed in the bosom of the Church, but
> 'in body' not 'in heart'.

Here the document refers, in a note, to St Augustine before
proceeding:

LG 14 | All children of the Church should remember
that their exalted condition results, not from
their own merits, but from the grace of Christ.
If they fail to respond in thought, word and deed
to that grace, not only shall they not be saved,
but they shall be the more severely judged.

This concerns those who belong to the Church, who are
'fully incorporated' in her society, and to whom the category
ad intra applies more specially. It is clear, however, that this
category manifests its deepest significance in the Council's
teaching in connection with the dimension of the People of
God and hence with the reality of grace and love itself. It is
clear that membership of the Church may itself be merely
external, lacking the interior elements which denote membership of the People of God and give man his place in the order of
salvation. So external membership without inner adherence
makes the Catholic's responsibility even more serious. Hence
the necessity for everyone to do his utmost in order that
external membership should be matched by inner loyalty. It can
also be seen that the whole Church must endeavour to realize
continuously 'in its visible body' the authentic reality of the
People of God, so as to rediscover and reaffirm itself in that
fundamental dimension.

As regards catechumens, *Lumen Gentium* expresses itself
as follows: 'Catechumens who, moved by the Holy Spirit,
desire with an explicit intention to be incorporated into the
Church, are by that very intention joined to her. With love

and solicitude mother Church already embraces them as her own' (LG 14).

Turning now to those *ad extra*, Vatican II considers first our separated Christian brethren.

LG 15 | The Church knows that she is joined in many ways to the baptized who are honoured by the name of Christian, but who do not however profess the Catholic faith in its entirety or have not preserved unity or communion under the successor of Peter. For there are many who hold sacred scripture in honour as a rule of faith and of life, who have a sincere religious zeal, who lovingly believe in God the Father Almighty and in Christ, the Son of God and the Saviour, who are sealed by baptism which unites them to Christ, and who indeed recognize and receive other sacraments in their own Churches or ecclesiastical communities. Many of them possess the episcopate, celebrate the holy Eucharist and cultivate devotion to the Virgin Mother of God. There is furthermore a sharing in prayer and spiritual benefits; these Christians are indeed in some real way joined to us in the Holy Spirit for, by his gifts and graces, his sanctifying power is also active in them and he has strengthened some of them even to the shedding of their blood.

This subject is dealt with in more detail in the Decree on Ecumenism (cf. *Unitatis Redintegratio* 3), to which we shall return. In *Lumen Gentium*, having spoken of the circle made up of Christians separated from the Catholic Church, the Council turns to consider those 'related to the People of God': it thus implies that all Christians belong in some way to God's People, while bearing in mind the 'separation of the brethren' as it is spoken of in *Lumen Gentium* and in greater detail the

Decree on Ecumenism. What we read concerning them in the Constitution *Lumen Gentium* is expanded on in the Declaration in the Relations of the Church to Non-Christian Religions. In *Lumen Gentium* we read:

> LG 16 | Finally, those who have not yet received the Gospel are related to the People of God in various ways. There is, first, that people to which the covenants and promises were made, and from which Christ was born according to the flesh (cf. Rom. 9:4–5): in view of the divine choice, they are a people most dear for the sake of the fathers, for the gifts of God are without repentance (cf. Rom. 11:28–9).

These words refer to the Jews who have not accepted Christ. The Council then speaks of the Moslems:

> LG 16 | But the plan of salvation also includes those who acknowledge the Creator, in the first place amongst whom are the Moslems: these profess to hold the faith of Abraham, and together with us they adore the one, merciful God, mankind's judge on the last day.

The expression 'together with us' should be noted here. It seems not only to denote the fact that we are all monotheists, but also to imply that we have something in common where Revelation is concerned.

The Constitution does not express itself in this way as regards other non-Christian religions. As to them it says:

> LG 16 | Nor is God remote from those who in shadows and images seek the unknown God, since he gives to all men life and breath and all things (cf. Acts 17:25–8), and since the Saviour wills all men to be saved (cf. 1 Tim. 2:4).

The Declaration on the Church's relations with non-Christian religions devotes special attention to the spiritual and moral values to be found in religions of the Far East such as Hinduism and Buddhism. In *Lumen Gentium*, which considers this matter from the point of view of 'ordination' to the People of God, the main emphasis is laid on the search for God which for man is the core of religion, and which seems to constitute the basis of 'ordination' between the People of God.

> LG 16 | Those who, through no fault of their own, do not know the Gospel of Christ or his Church, but who nevertheless seek God with a sincere heart, and, moved by grace, try in their actions to do his will as they know it through the dictates of their conscience – those too may achieve eternal salvation.

This search for God, as we see, is expressed primarily in right conduct and obedience to one's conscience.

Among those 'related' to the People of God, the Council also places all who seek God although ignorant of the Gospel and the Church. The passage already quoted continues:

> LG 16 | Nor shall divine providence deny the assistance necessary for salvation to those who, without any fault of theirs, have not yet arrived at an explicit knowledge of God, and who, not without grace, strive to lead a good life.

We have already spoken of those who, while seeking God, endeavour to do his will according to the dictates of their conscience. Their attitude towards moral values expresses their aspiration towards God, in whose existence they believe although they do not know it from revelation. But the Constitution also relates to God's People all those 'have not yet arrived at an explicit knowledge of God' yet 'strive to lead a good life' (LG 16). Vatican II, basing itself on Tradition, affirms that they cannot do so without the aid of divine grace. Hence, although such men do not seem to have God in mind as the purpose of their righteous acts, God himself draws them to him by means of those acts. Are these the 'anonymous Christians' of whom contemporary theologians write?

LG 16 | Whatever good or truth is found amongst them is considered by the Church to be a preparation for the Gospel and given by him who enlightens all men that they may at length have life.

This last sentence clearly indicates the essential criterion whereby the Council in its teaching envisages the reality of the People of God. This criterion is based on the action of God himself in the soul: the action of God and its efficacy are, essentially and finally, the determining factor in membership of the People of God. It is this action too which associates individuals with the People of God, even if they fail to display many of the outward signs that might permit one to judge of such a relationship. Vatican II, relying on the whole of Tradition, presents the reality of the People of God in such a way that, while on the one hand it may be feared that some men belong to it externally but not internally, on the other hand it cannot be excluded that others belong or are related to it inwardly although there is no outward sign that they are members of any religious community. It is a task for the theologians, and difficult to attempt here, to show how this picture of the People of God corresponds to the most ancient texts of revelation and to the whole Christian tradition.

We must, however, take note that at the very foundation of the revealed truth concerning the People of God we constantly find the interpersonal relationship of God to man and man to God in its most authentic biblical form. God converts human beings into his People by choosing, calling and leading to himself each individual separately in the unique way appropriate to him. While the reality of the People of God is, in

God's design and its realization, no less primary than the calling of an individual human being, for each individual it is equally primary that he is a person and that he enters into communion with other men. God alone has knowledge of the bond which unites human beings in the communion of his People. Vatican II teaches that this bond is more far-reaching than the 'Church' community as such, although at the same time it constitutes the fundamental dimension of the Church. This also explains how the consciousness of the Church as the People of God is both *ad intra* and *ad extra*. While declaring all this, Vatican II recognizes that there is a difference between belonging to the People of God and being 'related' to it: in other words, there are distinct graduations in the bond which constitutes God's communion with mankind.

The last part of our reflections on *Lumen Gentium* should no doubt be compared with what the Pastoral Constitution *Gaudium et Spes* has to say about atheism. On the one hand *Lumen Gentium* speaks of those who 'without any fault of theirs, have not yet arrived at an explicit knowledge of God, and who, not without grace, strive to lead a good life' (LG 16): such people, it declares, are related to the People of God. On the other hand we read in *Gaudium et Spes*: 'Without doubt those who wilfully try to drive God from their heart and to avoid all questions about religion, not following the biddings of their conscience, are not free from blame' (GS 19). These texts present an explicit antithesis, from which we must conclude that while the first category of people are related to the People of God, the others are not. But here also Vatican II formulates its judgement with the utmost care. As it goes on to say:

> GS 19 | Believers can thus have more than a little to do with the rise of atheism. To the extent that they are careless about their instruction in the faith, or present its teaching falsely, or even fail in their

> religious, moral, or social life, they must be said
> to conceal rather than to reveal the true nature
> of God and of religion.

These words evidently modify the basic contrast expressed
in the terms 'without any fault of theirs' and 'are not free from
blame'. Vatican II does not seek to obliterate the boundary
between those who are related to the People of God and those
who are not; but it defines the matter only as far as human
judgement can reach, while leaving the verdict to God alone,
who is the only *scrutator cordium* or searcher of hearts. Even
so the Council states:

> LG 16   Whatever good or truth is found amongst them
> is considered by the Church to be a preparation
> for the Gospel and given by him who enlightens
> all men that they may at length have life.

If this point in our consideration of the consciousness of the
Church as People of God can be called a 'point of arrival', we
must also state, as we did at the 'point of departure', that the
consciousness of the Church is in the last analysis a consciousness of mystery. At the starting-point was the reality of God
'who revealed himself' (*Dei Verbum* 3), and that reality, notwithstanding Revelation, continues to be a mystery. At the
point of arrival is the reality of man who 'freely commits his
entire self to God' (DV 5), and this reality too is in the last
analysis a mystery known to God alone.

3.   Communio, *the link uniting the Church as
     People of God*

> LG 13   The one People of God is accordingly present in
> all the nations of the earth, since its citizens,
> who are taken from all nations, are of a kingdom

whose nature is not earthly but heavenly. All
the faithful scattered throughout the world are
in communion with each other in the Holy Spirit,
so that 'he who dwells in Rome knows those in
most distant parts to be his members' (*qui
Romae sedet, Indos scit membrum suum esse*).
. . . This character of universality which adorns
the People of God is a gift from the Lord himself
whereby the Catholic ceaselessly and effica-
ciously seeks for the return of all humanity and
all its goods under Christ the Head in the unity
of his Spirit.

'Catholicity' signifies the universality of the Church. It
would seem that the foregoing analysis of the People of God
ad intra and *ad extra* has provided a large background against
which this universality can be perceived. At the same time this
extensive universality or catholicity is a permanent objective
for the Church:

LG 17 | Thus the Church prays and likewise labours so
that into the People of God, the Body of the
Lord and the Temple of the Holy Spirit, may
pass the fullness of the whole world, and that in
Christ, the head of all things, all honour and
glory may be rendered to the Creator, the
Father of the universe.

The dimensions of catholicity thus extend not only to all
mankind but also to the universe. Through redemption, the
consciousness of the Church, together with all humanity,
enters continuously but always anew into the work of creation
and draws from it praise to the Creator and Father.

However, this first significance of the catholicity of the
Church is completed in the Council's teaching by another
significance which enables us to conceive the universality of
the Church not only extensively, but also from the point of

view of that kind of union and unity which is proper to the
Church as the People of God, that People 'whose law is the new
commandment to love as Christ loved us (cf. John 13:34)'
(LG 9). Based on this law, the catholicity of the Church manifests and explains itself through *communio*, that is to say
community and social unity after the likeness of the community of persons which, as *Gaudium et Spes* tells us, can
only be fully realized in 'sincere self-giving' (GS 24).

The Church is the People of God, composed of human
individuals. However, on the basis of this fundamental
composition we may discover other characteristics, as *Lumen
Gentium* indicates. Composition implies an essential relationship between the parts and the whole and vice versa; and it is
here that we discern the second significance of the Church's
catholicity, which is concerned with the kind of union and
unity proper to the community of the People of God.

LG 13 | In virtue of this catholicity each part contributes
its own gifts to other parts and to the whole
Church, so that the whole and each of the parts
are strengthened by the common sharing of all
things and by the common effort to attain to
fullness in unity.

The kind of union and unity proper to the Church as the
People of God composed of human individuals corresponds
to the personal character of the whole community; it carries
in itself and expresses the very profile of interpersonal
relations. As individuals find themselves in self-giving,
through the interpersonal relationship which we call *communio*, so too the individual 'parts' find and affirm themselves
in the community of the Church in so far as they 'bring
their own gifts to the other parts and to the whole Church'.
The reality we call *communio* corresponds in this case
not only to a restricted community of persons but to the
whole People, whose unity springs from the Spirit of God
and from what is most essentially personal. Thus both the

Church as a whole and its individual parts are strengthened by the gift which each of its parts brings to every other and to the whole Church. All this springs from catholicity and is its expression and its fruit. While catholicity signifies universality, in this case we understand it not in an extensive but rather in an intensive sense. Through each person's gift of self, the good of one part becomes in a certain sense that of all and takes on a universal dimension. Everybody draws something from it and shares in it, precisely because that good has become a gift. Thus *communio* is in this sense the foundation of catholicity.

The Council, pointing to this type of union and unity that is proper to the People of God, directs our attention to the multiform composition of the Church.

| LG 13 | Hence it is that the People of God is not only an assembly of various peoples, but in itself is made up of different ranks. This diversity among its members is either by reason of their duties – some exercise the sacred ministry for the good of their brethren – or it is due to their condition and manner of life – many enter the religious state and, aiming at sanctity by a narrower way, spur on their brethren by their example. Holding a rightful place in the communion of the Church there are also particular Churches that retain their own traditions, without prejudice to the Chair of Peter which presides over the whole assembly of charity, and protects their legitimate variety while at the same time taking care that these differences do not hinder unity, but rather contribute to it. Finally, between the various parts of the Church there is a bond of close communion whereby spiritual riches, apostolic workers and temporal resources are shared. |

This text may be taken as a concise summary of the whole of *Lumen Gentium*, or at any rate most of its chapters. In the community of the People of God are many peoples, each of which contributes some special gift to enrich the others. We shall return to this in the next chapter. On the basis of the diversity and historical multiplicity of the peoples who have entered the universal Church and continue to do so, there has come to be a multiplicity of individual churches: we shall return to this point also.

Besides the *communio* thus outlined as the communion of the peoples and the Churches, *Lumen Gentium* indicates another when it says that 'the People of God is composed of many orders within itself'. Here we enter another dimension of the structure of the Church, one which is closer to the vocation of individuals and at the same time delineates *ad intra* a certain composition of the Church as a community and society of an altogether special kind. The passage quoted from *Lumen Gentium* speaks of estates and offices as elements distinguishing individuals within the church community. These estates and offices, i.e. the human beings who occupy or belong to them, serve the community and thereby serve other men, or, in the language of *Lumen Gentium*, they bring their own gifts to the complex structure of the Church. One kind of gift is brought by those 'exercising the sacred ministry for the good of their brethren' (LG 13), and another by those who 'aim at sanctity by a narrower way, and spur on the brethren by their example' (LG 13). In the first case we are clearly concerned with the hierarchy, to whom Chapter III of the Constitution is devoted, and in the second case with men and women in the religious state (Chapter VI). Vatican II also analyses with special profundity the gift brought to the community of the Church by laymen and laywomen (Chapter IV of the same Constitution).

If we want to follow the main thread of the Council's thought, all that it says concerning the hierarchy, the laity and the religious orders in the Church should be re-read in the light of the reality of *communio* for the community of the People of God.

> LG 13 | For the members of the People of God are called upon to share their goods, and the words of the apostle apply also to each of the Churches, 'according to the gift that each has received, administer it to one another as good stewards of the manifold grace of God' (1 Pet. 5:10).

Thus we have the *communio ecclesiarum* and the *communio munerum* and, through these, the *communio personarum*. Such is the image of the Church presented by the Council. The type of union and unity that is proper to the community of the Church as People of God essentially determines the nature of that community. The Church as People of God, by reason of its most basic premises and its communal nature, is oriented towards the resemblance there ought to be between 'the union of the sons of God in truth and charity' and the essentially divine unity of the divine persons *in communione Sanctissimae Trinitatis*. Even though the realization of this divine type of union suffers various distortions and deficiences because it is lived by man, in the human order, nevertheless it remains the special principle of the social unity of the Church as the People of God.

We shall not discuss here in detail Chapters III, IV and VI, already mentioned, of *Lumen Gentium*. As we explained at the outset, the present study is not intended as a commentary but as a kind of *vade mecum* in which, by describing systematically the wealth of doctrine imparted by Vatican II, we endeavour to trace the ways of enrichment of faith that the Council marked out for the future. The expression of that enrichment is both the consciousness of man's vocation in general, to which the Council devoted great attention, and the concrete and particular vocations delineated in the structure of the Church as the People of God. In this connection it may be of help to take another look at each of the above-mentioned chapters of

Lumen Gentium from the point of view of these manifold vocations. Even though it speaks of 'estates' and 'offices' it is easy to discover and identify a content which firmly emphasizes the personal element. It was not without reason that we began the present analysis of the consciousness of the Church as the People of God by illustrating, in accordance with the thought of Vatican II, the relationship of the person to the community and vice versa. If the concept of 'estate' or 'office' in the Church has a content, which indirectly expresses a personalistic reciprocal relationship between person and community, this is precisely because of the reality of *communio* as the union which constitutes the community of the Church as People of God. The *communio* thus indicates the proper place in that community not only of particular estates or social groups like the hierarchy, the laity and religious orders, but also of individuals in the Church.

All that we read about these groups in the relevant chapters of *Lumen Gentium* is of a general nature, but not so much so as to prevent our identifying the vocation of the individual and the reality of the communion between persons and groups. We can thus understand that in the community of the Church as People of God every man imparts his gifts to others, above all thanks to who and what he is.

LG 33 | Gathered together in the People of God and established in the one Body of Christ under one head, the laity – no matter who they are – have, as living members, the vocation of applying to the building up of the Church and to its continual sanctification all the powers which they have received from the goodness of the Creator and from the grace of the Redeemer.

The reality of *communio* results from the multiplicity of vocations and, as it were, provides room in which they can form and develop properly. These vocations constitute the Church as a community, but on the other hand the Church as the People of God itself constitutes each one of them. *Communio* signifies a stable immanent dynamism of the community, working from multiplicity and complexity towards unity – not only of the People, but of the Body itself – while at the same time, with the same force and efficacy, it upholds the complexity and multiplicity in that unity of the People and the Body. All this, we may add, indicates the reality of redemption as it abides in the Church.

With all this in mind we can see that Vatican II has become a particular source of the enrichment of faith which can be defined as that of 'communion'. This enrichment is the expression of an attitude which is in turn inspired by that aspect of the Church's consciousness which can be strictly defined as *communio*. This aspect is of great importance for the deepening and enrichment of faith in the manner understood by Vatican II. To God's revelation of himself (DV 2) man replies by a free commitment of himself (DV 5). This is not a merely intellectual response, but above all an existential one in the strict sense of the term. With this response the human individual enters the community of the People of God: this is in fact the response to his vocation in and to the community. By abandoning himself wholly to God the individual at the same time gives himself to the community of the Church. The reality of *communio* is decisive for the deeper significance of all the 'estates' and 'offices' in the Church, and hence also of all vocations in the community of the People of God. This is essential to the consciousness of the Church as a community and society, and it is also essential for each and every member of the Church.

Let us now see how the Council documents express this truth by taking the religious vocation as an example.

LG 44 | Being means to and instruments of love, the evangelical counsels unite those who practice them to the Church and her mystery in a special way. If follows that the spiritual life of such

Christians should be dedicated also to the welfare of the entire Church. To the extent of their capacities and in keeping with the particular kind of religious life to which they are individually called, whether it be one of prayer or of active labour as well, they have the duty of working for the implanting and strengthening of the kingdom of Christ in souls and for spreading it to the four corners of the earth.

LG 46 | Let no one think either that their consecrated way of life alienates religious from other men or makes them useless for human society. Though in some cases they have no direct relations with their contemporaries, still in a deeper way they have their fellow men present with them in the heart of Christ and cooperate with them spiritually, so that the building up of human society may always have its foundation in the Lord and have him as its goal: otherwise those who build it may have laboured in vain.

We can see here how vocation in and to the community is the authentic vocation of the person, a vocation to fulfil himself or herself.

LG 46 | At the same time let all realize that while the profession of the evangelical counsels involves the renunciation of goods that undoubtedly deserve to be highly valued, it does not constitute an obstacle to the true development of the human person but by its nature is supremely beneficial to that development. For the counsels, when willingly embraced in accordance with each one's personal vocation, contribute in no small degree to the purification of the heart and to spiritual freedom: they continually

> stimulate one to ardour in the life of love; and above all they have the power to conform the Christian more fully to that kind of poor and virginal life which Christ the Lord chose for himself and which his Virgin Mother embraced also.

Let us return, however, to the reality of *communio* as the type of union which is proper to the Church as People of God and constitutes the specific link of this community.

LG 32 | In the Church not everyone marches along the same path, yet all are called to sanctity and have obtained an equal privilege of faith through the justice of God (cf. 2 Pet. 1:1). Although by Christ's will some are established as teachers, dispensers of the mysteries and pastors for the others, there remains, nevertheless, a true equality between all with regard to the dignity and to the activity which is common to all the faithful in the building up of the Body of Christ. The distinction which the Lord has made between the sacred ministers and the rest of the People of God involves union, for the pastors and the other faithful are joined together by a close relationship: the pastors of the Church – following the example of the Lord – should minister to each other and to the rest of the faithful; the latter should eagerly collaborate with the pastors and teachers. And so amid variety all will bear witness to the wonderful unity in the Body of Christ: this very diversity of graces, of ministries and of works gathers the sons of God into one, for 'all these things are the work of the one and the same Spirit' (1 Cor. 12:11).

Thus *communio* as the specific link of the community of the People of God in the Church is expressed in a distinction which 'includes a bond', thus producing that 'witness to the marvellous unity' in the Body of Christ which is presented by the diversity of pastors and people. Moreover, the hierarchical constitution of the Church, of which we shall speak presently, presupposes a 'true equality' among all members of the People of God. This equality manifests itself 'with regard to the dignity of all the faithful and their share in building up the Body of Christ'. This dignity is at one and the same time human dignity, which belongs to each man as an individual, and Christian dignity in the order of grace. But it is not only in this field and on this account that Vatican II speaks of 'true equality' among all members of the Church, but also on account of the essential task of 'building up the Body of Christ'. All take part equally in this task, each with his own specific ability; and the action of a lay member of the People of God may be more effective than that of a member of the hierarchy or of a religious order. The history of the Church seems to give ample evidence of this, even though we can perhaps never exactly measure the effectiveness of action to 'build up the Body of Christ': the Church in its supernatural reality always remains a mystery.

The 'true equality' of all members of the People of God is identified with the brotherhood proclaimed by Christ the Lord. Vatican II recalls this teaching in *Lumen Gentium*:

LG 32 | As the laity through the divine choice have Christ as their brother, who, though Lord of all, came not to be served but to serve (cf. Mt. 20:28), they also have as brothers those in the sacred ministry who by teaching, by sanctifying and by ruling with the authority of Christ so nourish the family of God that the new commandment of love may be fulfilled by all. As St Augustine very beautifully puts it: 'When I am

> frightened by what I am to you, then I am
> consoled by what I am with you. To you I am
> the bishop, with you I am a Christian. The first
> is an office, the second a grace; the first a danger,
> the second salvation.'

The order of grace is more fundamental to the constitution
of the People of God than is the order of authority on which
the hierarchy of the Church is based. The order of grace is also
the source of the final equality of all members of the Church in
regard to the reality of salvation, to which all are equally
called.

The Council devotes much attention to making the faithful
conscious of *communio* as the link binding together the community of the People of God. Thus it appears that the internal
development and renewal of the Church in the spirit of Vatican
II depends to a very great extent on the authentic deepening
of faith in the Church as a community whose essential bond
is that of *communio*. It is here too that we should maybe
seek the foundation and root of the need for a dialogue
within the Church, pointed out both by the Council and by
Paul VI. *Lumen Gentium* has some eloquent words on this
subject:

LG 37 | Like all Christians, the laity have the right to
receive in abundance the help of the spiritual
goods of the Church, especially that of the word
of God and the sacraments from the pastors.
To the latter the laity should disclose their
needs and desires with that liberty and confidence which befits children of God and brothers
of Christ. By reason of the knowledge, competence or pre-eminence which they have, the laity
are empowered – indeed sometimes obliged – to
manifest their opinion on those things which
pertain to the good of the Church. If the occasion
should arise, this should be done through the

> institutions established by the Church for that
> purpose and always with truth, courage and
> prudence and with reverence and charity towards
> those who, by reason of their office, represent
> the person of Christ.

The Constitution next recalls the duty of obedience to 'what
is decided by the pastors who, as teachers and rulers of the
Church, represent Christ' (LG 37). This duty derives in a
special manner from the example of Christ himself. We then
read of the necessity to pray for our superiors in the Church:

LG 37 | The pastors, indeed, should recognize and pro-
> mote the dignity and responsibility of the laity
> in the Church. They should willingly use their
> prudent advice and confidently assign duties
> to them in the service of the Church, leaving
> them freedom and scope for acting. Indeed, they
> should give them the courage to undertake works
> on their own initiative. They should with
> paternal love consider attentively in Christ
> initial moves, suggestions and desires proposed
> by the laity. Moreover the pastors must respect
> and recognize the liberty which belongs to all
> in the terrestrial city.
>
> Many benefits for the Church are to be
> expected from this familiar relationship between
> the laity and the pastors. The sense of their own
> responsibility is strengthened in the laity, their
> zeal is encouraged, they are more ready to unite
> their energies to the work of their pastors.

Gaudium et Spes speaks thus of the need for a dialogue
within the Church:

GS 92 | Such a mission requires us first of all to create
> in the Church itself mutual esteem, reverence
> and harmony, and acknowledge all legitimate

> diversity; in this way all who constitute the one
> people of God will be able to engage in ever
> more fruitful dialogue, whether they are pastors
> or other members of the faithful. For the ties
> which unite the faithful together are stronger
> than those which separate them: let there be
> unity in what is necessary, freedom in what is
> doubtful, and charity in everything.

The most important thing is that all members of the Church should fully share fully in the awareness of 'communion'. This concept also has a profound ethical significance, and from this point of view it serves authentically to form Christian social morality. The Church, which in the reality of the People of God embraces its own social essence both *ad intra* and *ad extra*, must also, both *ad intra* and *ad extra*, seek ways of realizing 'communion' among human beings. Above all, however, in the society of the Church itself all must measure their behaviour according to the principle of communion whose theological meaning and importance have been re-emphasized by Vatican II.

4.   Koinonia *and* diakonia: *the hierarchical order of the Church*

> LG 18 | This sacred synod, following in the steps of the
> First Vatican Council, teaches and declares with
> it that Jesus Christ, the eternal pastor, set up the
> holy Church by entrusting the apostles with their
> mission as he himself had been sent by the Father
> (cf. Jn. 20:21). He willed that their successors,

the bishops namely, should be the shepherds in his Church until the end of the world. In order that the episcopate itself, however, might be one and undivided he put Peter at the head of the other apostles, and in him he set up a lasting and visible source and foundation of the unity both of faith and of communion. This teaching concerning the institution, the permanence, the nature and import of the sacred primacy of the Roman Pontiff and his infallible teaching office, the sacred synod proposes anew to be firmly believed by all the faithful, and, proceeding undeviatingly with this same undertaking, it proposes to proclaim publicly and enunciate clearly the doctrine concerning bishops, successors to the apostles, who together with Peter's successor, the Vicar of Christ and the visible head of the whole Church, direct the house of the living God.

The whole of Chapter III of *Lumen Gentium* is devoted to an exposition of the doctrine concerning the hierarchical constitution of the Church and in particular the Episcopate. It is worth while combining a detailed study of this chapter with an analysis of the Decree on the Pastoral Office of Bishops in the Church. These two texts are of basic importance to the theology of the episcopate. However, we shall not study these documents here in detail, but rather try to throw further light on the communion (*communio, koinonia*) of the People of God as it is fostered in the Church by the vocation and ministry of bishops, which are likewise a form of service (*diakonia*) to the community. It is significant that the Council Fathers placed the chapter on the hierarchy immediately after the chapter on the People of God, so as to bring out the fact of the organic link between them. The truth that authority is a form of service is one that we find in the Gospel and that

Christ taught with word and example, and accordingly Vatican II insists on the link between *diakonia* and *koinonia*. The Church rediscovers its own communal nature not only in the universal reality of the People of God but also in the authority over that People which was set up by Christ and wholly subordinated to the task of preaching the Gospel.

LG 21 | In order to fulfil such exalted functions, the apostles were endowed by Christ with a special outpouring of the Holy Spirit coming upon them (cf. Acts 1:8; 2:4; Jn. 20:22–3), and, by the imposition of hands, (cf. 1 Tim 4:14; 2 Tim. 1:6–7) they passed on to their auxiliaries the gift of the Spirit, which is transmitted down to our day through episcopal consecration.

'Thus the Apostles were both the seeds of the new Israel and the beginning of the sacred hierarchy' (AGD 5).

LG 20 | That divine mission, which was committed by Christ to the apostles, is destined to last until the end of the world (cf. Mt. 28:20), since the Gospel, which they were charged to hand on, is, for the Church, the principle of all its life for all time. For that very reason the apostles were careful to appoint successors in this hierarchically constituted society . . . Moreover, just as the office which the Lord confided to Peter alone, as first of the apostles, destined to be transmitted to his successors, is a permanent one, so also endures the office, which the apostles received, of shepherding the Church, a charge destined to be exercised without interruption by the sacred order of bishops. The sacred synod consequently teaches that the bishops have by divine institution taken the place of the apostles as pastors of the Church, in such wise that whoever listens to them is listening to Christ and whoever despises them despises Christ and him who sent Christ (cf. Lk. 10:16).

LG 21 | In the person of the bishops, then, to whom the priests render assistance, the Lord Jesus Christ, supreme high priest, is present in the midst of the faithful. Though seated at the right hand of God the Father, he is not absent from the assembly of his pontiffs. On the contrary indeed, it is above all through their signal service that he preaches the Word of God to all peoples and administers without cease to the faithful the sacraments of faith; that through their paternal care (cf. 1 Cor. 4:15) he incorporates, by a supernatural rebirth, new members into his body; that finally, through their wisdom and prudence he directs and guides the people of the New Testament on their journey towards eternal beatitude.

LG 21 | . . . [The] bishops, in a resplendent and visible manner, take the place of Christ himself, teacher, shepherd and priest, and act as his representatives (*in eius persona*). It is the right of bishops to admit newly elected members into the episcopal body by means of the sacrament of Orders.

The special theme of the Council's teaching is the community of Bishops, the links uniting them with one another and above all with the Successor of St Peter.

LG 22 | Just as, in accordance with the Lord's decree, St Peter and the rest of the apostles constitute a unique apostolic college, so in like fashion the Roman Pontiff, Peter's successor, and the bishops, the successors of the apostles, are related with and united to one another.

Here is the starting-point of the teaching on the collegiality of the Episcopate.

LG 22 | The college or body of bishops has for all that no authority unless united with the Roman Pontiff, Peter's successor, as its head, whose primatial authority, let it be added, over all, whether pastors or faithful, remains in its integrity. For the Roman Pontiff, by reason of his office as Vicar of Christ, namely, and as pastor of the entire Church, has full, supreme and universal power over the whole Church, a power which he can always exercise unhindered. The order of bishops is the successor to the college of the apostles in their role as teachers and pastors, and in it the apostolic college is perpetuated. Together with their head, the Supreme Pontiff, and never apart from him, they have supreme and full authority over the universal Church.

These are the Council's formulations regarding the principle of collegiality:

LG 22 | This college, in so far as it is composed of many members, is the expression of the multifariousness and universality of the People of God; and of the unity of the flock of Christ, in so far as it is assembled under one head.

LG 23 | The Roman Pontiff, as the successor of Peter, is the perpetual and visible source and foundation of the unity both of the bishops and of the whole company of the faithful. The individual bishops are the visible source and foundation of unity in their own particular Churches, which are constituted after the model of the universal Church; it is in these and formed out of them that the one and unique Catholic Church exists.

> And for that reason precisely each bishop
> represents his own Church, whereas all, together
> with the pope, represent the whole Church in a
> bond of peace, love and unity.

The principle of collegiality itself defines the way, instituted by Christ himself, in which authority is exercised in the Church. At the same time, this principle indirectly expresses the reality of the Church itself as a *koinonia*. A universal Church exists in the numerous individual churches. The bishops, successors of the Apostles, through their union with St Peter's successor, the Bishop of Rome, express together multiplicity and unity, universality and particularity. This brings to light the essence of the 'communion' of the Church as the community of God's people on earth. The People of God is the Church, and the Church is also a communion of the churches – *communio Ecclesiarum* – constituted by the communion of bishop-pastors. To recall the words we have already quoted:

LG 13 | Holding a rightful place in the communion of the
> Church there are also particular Churches that
> retain their own traditions, without prejudice
> to the Chair of Peter which presides over the
> whole assembly of charity.

The principle of collegiality in a special way emphasizes the principle of primacy: both were instituted by Christ, both express and serve to realize the structure of the Church as a communion of the People of God.

Christ is constantly building the Church on earth as his Body, through that nucleus which Vatican II calls the *Corpus seu Collegium* of bishops as successors of the Apostles. That Body which is the Church, in its hierarchical constitution, exists and lives by virtue of the reciprocal 'communion' of all bishops in the Church, which demands in turn on their 'communion' with their common centre, the See of Peter.

LG 23 | Consequently, the bishops, each for his own part, in so far as the due performance of their own duty permits, are obliged to enter into collaboration with one another and with Peter's successor, to whom, in a special way, the noble task of propagating the Christian name was entrusted. Thus, they should come to the aid of the missions by every means in their power, supplying both harvest workers and also spiritual and material aids, either directly and personally themselves, or by arousing the fervent cooperation of the faithful. Lastly, in accordance with the venerable example of former times, bishops should gladly extend their fraternal assistance, in the fellowship of an all-pervading charity, to other Churches, especially to neighbouring ones and to those most in need of help.

In the Decree on the Pastoral Office of Bishops (*Christus Dominus*) we read:

CD 36 | From the earliest ages of the Church, bishops in charge of particular churches, inspired by a spirit of fraternal charity and by zeal for the universal mission entrusted to the apostles, have pooled their resources and their aspirations in order to promote both the common good and the good of individual churches. With this end in view synods, provincial councils and, finally, plenary councils were established in which the bishops determined on a common programme to be followed in various churches both for teaching the truths of the faith and for regulating ecclesiastical discipline.

This passage comes from Chapter III of the Decree, which speaks of the cooperation of bishops for the common good of the greater number of churches. Chapter II is concerned with the duties of bishops in regard to particular churches, i.e. dioceses, while Chapter I speaks of their relations with the universal Church.

The same regard for the principle of collegiality and cooperation among bishops for the good of the greatest number of particular churches within the universal Church finds expression in our day in the institution of episcopal conferences. As we read in *Lumen Gentium*, these conferences 'are in a position to contribute in many and fruitful ways to the concrete realization of the collegiate spirit' (LG 23).

We have sufficiently emphasized the link established by the Council's teaching between *koinonia* and *diakonia*, the community of the People of God and the fact that authority in the Church is by its nature service. This link appears in all its clarity in the light of *communio*, which is a still more fundamental reality and links the individual still more directly with the community. Naturally this is an ideal and a standard to be realized, not simply a reality that exists of its own accord. But within this general picture, dominated by *communio* as the proper link uniting the People of God, it is easy to find the proper place of the hierarchical *diakonia*. If all are oriented towards mutual service, towards an act of giving by which they are reciprocally enriched, then authority or hierarchy can most simply be interpreted as ministry or service. This does not mean that the Council disregards the hierarchical nature of authority in the Church, without which it would not be authority: but authority itself is necessary if those concerned are to be able to serve.

> LG 24 | The bishops, inasmuch as they are the successors of the apostles, receive from the Lord, to whom all power is given in heaven and on earth, the mission of teaching all peoples, and of preaching the Gospel to every creature, so that all men may attain to salvation through faith,

baptism and the observance of the command-
ments (cf. Mt. 28:18; Mk. 16:15–16; Acts
26:17 f.). For the carrying out of this mission
Christ promised the Holy Spirit to the apostles
and sent him from heaven on the day of Pentecost,
so that through his power they might be witnesses to him in the remotest parts of the earth,
before nations and peoples and kings (cf. Acts
1:8; 2:1 ff.; 9:15). That office, however, which
the Lord committed to the pastors of his people,
is, in the strict sense of the term, a service, which
is called very expressively in sacred scripture a
diakonia or ministry (cf. Acts 1:17 and 25; 21:19;
Rom. 11:13; 1 Tim. 1:12).

As regards the hierarchy of office *Lumen Gentium* says:

LG 28 | Thus the divinely instituted ecclesiastical minis-
try is exercised in different degrees by those who
even from ancient times have been called bishops,
priests and deacons.

We have tried here to show how Vatican II expressed not
only the structure of the ministry, i.e. the hierarchical authority
instituted by Christ in the Church, but also the spirit of that
institution. This becomes still clearer in the light of present-
day realities.

LG 28 | Since the human race today is tending more and
more towards civil, economic and social unity,
it is all the more necessary that priests should
unite their efforts and combine their resources
under the leadership of the bishops and the
Supreme Pontiff and thus eliminate division and
dissension in every shape and form, so that all
mankind may be led into the unity of the family
of God.

CHAPTER V

The historical and eschatological consciousness of the Church as the People of God

Continuing our study of the ways of enriching faith that have been pointed out by the Council, we must draw attention to both the historical and the eschatological aspects of the Church as essential components of the reality of the People of God, of its very existence. This is how the Church exists as the People of God, and the mind of the Church corresponds to these characteristics of objective existence in faith.

GS 40 | Proceeding from the love of the eternal Father, the Church was founded by Christ in time and gathered into one by the Holy Spirit. It has a saving and eschatological purpose which can be fully attained only in the next life. But it is now present here on earth and is composed of men; they, the members of the earthly city, are called to form the family of the children of God even in this present history of mankind and to increase it continually until the Lord comes. Made one in view of heavenly benefits and enriched by them, this family has been 'constituted and organized as a society in the present world' by Christ and 'provided with means adapted to its visible and social union'. Thus the Church, at once 'a visible organization and a spiritual community,' travels the same journey as all mankind and shares the same earthly lot with the world: it is to be a leaven and, as it were. the soul of human society in its renewal by Christ and transformation into the family of God.

That the earthly and heavenly city penetrate one another is a fact open only to the eyes of faith; moreover, it will remain the mystery of human history, which will be harassed by sin until the perfect revelation of the splendour of the sons of God.

Following the thought of Vatican II, we shall try to clarify in analytical form the double content and significance of the Church's existence and its consciousness, expressed in summary form in the above passage of *Gaudium et Spes*. Although this dual aspect of the Church's existence and the interpenetration of faith and doctrine, it is clear that Vatican II emphasizes these aspects strongly in a new way, reflecting its fundamental precepts for the enriching and deepening of faith. This emphasis has already found ample expression and diffusion in the works of theologians and catechists. This applies in particular to the history of salvation, especially when we see that the consciousness of the Church as the People of God is 'historical'.

1.   *The history of salvation*

We must first note that the 'historical' consciousness of the Church as the People of God is closely linked with faith in the Truine God who came to man and continually comes to him and to mankind through the saving mission of the Word and the Holy Spirit. That which the Council clearly expressed in Chapter I of *Lumen Gentium* brings it about that the consciousness of salvation is linked, in the faith of the Church, not only with the existence of God in his transcendence or with his call to man, but still more closely with God's approach to man and to the human community. This approach or advent has a historical character above all in the sense that it took place in human history and continues to do so. The history of salvation does not and cannot mean a reduction of God's action and the mission of the divine Persons, to the dimensions of an ordinary human history (nor is it a question here of a simple 'historicization' of theology); but it shows that that action and mission, while fully preserving the divine transcendency, take place within time and in the sight of man and of humanity in the course of history, and therefore become history themselves.

LG 2 | [All the elect] the Father foreknew and predestined before time began 'to become conformed to the image of his Son, that he should be the first-born among many brethren' (Rom. 8:29). He determined to call together in a holy Church those who should believe in Christ. Already present in figure at the beginning of the world, this Church was prepared in marvellous fashion in the history of the people of Israel and in the old Alliance. Established in this last age of the world, and made manifest in the outpouring of the Spirit, it will be brought to glorious completion at the end of time. At that moment, as the Fathers put it, all the just from the time of Adam, 'from Abel, the just one, to the last of the elect' will be gathered together with the Father in the universal Church.

Thus salvation, the source and accomplishment of which are in God, in the Holy Trinity, has its history from the standpoint of the People of God. God's advent determines the issue of salvation in the historical context also, that of the

history of salvation. This advent is above all God's revelation
of himself. 'The invisible God (cf. Col. 1:15; 1 Tim. 1:17),
from the fullness of his love, addresses men as his friends (cf.
Exod. 33:11; John 15:14–15), and moves among them (cf.
Baruch 3:38), in order to invite and receive them into his own
company' (DV 2). These men are indeed 'historical' in the
sense that each of them has his own history, while at the same
time all of them participate in the history of various societies
and of the whole human family.

DV 3 | God . . . wishing to open up the way to heavenly
salvation, manifested himself to our first parents
from the very beginning. After the fall, he
buoyed them up with the hope of salvation,
by promising redemption (cf. Gen. 3:15); and
he has never ceased to take care of the human
race. For he wishes to give eternal life to all
those who seek salvation by patience in well-
doing (cf. Rom. 2:6–7). In his own time God
called Abraham, and made him into a great
nation (cf. Gen. 12:2). After the era of the
patriarchs, he taught this nation, by Moses and
the prophets, to recognize him as the only
living and true God, as a provident Father and
just judge. He taught them, too, to look for the
promised Saviour. And so, throughout the ages,
he prepared the way for the Gospel.

DV 4 | After God had spoken many times and in
various ways through the prophets, 'in these
last days he has spoken to us by a Son' (Heb.
1:1–2). For he sent his Son, the eternal Word
who enlightens all men, to dwell among men
and to tell them about the inner life of God.
Hence, Jesus Christ, sent as 'a man among men',
'speaks the words of God' (Jn. 3:34), and

.accomplishes the saving work which the Father gave him to do (cf. Jn. 5:36; 17:4). As a result, he himself – to see whom is to see the Father (cf. Jn. 14:9) – completed and perfected Revelation and confirmed it with divine guarantees. He did this by the total fact of his presence and self-manifestation – by words and works, signs and miracles, but above all by his death and glorious resurrection from the dead, and finally by sending the Spirit of truth. He revealed that God was with us, to deliver us from the darkness of sin and death, and to raise us up to eternal life.

DV 2 | This economy of Revelation is realized by deeds and words, which are intrinsically bound up with each other. As a result, the works performed by God in the history of salvation show forth and bear out the doctrine and realities signified by the words; the words, for their part, proclaim the works, and bring to light the mystery they contain. The most intimate truth which this revelation gives us about God and the salvation of man shines forth in Christ, who is himself both the mediator and the sum total of Revelation.

God's advent to man is, first and foremost, revelation. The content of revelation, and the purpose of this advent which took place and continues to take place in time, is the salvation of man. The consciousness of salvation is closely bound up with the mission of the Son and the Holy Spirit in which is expressed the eternal design of the Father who 'created the whole universe and chose to raise up men to share in his own divine life' (LG 2). This design, the eternal divine plan, and, closely linked with it, the mission of the Son and the Holy Spirit, constitute the mystery of the Church: a mystery which consists in the salvation of which the Church is the bearer thanks to the 'advent' of God that has taken place and continues to do so. This advent means that the Church, immersed in its own mystery, is always inclined in the direction of history, since the salvation of mankind is a historical process. Some historical threads have to be distinguished here from others, although they are all intertwined so that the 'history of salvation' relates in some degree to every one of them. Thus the original thread is the story of revelation, and the thread which derives from it is the story of the People of God, for the latter presupposes revelation while speaking of salvation as something not only revealed but accepted in faith and realized in actual life. We have already seen that the Church, in accordance with the teaching of Vatican II, identifies itself with the reality of the People of God, and we have explained how this is to be understood. On the basis of this identification we must also take it that the history of the Church, like that of Israel under the old Covenant, is one of the threads to be taken into account in the history of salvation.

DV 14 | By his covenant with Abraham (cf. Gen. 15:18) and, through Moses, with the race of Israel (cf. Ex. 24:8), he did acquire a people for himself, and to them he revealed himself in words and deeds as the one, true, living God, so that Israel might experience the ways of God with men. Moreover, by listening to the voice of God speaking to them through the prophets, they had daily to understand his ways more fully and more clearly, and make them more widely known among the nations (cf. Ps. 21:28-9; 95:1-3; Is. 2:1-4; Jer. 3:17).

The Council has before its eyes the Church as the People of God, in which the advent of God and the mystery of salvation come into contact, all through history, with man and mankind.

Thus the Church is a historical reality with the historical consciousness that is proper to it and whose essential content is the history of salvation. In *Lumen Gentium* we read:

LG 9 | All those, who in faith look towards Jesus, the author of salvation and the principle of unity and peace, God has gathered together and established as the Church, that it may be for each and everyone the visible sacrament of this saving unity. Destined to extend to all regions of the earth, it enters into human history, though it transcends at once all times and all racial boundaries.

The historical reality of the Church, thus constituted, and the 'historical' consciousness that corresponds to it, are always considered by Vatican II in their eschatological dimension. The passage quoted above continues:

LG 9 | Advancing through trials and tribulations, the Church is strengthened by God's grace, promised to her by the Lord so that she may not waver from perfect fidelity, but remain the worthy bride of the Lord, until, through the cross, she may attain to that light which knows no setting.

History and eschatology complement each other 'substantially', and this enables us to appraise exactly the specific character of the story of salvation. Eschatology does not undo its historicity but gives it a sense other than the usual meaning of 'history'. This is because eschatology signifies the fullness of 'salvation', the history of which is at issue. On the road towards this fullness and ultimate realization, salvation has its history in men, mankind and nations, and 'the Church enters human history'. But all this happens 'on the way' towards the future revealed by God, and in view of that final reality. No other history, which belongs essentially to the past, can have this kind of relevance.

The Church's continued relation to human history is expressed in a penetrating manner by the Council in relation to individuals as well as peoples and nations.

LG 13 | Since the kingdom of Christ is not of this world (cf. Jn. 18:36), the Church or People of God which establishes this kingdom does not take away anything from the temporal welfare of any people. Rather she fosters and takes to herself, in so far as they are good, the abilities, the resources and customs of peoples. In so taking them to herself she purifies, strengthens and elevates them. The Church indeed is mindful that she must work with that king to whom the nations were given for an inheritance (cf. Ps. 2:8) and to whose city gifts are brought (cf. Ps. 71[72]: 10; Is. 60:4–7; Apoc. 21:24). This character of universality which adorns the People of God is a gift from the Lord himself whereby the Catholic ceaselessly and efficaciously seeks for the return of all humanity and all its goods under Christ the Head in the unity of his Spirit.

We have already spoken of the Conciliar significance of the Church's universality or catholicity; and it is evident that that universality is permeated by awareness of history. Reading the above passage, it is difficult not to feel that it contains a specific interpretation of the truth concerning the relationship between nature and grace – a truth which is seen not so much through the prism of the interior history of the soul, but rather through the history of all humanity and of individual peoples. On the occasion of the millennium of Polish Christianity (i.e. in 1966) we have read and re-read these Conciliar texts with the greatest care and emotion.

LG 17 | By her proclamation of the Gospel, she draws her hearers to receive and profess the faith, she prepares them for baptism, snatches them from the slavery of error, and she incorporates them into Christ so that in love for him they grow to full maturity. The effect of her work is that whatever good is found sown in the minds and hearts of men or in the rites and customs of peoples, these [sic] not only are preserved from destruction, but are purified, raised up, and perfected for the glory of God, the confusion of the devil, and the happiness of man.

The history of salvation leads through human souls but also finds expression in various communities, and within certain limits it also becomes the history of those communities.

Perhaps the most exact and concise statement of that historical reality and of the historical consciousness of the Church is to be found in the Decree *Ad gentes* on the Missionary Activity of the Church, where we read:

AGD 3 | [However, in] order to establish a relationship of peace and communion with himself, and in order to bring about brotherly union among men, being sinners, God decided to enter into the history of mankind in a new and definitive manner, by sending his own Son in human flesh, so that through him he might snatch men from the power of darkness and of Satan (cf. Col. 1:13; Acts 10:38) and in him reconcile the world to himself.

AGD 4 | To do this, Christ sent the Holy Spirit from the Father to exercise inwardly his saving influence, and to promote the spread of the Church. Without doubt, the Holy Spirit was at work in the world before Christ was glorified. On the day of Pentecost, however, he came down on the disciples that he might remain with them forever (cf. Jn. 14:16); on that day the Church was openly displayed to the crowds and the spread of the Gospel among the nations, through preaching, was begun.

AGD 8 | Even in the secular history of mankind the Gospel has acted as a leaven in the interests of liberty and progress, and it always offers itself as a leaven with regard to brotherhood, unity and peace. So it is not without reason that Christ is hailed by the faithful as the hope of the nations and their saviour.

Vatican II clearly emphasizes the historical consciousness of the Church, the origin of which is 'God's entry into history'; that entry, in the economy of the New Covenant, is linked to the Church's historical mission to mankind and to all peoples. Various Conciliar texts emphasize that 'the period between the first and second coming of the Lord is the time of missionary activity', which 'tends towards eschatological fullness' (AGD 9). The history of salvation, as we have said, is linked with eschatology. At the same time, the historical consciousness of the Church is expressed in a sincere recognition of the particular characteristics of every human subject and every environment in which the Church's mission and through it God's entry into history continue to take effect. This is evidenced by the Council texts already quoted, to which we may add another from the Constitution on the Sacred Liturgy:

SC 37 | [The Church respects and fosters] the qualities and talents of the various races and nations. Anything in these people's way of life which is not indissolubly bound up with superstition and error she studies with sympathy, and, if possible,

> preserves intact. She sometimes even admits such things into the liturgy itself, provided they harmonize with its true and authentic spirit.

Finally we should note that during the period of Vatican II the historical consciousness of the Church expressed itself in a special manner in *Gaudium et Spes*, the Constitution on the Church in the Modern World. The introduction to this Constitution, which sets out to describe the condition of man in today's world, states that the Church's mission and, through it, the entry of God into history requires a sincere recognition of all the individuals and societies which make up that history.

> GS 4 | At all times the Church carries the responsibility of reading the signs of the time and of interpreting them in the light of the Gospel, if it is to carry out its task. In language intelligible to every generation, she should be able to answer the ever recurring questions which men ask.

The category proper to history is time, that primary channel of the stream of history of men, mankind and peoples. God's entry into history, accomplished in and through the Church, constantly emphasizes contemporaneity as the specific summing-up of 'signs of the times'. These signs define closely all that is significant and important to the history of salvation, the entry of God into history and the mission of the Church. 'We must be aware of and understand the aspirations, the yearnings, and the often dramatic features of the world in which we live' (GS 4).

The notion of 'signs of the times' – one of those most frequently studied and analysed in the teaching of Vatican II – also brings into prominence the proper historical consciousness of the Church: for it expresses the fact that the Church's mission of salvation requires essentially to be rooted in time, which shapes its history.

2. *The evolution of the world and the increase of the Kingdom*

Gaudium et Spes underlines the fact that the course of history itself is important for the history of salvation. The Council is careful to take this into account.

> GS 5 | The accelerated pace of history is such that one can scarcely keep abreast of it. The destiny of the human race is viewed as a complete whole, no longer, as it were, in the particular histories of various peoples: now it merges into a complete whole. And so mankind substitues a dynamic and more evolutionary concept of nature for a static one, and the result is an immense series of new problems calling for a new endeavour of analysis and synthesis.

This passage speaks not only of the acceleration of history but of the tendency of modern man to give history a 'dynamic' sense. The sign of the times here consists in a conviction on his part that the whole object of his earthly history is development and temporal progress.

> GS 9 | Meanwhile there is a growing conviction of mankind's ability and duty to strengthen its mastery over nature, and of the need to establish a political, social and economic order at the service of man to assert and develop the dignity proper to individuals and to societies. . . . Man as an individual and as a member of society craves a life that is full, autonomous, and worthy of his nature as a human being; he longs to harness for his own welfare the immense

> resources of the modern world. Among nations
> there is a growing movement to set up a world-
> wide community.

The Church, with the consciousness of the history of
salvation that is proper to it, confronts this multiform evolution and the consciousness of modern man that goes with it:

GS 38 | The Word of God, through whom all things were
made, became man and dwelt among men: a
perfect man, he entered world history, taking
that history into himself and recapitulating it.

This text does much to clarify the 'historical' consciousness
of the Church as the People of God. Human activity in the
world, directed towards universal development and progress,
is compared by the Council to the *mysterium paschale*:

GS 38 | Constituted Lord by his resurrection and given
all authority in heaven and on earth, Christ
is now at work in the hearts of men by the
power of his Spirit; not only does he arouse in
them a desire for the world to come but he
quickens, purifies and strengthens the generous
aspirations of mankind to make life more
humane and conquer the earth for this purpose.

The paschal mystery of Christ lies open in the direction of
eschatology, since it awakes 'the desire of the age to come',
and also towards the evolution of the world which the Council
understands as devoted above all to 'humanizing' (GS 40) the
life of mankind and of human beings. Vatican II lays stress
on the ethical significance of evolution. The ideal of a 'more
human' world fits in with the Gospel, in which Christ teaches
us that:

GS 38 | The fundamental law of human perfection, and
consequently of the transformation of the world,
is the new commandment of love. He assures

those who trust in the charity of God that the
way of love is open to all men and that the effort
to establish a universal brotherhood will not be
in vain.

This love is not something reserved for
important matters, but must be exercised above
all in the ordinary circumstances of daily life.
Christ's example in dying for us sinners teaches
us that we must carry the cross, which the
flesh and the world inflict on the shoulders of all
who seek after peace and justice.

It will be seen that the Gospel not only proclaims the
ideal of a more human world but realistically points out the
practical means which lead to such a world. While the Council
explains how these ways are realized in human conduct.

GS 38 | The gifts of the Spirit are manifold: some men
are called to testify openly to mankind's yearn-
ing for its heavenly home and keep the awareness
of it vividly before men's minds; others are
called to dedicate themselves to the earthly
service of men and in this way to prepare the
way for the kingdom of heaven. But of all the
Spirit makes free men, who are ready to put
aside love of self and integrate earthly resources
into human life, in order to reach out to that
future day when mankind itself will become an
offering accepted by God.

Thus the ideal of a more and more human world which, as
we have said, is in accordance with the Gospel message, is
not its last word concerning man's vocation. Vatican II
carefully distinguishes the evolution of the world from the
history of salvation, while giving full weight to the links
between the two.

GS 39 | That is why, although we must be careful to distinguish earthly progress clearly from the increase of the kingdom of Christ, such progress is of vital concern to the kingdom of God, in so far as it can contribute to the better ordering of human society. When we have spread on earth the fruits of our nature and our enterprise – human dignity, brotherly communion, and freedom – according to the command of the Lord and in his Spirit, we will find them once again, cleansed this time from the stain of sin, illuminated and transfigured, when Christ presents to his Father an eternal and universal kingdom 'of truth and life, a kingdom of holiness and grace, a kingdom of justice, love and peace'. Here on earth the kingdom is mysteriously present; when the Lord comes it will enter into its perfection.

According to the teaching of Vatican II the Church shares in the evolution of the world not only because the ideal of a more and more human world is in accordance with the Gospel, but also because through the realization of such a world there runs the history of salvation in which ultimate reality takes shape. Moreover this reality, as it were in embryo and in a mysterious fashion, is already present in the world through the Church. It is worth while to pay attention first to the way in which the Church, according to the Council's teaching, shares in evolution and progress towards a more and more human world, and then how in its consciousness it continually transcends that evolution, directing itself towards the ultimate reality which will at the same time be the 'fullness of the Kingdom of God'.

Vatican II speaks in many places of the active participation of the Kingdom in the evolution of the world, but perhaps

most fully in Chapters III and IV of Part 1 of *Gaudium et Spes*.
In Chapter III we read several times that 'Individual and
collective activity, that monumental effort of man through the
centuries to improve the circumstances of the world, . . .
considered in itself, corresponds to the plan of God' (GS 34).
In Chapter IV we read:

GS 40 | In pursuing its own salvific purpose not only
does the Church communicate divine life to men
but in a certain sense it casts the reflected light
of that divine life over all the earth, notably
in the way it heals and elevates the dignity of
the human person, in the way it consolidates
society, and endows the daily activity of men
with a deeper sense and meaning. The Church,
then, believes it can contribute much to humanizing the family of man and its history through
each of its members and its community as a
whole.

Chapter IV of *Gaudium et Spes*, examining the tasks of the
Church in the modern world, observes that one of the chief
of these is to safeguard man's personal dignity and freedom.

GS 41 | There is no human law so powerful to safeguard
the personal dignity and freedom of man as the
Gospel which Christ entrusted to the Church;
for the Gospel announces and proclaims the
freedom of the sons of God, it rejects all bondage
resulting from sin, it scrupulously respects the
dignity of conscience and its freedom of choice,
it never ceases to encourage the employment of
human talents in the service of God and man,
and, finally, it commends everyone to the
charity of all.

Further on we read:

GS 41 | In virtue of the Gospel entrusted to it the Church proclaims the rights of man: she acknowledges and holds in high esteem the dynamic approach of today which is fostering these rights all over the world. But this approach needs to be animated by the spirit of the Gospel and preserved from all traces of false autonomy. For there is a temptation to feel that our personal rights are fully maintained only when we are exempt from every restriction of divine law. But this is the way leading to the extinction of human dignity, not its preservation.

The evolution towards recognition of the dignity of the human person is in accordance with the Gospel, in which it in fact finds a continuous 'leaven', so that in the realization of this aspiration we may see not only the fruit of the human spirit but also the fruit of the action of the divine Spirit in men's souls. Accepting this participation in the evolution of the 'world' and underlining what is essential in it, Vatican II at the same time utters a warning against any distortion: human dignity must not be identified with some misconceived 'autonomy' of man. Vatican II is at pains to express the true relationship between the Gospel and evolution and to see that the real meaning of many concepts that belong to the language of progress is not obscured.

GS 41 | Modern man is in a process of fuller personality development and of a growing discovery and affirmation of his own rights. But the Church is entrusted with the task of opening up to man the mystery of God, who is the last end of man; in doing so it opens up to him the meaning of his own existence, the innermost truth about himself.

GS 42 | The Church, moreover, acknowledges the good to be found in the social dynamism of today, particularly progress towards unity, healthy socialization, and civil and economic cooperation. The encouragement of unity is in harmony with the deepest nature of the Church's mission, for it 'is in the nature of a sacrament – a sign and instrument – that is of communion with God and of unity among all men'. It shows to the world that social and exterior union comes from a union of hearts and minds, from the faith and love by which its own indissoluble unity has been founded in the Holy Spirit. The impact which the Church can have on modern society amounts to an effective living of faith and love, not to any external power exercised by purely human means.

The Council understands the Church's participation in the evolution of the world in a double sense. For instance, in Chapter IV of *Gaudium et Spes* we read: 'The Church also realizes how much it needs the maturing influence of centuries of past experience in order to work out its relationship to the world' (GS 43). Or again:

GS 44 | The Church has a visible social structure, which is a sign of its unity in Christ: as such it can be enriched, and it is being enriched, by the evolution of social life – not as if something were missing in the constitution which Christ gave the Church, but in order to understand this constitution more deeply, express it better, and adapt it more successfully to our times . . . The Church itself also recognizes that it has benefited and is still benefiting from the opposition of its enemies and persecutors.

The Church, it will be seen, participates in the evolution of the world through its own evolution also. Vatican II expresses a mature consciousness of this truth, making it a fundamental principle of the whole programme of renewal.

Here the historical consciousness of the Church manifests itself with especial clarity. It may be said that the Council's whole concept of *aggiornamento* (*renovatio accommodata*) is above all an expression of that consciousness. As we have already pointed out, historical consciousness is distinguished by a particular understanding of the subject of history and of the various human environments in which it unfolds.

GS 44 | Indeed, this kind of adaptation and preaching of the revealed Word must ever be the law of all evangelization. In this way it is possible to create in every country the possibility of expressing the message of Christ in suitable terms and to foster vital contact and exchange between the Church and different cultures. Nowadays when things change so rapidly and thought patterns differ so widely, the Church needs to step up this exchange by calling upon the help of people who are living in the world, who are experts in its organizations and its forms of training, and who understand its mentality, in the case of believers and nonbelievers alike. With the help of the Holy Spirit, it is the task of the whole people of God, particularly of its pastors and theologians, to listen to and distinguish the many voices of our times and to interpret them in the light of the divine Word, in order that the revealed truth may be more deeply penetrated, better understood, and more suitably presented.

Emphasizing the participation of the Church in the evolution of the world through its own evolution, and proclaiming the necessity for this, Vatican II takes up a position *vis à vis* both the past and the future. This is a special expression of the historic consciousness of the Church: special, because the normal category of history is only the past, whereas the history of salvation, referring continuously to the eschatological dimension which is both essential and dynamic, contains within itself a particular reason for confronting the future.

Only in all these dimensions together does the Church retain full consciousness of its own identity, which is also the basis of renewal and *aggiornamento*. The Church can share in the evolution of the world only on this essential condition, that is to say through its own evolution. This, we may say, is the deepest substratum of the 'historical consciousness' of the Church and the fundamental premiss of the judgement which the Church, through the Council, has uttered concerning itself.

> GS 43   By the power of the Holy Spirit the Church is the faithful spouse of the Lord and will never fail to be a sign of salvation in the world; but she is by no means unaware that down through the centuries there have been among her members, both clerical and lay, some who were disloyal to the Spirit of God.

This judgement on the past also extends to the present: 'Today as well, the Church is not blind to the discrepancy between the message it proclaims and the human weakness of those to whom the Gospel has been entrusted' (GS 43). This in turn is an element in plans for the future, to some extent in the basic premisses of what must be a continuous renewal.

> GS 43 | Whatever is history's judgment on these shortcomings, we cannot ignore them and we must combat them earnestly, lest they hinder the spread of the Gospel. The Church also realizes how much it needs the maturing influence of

centuries of past experience in order to work out its relationship to the world. Guided by the Holy Spirit the Church ceaselessly 'exhorts her children to purification and renewal so that the sign of Christ may shine more brightly over the face of the Church'.

We have tried to draw together the chief strands of the teaching of Vatican II which serve to enrich the historical consciousness of the Church as the People of God. To arrange these themes in a fundamental order it is necessary to refer to all we have said on the subject of awareness of salvation in relation to the revelation of the Holy Trinity, and awareness of redemption in the mystery of Jesus Christ. These strata of consciousness, if we may so call them, are antecedents which condition the historical consciousness of the Church. Man's salvation is the plan and design of the Holy Trinity before it becomes the basis of history as a result of the advent of God, the mission of the divine Persons; supernatural salvation becomes the basis of history as a result of forming part of the history of men and peoples and developing along with it. Thus, not only do men 'lend' their history to the eternal plan and mystery of salvation, but salvation itself is accomplished in a historical manner which corresponds to that plan and mystery. The paschal mystery, the culmination of the history of salvation, was historically prepared before it took place, and since it became historical fact it has continued to realize itself in the history of the People of God on earth.

The consciousness of salvation (a 'conditioning stratum' of the historical consciousness of the Church) is closely linked with the consciousness of redemption. In the Council's teaching redemption, as we have tried to show, is a reality constantly turned towards the world and thus constantly present in the Church. This idea is confirmed by most of the Council texts on the subject of the evolution of the world of man in relation to the 'increase of the Kingdom of God'. In the mystery and reality of redemption there is a strong emphasis which comes from faith which calls on men to make a reality of dignity, freedom and brotherly concord. The Council, particularly in *Gaudium et Spes*, emphasizes that the fundamental content of that exhortation corresponds to real human aspirations in the world which are, so to speak, empirically knowable. In this way there is a profound connection and even a kind of elementary identity between the principal vectors of the history and evolution of the world, on the one hand, and the history of salvation on the other. The plan of salvation sinks its roots into the most real aspirations and purposes of human beings and humanity. Redemption is constantly directed towards man and humanity in the world, and the Church encounters the world against the background of those aspirations and purposes. In the same way the history of the world runs in the channel of the history of salvation, which in a sense it regards as its own. And, conversely, the true conquests of man and humanity, authentic victories in the history of the world, are also the 'substratum' of the kingdom of God on earth.

None the less, the history of salvation always embraces more than the history of the 'world'. This fact is confirmed and determined by redemption as a divine reality in Jesus Christ, addressed to man in the world and to mankind. Historical though it is, redemption is at the same time profoundly eschatological. It bears witness above all to the constant need for purification of the most human values, of man's aspirations and purposes, in which the history of the world in a sense encounters the history of salvation. The reality of redemption attests the need to find in these values, aspirations and purposes the divine dimension which is proper to them in order that they may become the 'substance' of the kingdom of God. At the same time redemption, by its own power, actually creates that divine dimension and carries out that fundamental purification of values, aspirations and purposes. It thus becomes the basis of renewal: it is a new beginning of the whole reality of creation. As a result of all this, redemption – a mystery and reality constantly present in the Church and always turned towards the world – with its profound and eloquent dynamism orients the world, through the Church, towards its ultimate fulfilment. The history of salvation is an authentic history and at the same time a history that constantly looks beyond itself: a history whose full meaning is found not in the past but rather in the future:

LG 6 | While on earth she journeys in a foreign land away from the Lord (cf. 2 Cor. 5:6), the Church sees herself as an exile. She seeks and is concerned about those things which are above, where Christ is seated at the right hand of God, where the life of the Church is hidden with Christ in God until she appears in glory with her Spouse (cf. Col. 3:1–4).

GS 45 | The Word of God, through whom all things were made, was made flesh, so that as a perfect man he could save all men and sum up all things in himself. The Lord is the goal of human history, the focal point of the desires of history and civilization, the centre of mankind, the joy of all hearts, and the fulfilment of all aspirations. It is he whom the Father raised from the dead, exalted and placed at his right hand, constituting him judge of the living and the dead. Animated and drawn together in his Spirit we press onwards on our journey towards the consummation of history which fully corresponds to the plan of his love: 'to unite all things in him, things in heaven and things on earth' (Eph. 1:10).

The Lord himself said: 'Behold, I am coming soon, bringing my recompense, to repay every one for what he has done. I am the alpha and the omega, the first and the last, the beginning and the end' (Apoc. 22:12–13).

3.   *The eschatological character of the Church and the renewal of the world*

GS 18 | It is in regard to death that man's condition is most shrouded in doubt. Man is tormented not only by pain and by the gradual breaking-up of his body but also, and even more, by the dread of forever ceasing to be. But a deep instinct leads him rightly to shrink from and to reject the utter ruin and total loss of his personality. Because he bears in himself the seed of eternity, which cannot be reduced to mere matter, he rebels against death. All the aids made available by technology, however useful they may be, cannot set his anguished mind at rest. They may prolong his life-span; but this does not satisfy his heartfelt longing, one that can never be stifled, for a life to come.

Eschatology – that branch of the science of faith, and before it of revelation, which treats of the 'last things' – traditionally has its beginning in the contemplation of the necessity of death to which man is subject. In the passage quoted above Vatican II expresses the same truth as it appears to the consciousness of present-day man. At the same time, however, in accordance with the long tradition of faith and of human thought, the Council explains that 'rebellion' against death, the resistance that man opposes to it with his longing for immortality. Christian eschatology starts from these two fundamental truths: the death of the body and the immortality of the soul.

GS 18 | While the mind is at a loss before the mystery of death, the Church, taught by divine Revelation, declares that God has created man in view of a blessed destiny that lies beyond the limits of his sad state on earth. Moreover, the Christian faith teaches that bodily death, from which man would have been immune had he not sinned, will be overcome when that wholeness which he lost through his own fault will be given once again to him by the almighty and merciful Saviour. For God has called man, and still calls him, to cleave with all his being to him in sharing for ever a life that is divine and free from all decay. Christ won this victory when he rose to life, for by his death he freed man from death. Faith, therefore, with its solidly based teaching, provides every thoughtful man with an answer to his anxious queries about his future lot. At the same time it makes him able to be united in Christ with his loved ones who have already died, and gives hope that they have found true life with God.

These truths include everything that, according to Revelation, comprises the reality of eternal life to which man is called. The Council's teaching presents the eschatology of man in the light of the full truth concerning the Church, understood as the universal sacrament of eternal salvation.

LG 48 | So it is, united with Christ in the Church and marked with the Holy Spirit 'who is the guarantee of our inheritance' (Eph. 1:14) that we are truly called and indeed are children of God (cf. 1 Jn. 3:1), though we have not yet appeared with Christ in glory (cf. Col. 3:4) in which we will be like to God, for we will see him as he is (cf. 1 Jn. 3:2).

Eternal life is the fruit of the saving mission of Jesus Christ, the Son of God, and of the Holy Spirit, which implants in man's immortal soul the grace of divine sonship as a 'pledge of inheritance'. According to Revelation and to the immutable doctrine of the Church there is a close link between sanctifying grace – i.e. sonship by divine adoption, and the resemblance to Christ that this implies – and the beatific vision of God 'as he truly is' (1 John 3:2). This beatific vision is founded in the supernatural likeness of man to God, thanks to which he is to 'appear' with Christ in glory. Eternal life is the final fulfilment of man's vocation, towards which his spiritual nature tends under the influence of grace.

> LG 48   'While we are at home in the body we are away from the Lord' (2 Cor. 5:6) and having the first fruits of the Spirit we groan inwardly (cf. Rom. 8:23) and we desire to be with Christ (cf. Phil. 1:23).

These 'first fruits of the Spirit' turn our steps towards Christ here on earth, and this turning to Christ has an eschatological, other-worldly character. It is that character which causes us to think of the whole of life as a test which will have its final reward in the 'future glory' which is to be revealed to us' (Rom. 8:18). Further we read:

> LG 48   That same charity urges us to live more for him who died for us and who rose again (cf. 2 Cor. 5:15). We make it our aim, then, to please the Lord in all things (cf. 2 Cor. 5:9) and we put on the armour of God that we may be able to stand against the wiles of the devil and resist in the evil day (cf. Eph. 6:11–13). Since we know neither the day nor the hour, we should follow the advice of the Lord and watch constantly so that when the single course of our earthly life is

> completed (cf. Heb. 9:27), we may merit to
> enter with him into the marriage feast and be
> numbered among the blessed (cf. Mt. 25:31–46)
> and not, like the wicked and slothful servants
> (cf. Mt. 25:26), be ordered to depart into the
> eternal fire (cf. Mt. 25:41), into the outer
> darkness where 'men will weep and gnash their
> teeth' (Mt. 22:13 and 25:30). Before we reign
> with Christ in glory we must all appear 'before
> the judgment seat of Christ, so that each one
> may receive good or evil, according to what he
> has done in the body' (2 Cor. 5:10), and at the
> end of the world 'they will come forth, those
> who have done good, to the resurrection of life,
> and those who have done evil, to the resurrection
> of judgment' (Jn. 5:29; cf. Mt. 25:46).

Christian eschatology is Christocentric. It is easy to see in
it the fulfilment of redemption as a reality which, being continually present in the Church, is always directed towards
man in the world. Thanks to the mystery of redemption, man
in a sense shares divine sonship with Christ, and is to share
his glory for ever. On the road towards this glorification
of man in Christ is Judgement, which is also Christ's tribunal.
Vatican II presents the eschatology of man as a consequence of
redemption, fruit of the paschal mystery of Christ acting in
man and bringing him through the 'sufferings of this present
time' (Rom. 8:18) to future glory. In *Lumen Gentium* we read:

LG 48 | We reckon then that 'the sufferings of this
> present time are not worth comparing with the
> glory that is to be revealed to us' (Rom. 8:18;
> cf. 2 Tim. 2.11–12); and strong in faith we look
> for 'the blessed hope, the appearing of the glory
> of our great God and Saviour Jesus Christ'
> (Tit. 2:13) 'who will change our lowly body

> to be like his glorious body' (Phil. 3:21) and
> who will come 'to be glorified in his saints, and
> to be marvelled at in all who have believed'
> (2 Th. 1:10).

The resurrection of the body, which is the very centre of the earthly *mysterium paschale* of Jesus Christ, appears in the eschatological view as the fullness of resemblance to Christ: a resemblance in the Spirit through the grace of divine sonship, which is to lead to the ultimate reality of bodily resemblance, 'to be like his glorious body' (Phil 3:21).

However, before attaining final victory and the kingdom of Christ, the pilgrim Church on earth remains in union not only with the Church of glory but also with the Church of purification. As we read in *Lumen Gentium*:

LG 49 | When the Lord will come in glory, and all his
> angels with him (cf. Mt. 25:31), death will be
> no more and all things will be subject to him (cf.
> 1 Cor. 15:26–7). But at the present time some
> of his disciples are pilgrims on earth. Others
> have died and are being purified, while still
> others are in glory, contemplating 'in full light,
> God himself triune and one, exactly as he is'.
> All of us, however, in varying degrees and in
> different ways share in the same charity towards
> God and our neighbours, and we all sing the one
> hymn of glory to our God.

It is significant that in the Conclusion to *Gaudium et Spes* the Council appeals to the judgement of God on all Christians, reminding them that 'they have shouldered a weighty task here on earth and must render an account of it to him who will judge all men on the last day. Not everyone who says "Lord, Lord" will enter the kingdom of heaven, but those who do the will of the Father and who manfully put their hands to the work' (GS 93).

In the Council's teaching as a whole can be found all that which we here call the 'eschatology of man' and which in catechetical or homiletic tradition has been styled the doctrine of 'last things'. However, the foregoing analysis of the consciousness of the Church as the People of God will have shown what attention the Council pays to society and the mutual relationship between it and individuals; and we find this communal dimension of the Church repeated in the field of eschatology. The Council deals with the eschatology of the Church more fully than that of man; none the less, as there are basic links between the community and the individual, the eschatology of the Church enables us to penetrate more profoundly into that of man as well.

LG 48 | Christ, lifted up from the earth, has drawn all men to himself (cf. Jn. 12:32). Rising from the dead (cf. Rom. 6:9) he sent his life-giving Spirit upon his disciples and through him set up his Body which is the Church as the universal sacrament of salvation. Sitting at the right hand of the Father he is continually active in the world in order to lead men to the Church and, through it, join them more closely to himself; and, by nourishing them with his own Body and Blood, make them partakers of this glorious life.

LG 49 | All, indeed, who are of Christ and who have his Spirit form one Church and in Christ cleave together (Eph. 4:16).

In Jesus Christ both dimensions of the Church, the temporal and the eschatological, are not only united but interpenetrate each other. The eschatological community of the Church is formed continually in a lively union with the aims of the pilgrim Church on earth. The centre and source of that union is Christ.

LG 49 | So it is that the union of the wayfarers with the brethren who sleep in the peace of Christ is in no way interrupted, but on the contrary, according to the constant faith of the Church, this union is reinforced by an exchange of spiritual goods. Being more closely united to Christ, those who dwell in heaven fix the whole Church more firmly in holiness, add to the nobility of the worship that the Church offers to God here on earth, and in many ways help in a broader building up of the Church (cf. 1 Cor. 12:12–27). Once received into their heavenly home and being present to the Lord (cf. 2 Cor. 5:8), through him and with him and in him they do not cease to intercede with the Father for us, as they proffer the merits which they acquired on earth through the one mediator between God and men, Christ Jesus (cf. 1 Tim. 2:5), serving God in all things and completing in their flesh what is lacking in Christ's afflictions for the sake of his Body, that is, the Church (cf. Col. 1:24). So by their brotherly concern is our weakness greatly helped.

Christ is the centre and source of the Communion of Saints, through which the whole Church finds itself in intimate union and communion. Not only does the eschatological dimension of the Church create itself continuously in connection with its earthly pilgrimage, but it also enters into this pilgrimage because of a specific foreshadowing which manifests itself in the history of salvation and the life of the Church within time. There is both an ascending and a descending rhythm between that history and eschatology, between pilgrimage and fulfilment. The ascending rhythm corresponds to the earthly pilgrimage and the Church's striving towards its goal: we shall see this more clearly when meditating on the meaning of sanctity in the light of the Council's teaching. But the Church's earthly pilgrimage and striving towards its goal already bear the mark of ultimate fulfilment:

LG 48 | Already the final age of the world is with us (cf. 1 Cor. 10:11) and the renewal of the world is irrevocably under way; it is even now anticipated in a certain real way, for the Church on earth is endowed already with a sanctity that is real though imperfect. However, until there be realized new heavens and a new earth in which justice dwells (cf. 2 Pet. 3:13) the pilgrim Church, in its sacraments and institutions, which belong to this present age, carries the mark of this world which will pass, and she herself takes her place among the creatures which groan and travail yet and await the revelation of the sons of God (cf. Rom. 8:19–22).

Vatican II has done much to enrich the eschatological consciousness of the Church – a consciousness that I would say fully expresses the basic relationship between the Church and the world, which plays such a prominent part in all the Council's thinking. 'The world which the Council has in mind is that which . . . in the Christian vision has been created and is sustained by the love of its maker, which has been freed from the slavery of sin by Christ, who was crucified and rose again in order to break the stranglehold of the Evil One, so that it might be fashioned anew according to God's design and brought to its fulfilment' (GS 2). The eschatological consciousness of the Church is closely united to the consciousness of creation and redemption. It embraces the world as the universal created reality, at the centre of which man has been placed by God: this reality, including man, must be renewed once and for all in Christ.

LG 48 | The Church, to which we are all called in
Christ Jesus, and in which by the grace of God
we acquire holiness, will receive its perfection
only in the glory of heaven, when will come
the time of the renewal of all things (Acts 3:21).
At that time, together with the human race, the
universe itself, which is so closely related to
man and which attains its destiny through him,
will be perfectly reestablished in Christ (cf.
Eph. 1:10; Col. 1:20; 2 Pet. 3:10–13).

The eschatological renewal of the world began with
redemption by Christ, and it is that redemption of the world
that continues in the Church. The Church participates in the
evolution of the world. More, the pilgrim Church bears
on its face the 'transient image of this world' – for evolution
must signify transience. None the less, in the depths of the
evolution of the transitory world, the Church recognizes,
thanks to its faith based on the Word of God, which goes
beyond those creatures which, groaning in travail, 'wait with
eager longing for the revealing of the sons of God' (cf. Rom.
8:19–22). This revelation constitutes man's final prospect,
not 'outside the world' but together with it. Vatican II,
following Holy Scripture, presents to us the eschatology of
man, the 'revealing of the sons of God', as the root and basis
of the final renewal of the world, and in this the eschatological
character of the Church is expressed in all its fullness. This
is the final fulfilment of the relationship, of which the Council
speaks, between the Church and the world. The eschatology
of the Church is at the same time the fulfilment of the world,
a great cosmic consummation. It is Christ who is to bring the
world to that fulfilment.

GS 45 | Animated and drawn together in his Spirit we
press onwards on our journey towards the
consummation of history which fully corres-

> ponds to the plan of his love: 'to unite all things in him, things in heaven and things on earth' (Eph. 1:10).

The fulfilment of human history in Christ is, as it were, the very nucleus of the fulfilment of the world. The cosmic consummation is based on *Christus-Consummator* and must effect itself through him. The fulfilment of the world corresponds to the redemption of the world.

GS 48 | The promised and hoped-for restoration, therefore, has already begun in Christ. It is carried forward in the sending of the Holy Spirit and through him continues in the Church in which, through our faith, we learn the meaning of our earthly life, while we bring to term, with hope of future good, the task allotted to us in the world by the Father, and so work out our salvation (cf. Phil. 2:12).

Vatican II sees, especially in the Church's liturgy, the prelude to the eternal glory of God in which the eschatological Church will live, which will unite in Christ all men who have been saved and all the renewed world.

LG 51 | For if we continue to love one another and to join in praising the Most Holy Trinity – all of us who are sons of God and form one family in Christ (cf. Heb. 3:6) – we will be faithful to the deepest vocation of the Church and will share in a foretaste of the liturgy of perfect glory.

LG 50 | It is especially in the sacred liturgy that our union with the heavenly Church is best realized; in the liturgy, through the sacramental signs, the power of the Holy Spirit acts on us, and with community rejoicing we celebrate together the praise of the divine majesty, when all those of every tribe and tongue and people and nation (cf. Apoc. 5:9) who have been redeemed by the blood of Christ and gathered together into one Church glorify, in one common song of praise, the one and triune God.

The glory of God is the end of all creation. The final fulfilment of that glory is the salvation of man and the renewal of the world in Christ.

GS 39 | We know neither the moment of the consummation of the earth and of man nor the way the universe will be transformed. The form of this world, distorted by sin, is passing away and we are taught that God is preparing a new dwelling and a new earth in which righteousness dwells, whose happiness will fill and surpass all the desires of peace arising in the hearts of men. Then, with death conquered, the sons of God will be raised in Christ and what was sown in weakness and dishonour will put on the imperishable: charity and its works will remain, and all of creation, which God made for man, will be set free from its bondage to decay.

We have been warned, of course, that it profits man nothing if he gains the whole world and loses or forfeits himself. Far from diminishing our concern to develop this earth, the expectation of a new earth should spur us on, for it is here that the body of a new human family grows, foreshadowing in some way the age which is to come.

4. *The meaning of holiness. Mary as a figure of the Church*

The meaning of holiness in the teaching of Vatican II is brought out in the context of the earthly history of salvation and of the eschatology of the Church, as we have already outlined. Chapter VII of *Lumen Gentium* speaks of the 'eschatological nature of the pilgrim Church and its union with the Church in heaven', while Chapter V is entitled 'The Call to Holiness'. Christian holiness is the central theme of faith and the fulness of its realization, that is to say of the 'life of faith'. This meaning must be sought, above all in a study of Chapters V and VII of *Lumen Gentium*.

So far we have considered especially the 'eschatological' Chapter VII, which defines sanctity from the point of view of the Church's fulfilment in heaven. In the communion of the saved, the Blessed and the Saints we have before us all those who first shared the hardships of the Church's earthly pilgrimage.

> LG 50 | God shows to men, in a vivid way, his presence and his face in the lives of those companions of ours in the human condition who are more perfectly transformed into the image of Christ (cf. 2 Cor. 3:18). He speaks to us in them and offers us a sign of this kingdom, to which we are powerfully attracted, so great a cloud of witnesses is there given (cf. Heb. 12:1) and such a witness of the truth of the Gospel.

Human sanctity brings God into man's presence in a particular way, becomes a living witness to him and confirms the truth of the Gospel. Thus it does more than anything else else to attract others to the way of salvation.

LG 50 | To look on the life of those who have faithfully followed Christ is to be inspired with a new reason for seeking the city which is to come (cf. Heb. 13:14 and 11:10), while at the same time we are taught to know a most safe path by which, despite the vicissitudes of the world, and in keeping with the state of life and condition proper to each of us, we will be able to arrive at perfect union with Christ, that is, holiness.

The history of salvation is the history of the whole people of God, which also pervades the lives of individuals and takes a new specific form in each. The essential meaning of holiness is that it is always personal, and that each and every man is called to it. All members of the People of God are called, but each is called in a unique and unrepeatable manner.

Holiness is consequently the fundamental basis on which the formation of the community of the People of God must rest. *Lumen Gentium* shows this to be so in terms of the earthly history of salvation as well as in the eschatological dimension. To begin with the latter:

LG 50 | It is not merely by the title of example that we cherish the memory of those in heaven; we seek, rather, that by this devotion to the exercise of fraternal charity the union of the whole Church in the Spirit may be strengthened (cf. Eph. 4:1–6). Exactly as Christian communion between men on their earthly pilgrimage brings us closer to Christ, so our community with the saints joins us to Christ, from whom as from its fountain and head issues all grace and the life of the People of God itself. It is most fitting, therefore, that we love those friends and co-heirs of Jesus Christ who are also our brothers and outstanding benefactors, and that we give due thanks to God for them, 'humbly invoking

> them, and having recourse to their prayers, their aid and help in obtaining from God through his Son, Jesus Christ, Our Lord, our only Redeemer and Saviour, the benefits we need'. Every authentic witness of love, indeed, offered by us to those who are in heaven tends to and terminates in Christ, 'the crown of all the saints,' and through him in God, who is wonderful in his saints and is glorified in them.

The meaning of holiness for the community of the People of God is expressed in all the richness of the mystery of the communion of saints, which Vatican II recalls in the above passages from *Lumen Gentium*. In that mystery is revealed in its fullness also the kind of union proper to the Church as the People of God, that is to say *communio*. In this communion the individual makes a perfect gift of himself to others while at the same time fully realizing himself: thus sanctity seen in its eschatological dimension is fulfilment.

In the dimension of the earthly history of salvation, holiness is a vocation and an aspiration. The call to holiness comes from Christ the Lord and becomes a characteristic as well as a duty of the Church. Vatican II recalls that holiness is an essential content of the Christian vocation.

LG 40 | The Lord Jesus, divine teacher and model of all perfection, preached holiness of life (of which he is the author and maker) to each and every one of his disciples without distinction: 'You, therefore, must be perfect, as your heavenly Father is perfect' (Mt. 5:48). For he sent the Holy Spirit to all to move them inwardly to love God with their whole heart, with their whole soul, with their whole understanding, and with their whole strength (cf. Mk. 12:30), and to love one another as Christ loved them (cf. Jn. 13:34; 15:12). The followers of Christ, called by God

not in virtue of their works but by his design and
grace, and justified in the Lord Jesus, have been
made sons of God in the baptism of faith and
partakers of the divine nature, and so are truly
sanctified. They must therefore hold on to and
perfect in their lives that sanctification which
they have received from God. They are told
by the apostle to live 'as is fitting among saints'
(Eph. 5:3), and to put on 'as God's chosen ones,
holy and beloved, compassion, kindness, lowli-
ness, meekness, and patience' (Col. 3:12), to
have the fruits of the Spirit for their sanctification
(cf. Gal. 5:22; Rom. 6:22). But since we all
offend in many ways (cf. Jas. 3:2), we constantly
need God's mercy and must pray every day:
'And forgive us our debts' (Mt. 6:12).

Such is a brief summary of Christ's call to holiness, a call
addressed to mankind by word and example. The call is
effective because it is accompanied by a gift of the Holy
Spirit, that is by grace, which constitutes the real foundation
of man's santification notwithstanding his weak and sinful
nature. On man's part, holiness, which is always a response
in faith to the divine gift of grace, takes the form of moral
perfection, the mainspring of which is charity.

LG 42 | 'God is love, and he who abides in love abides
in God, and God abides in him' (1 Jn. 4:16). God
has poured out his love in our hearts through the
Holy Spirit to all to move them interiorly to love
5:5); therefore the first and most necessary gift
is charity, by which we love God above all things
and our neighbour because of him.

Christian perfection, or holiness, corresponds fully to the
dignity of the individual, of which we read so often in the
Council documents and particularly in *Gaudium et Spes*.

LG 40 | It is therefore quite clear that all Christians in any state or walk of life are called to the fullness of Christian life and to the perfection of love, and by this holiness a more human manner of life is fostered also in earthly society.

Holiness has always profoundly united the Church with man and with humanity: accordingly Vatican II prescribes it in the following words:

LG 40 | In order to reach this perfection the faithful should use the strength dealt out to them by Christ's gift, so that, following in his footsteps and conformed to his image, doing the will of God in everything, they may wholeheartedly devote themselves to the glory of God and to the service of their neighbour. Thus the holiness of the People of God will grow in fruitful abundance, as is clearly shown in the history of the Church through the life of so many saints.

The universal call to holiness is also, as the Council teaches, the primary inspiration of the sanctity of the Church.

LG 39 | The Church, whose mystery is set forth by this sacred Council, is held, as a matter of faith, to be unfailingly holy. This is because Christ, the Son of God, who with the Father and the Spirit is hailed as 'alone holy', loved the Church as his Bride, giving himself up for her so as to sanctify her (cf. Eph. 5:25–6); he joined her to himself as his body and endowed her with the gift of the Holy Spirit for the glory of God. Therefore all in the Church, whether they belong to the hierarchy or are cared for by it, are called to holiness, according to the apostle's saying: 'For this is the will of God, your santification' (1 Th. 4:3; cf. Eph. 1:4). This holiness of the

Church is constantly shown forth in the fruits
of grace which the Spirit produces in the faithful,
and so it must be; it is expressed in many ways
by the individuals who, each in his own state of
life, tend to the perfection of love, thus sanctifying
others; it appears in a certain way of its own in
the practice of the counsels which have been
usually called 'evangelical'. This practice of the
counsels prompted by the Holy Spirit, undertaken by many Christians whether privately or
in a form or state sanctioned by the Church,
gives and should give a striking witness and
example of that holiness.

This passage is also a concise exposition of what constitutes
the essence of sanctity according to the Gospel, namely
charity, which develops with the aid of grace and reaches
perfection according to the particular vocation of every
Christian. Accordingly Vatican II indicates various ways to
sanctity: through conjugal life as well as that of single or
widowed persons, and through various activities and obligations (cf. LG 41). The Council then recalls the significance and
value of the evangelical counsels, of which the same document
speaks more fully in Chapter VI on the religious vocation.
While emphasizing the importance of chastity (virginity and
celibacy 'for love of the kingdom of heaven'), the Council
seems to lay special stress on the value of poverty in a broad
sense.

LG 42 | Therefore all the faithful are invited and obliged
to holiness and the perfection of their own state
of life. Accordingly let all of them see that they
direct their affections rightly, lest they be
hindered in their pursuit of perfect love by the
use of worldly things and by an adherence to
riches which is contrary to the spirit of evangelical poverty, following the apostle's advice:

> Let those who use this world not fix their abode
> in it, for the form of this world is passing away
> (cf. 1 Cor. 7:31, Greek text).

The Apostle's words here quoted are particularly apposite
in the context of the Council's doctrine concerning the
Church, which seeks in the contemporary world to rediscover
its own original image of a 'Church of the poor', closely
attuned to the beatitudes of Christ.

The evangelical counsels, even more than the command-
ments, should serve to promote charity. Charity is the essence
of holiness in a Christian, and his progress towards sanctity is
measured by the increase of his charity. This principle enables
us to perceive a unity in the multiplicity of ways which, within
the general call to sanctity, lead individuals to attain it in their
different fashions.

LG 41
> The forms and tasks of life are many but holiness
> is one – that sanctity which is cultivated by all
> who act under God's Spirit and, obeying the
> Father's voice and adoring God the Father in
> spirit and in truth, follow Christ, poor, humble
> and cross-bearing, that they may deserve to be
> partakers of his glory. Each one, however,
> according to his own gifts and duties must
> steadfastly advance along the way of a living
> faith, which arouses hope and works through
> love.

Jesus Christ is the sole 'author' of the holiness of his
disciples and followers, and is he who brings it to fulfilment.
Although the facets of sanctity are different in different
people, they can all be discerned and related to their common
Source and Model. Through all the imitators of a single
Master, as well as through himself, there is revealed in the
world 'the love with which God loved the world'.

LG 41 | Accordingly all Christians, in the conditions, duties and circumstances of their life and through all these, will sanctify themselves more and more if they receive all things with faith from the hand of the heavenly Father and co-operate with the divine will, thus showing forth in that temporal service the love with which God has loved the world.

The most perfect witness to this love is martyrdom. Such has been the conviction of all Tradition, and it is reaffirmed by Vatican II.

LG 42 | Since Jesus, the Son of God, showed his love by laying down his life for us, no one has greater love than he who lays down his life for him and for his brothers (cf. 1 Jn. 3:16, Jn. 15:13). Some Christians have been called from the beginning, and will always be called, to give this greatest testimony of love to all, especially to persecutors. Martyrdom makes the disciple like his master, who willingly accepted death for the salvation of the world, and through it he is conformed to him by the shedding of blood. Therefore the Church considers it the highest gift and supreme test of love. And while it is given to few, all however must be prepared to confess Christ before men and to follow him along the way of the cross amidst the persecutions which the Church never lacks.

Having spoken of martyrdom, which is the supreme witness of love, the Council document also describes the more ordinary ways to holiness and speaks of those means of sanctification which have been confirmed by long experience.

LG 42 | But if charity is to grow and fructify in the soul like a good seed, each of the faithful must

> willingly hear the word of God and carry out his
> will with deeds, with the help of his grace; he
> must frequently partake of the sacraments,
> chiefly the Eucharist, and take part in the
> liturgy; he must constantly apply himself to
> prayer, self-denial, active brotherly service and
> the practice of all virtues.

The consciousness of the Church as the People of God is
both historical and eschatological: this is shown by the clear
teaching of Vatican II. Against this background we perceive
the significance of holiness, which illustrates more clearly and
confirms that which lies between the history of salvation and
eschatology, between the Church's aim and its fulfilment. The
saints in the Church cooperate in forming the historical and
eschatological consciousness of the People of God, which is in
a sense the last word of the response of faith to God's self-
revelation. In fact through Revelation 'The invisible God
(cf. Col. 1:15; 1 Tim. 1:17) from the fullness of his love
addresses men as his friends (cf. Exod. 33:11; John 15:14–15)
and moves among them (cf. Baruch 3:38), in order to invite
and receive them into his own company' (DV 2).

Vatican II teaches that among all the saints and Blessed a
special place belongs to the Virgin Mother of God. This
doctrine, inherited from unchanging tradition and enriched
by new arguments, is set forth in Chapter VIII of *Lumen
Gentium.*

LG 63 | By reason of the gift and role of her divine
> motherhood, by which she is united with her
> Son, the Redeemer, and with her unique graces
> and functions, the Blessed Virgin is also inti-
> mately united to the Church. As St Ambrose
> taught, the Mother of God is a type of the
> Church in the order of faith, charity, and perfect
> union with Christ. For in the mystery of the
> Church, which is itself rightly called mother

and virgin, the Blessed Virgin stands out in eminent and singular fashion as exemplar both of virgin and mother. Through her faith and obedience she gave birth on earth to the very Son of the Father, not through the knowledge of man but by the overshadowing of the Holy Spirit, in the manner of a new Eve who placed her faith, not in the serpent of old but in God's messenger without wavering in doubt. The Son whom she brought forth is he whom God placed as the first born among many brethren (Rom. 8:29), that is, the faithful, in whose generation and formation she cooperates with a mother's love.

The spiritual motherhood of the Church is prefigured in the divine motherhood of Mary. The Church sees its own resemblance to her in motherhood and also in the virginal gift of self to God, the Bridegroom.

LG 64 | The Church indeed contemplating her hidden sanctity, imitating her charity and faithfully fulfilling the Father's will, by receiving the word of God in faith becomes herself a mother. By preaching and baptism she brings forth sons, who are conceived of the Holy Spirit and born of God, to a new and immortal life. She herself is a virgin, who keeps in its entirety and purity the faith she pledged to her spouse. Imitating the mother of her Lord, and by the power of the Holy Spirit, she keeps intact faith, firm hope and sincere charity.

The mysterious union of motherhood and virginity, which Vatican II sees as the basis of the resemblance between Our Lady and the Church, profoundly penetrates the historical and eschatological consciousness of the Church and expresses itself in it. In *Lumen Gentium* we read that the Mother of Christ 'advanced in her pilgrimage of faith' (LG 58), but at the same time it is in her alone that the Church sees the fulfilment of that for which it was prepared by the Bridegroom and Redeemer and towards which it is constantly led by the Holy Spirit. As we read in Chapter VIII:

> LG 65 | But while in the most Blessed Virgin the Church has already reached that perfection whereby she exists without spot or wrinkle (cf. Eph. 5:27), the faithful still strive to conquer sin and increase in holiness. And so they turn their eyes to Mary, who shines forth to the whole community of the elect as the model of virtues.

Mary's role as a Mother and Bride makes her an archetype of the Church and, by the same token, of the People of God. She is an example of holiness to all, and to every member of God's people – an example expressing both aspiration and fulfilment. Thanks to the fullness of grace which belongs to the Mother of God, the fulfilment is already contained in the aspiration.

> LG 68 | In the meantime the Mother of Jesus in the glory which she possesses in body and soul in heaven is the image and beginning of the Church as it is to be perfected in the world to come. Likewise she shines forth on earth until the day of the Lord shall come (cf. 2 Pet. 3:10), a sign of certain hope and comfort to the pilgrim People of God.

It is in Mary that we see revealed in all its fullness the way that leads to Christ, the *Auctor et Consummator* of her particular holiness and of every other form of holiness that is realized in the People of God.

> LG 65 | Devoutly meditating on her and contemplating her in the light of the Word made man, the

Church reverently penetrates more deeply into the great mystery of the Incarnation and becomes more and more like her spouse. Having entered deeply into the history of salvation, Mary, in a way, unites in her person and re-echoes the most important doctrines of the faith: and when she is the subject of preaching and worship she prompts the faithful to come to her Son, to his sacrifice and to the love of the Father. Seeking after the glory of Christ, the Church becomes more like her lofty type, and continually progresses in faith, hope and charity, seeking and doing the will of God in all things.

PART III

The Formation of
Attitudes

CHAPTER I

Mission and testimony as the basis of the enrichment of faith

As we explained at the outset, it is not our intention here to expound the teaching of Vatican II as such, but rather to seek in it the reply to the existential question: What does it mean to be a believer, to be a Christian, to be in the Church? This question, we believe, is implicit in the central question that the Council put to itself as to the nature of the Church: *Ecclesia, quid dicis de te ipsa*? ('Church, What do you say of yourself?').

It appears to us, moreover, that this involvement of the two questions determined the pastoral orientation of Vatican II. The effort to implement the Council's teaching must therefore have the same orientation. Accordingly it is our business here to study the fundamental significance of the Council's initiative and the more specific ways of 'initiation' which, as we have pointed out more than once, are to lead to the enrichment and deepening of faith. In individuals and communities, the enrichment of faith is expressed in terms of consciousness and attitude. For this reason we have studied the matter firstly from the point of view of the formation of the believer's consciousness in accordance with the Council's teaching; we now propose to consider the attitudes in which the Conciliar enrichment should find expression.

Stating the problem in this way, we endeavoured in Chapter I to indicate, as it were, the true proportions of the subject. Faith and the enrichment of faith is a supernatural gift of God and is not subject to human planning or causation; but man, and the Church as a human community, can and must

cooperate with the grace of faith and contribute to its enrichment. The Council itself acted in this way, and its action,
considering the level on which it took place, may be considered a plan of action for the whole Church. Thus the
implementation of the Council in the Church can and should be
understood as the enrichment of faith in accordance with the
plan delineated by the Council. While expressing the human
order of action in these terms, we believe that it is subordinate
to the divine action of the Holy Spirit in the Church. We must
therefore be concerned to see that the implementation of the
Council corresponds to its authentic doctrine, in which can be
discerned an almost historical plan of action of the whole
Church towards the enrichment of faith; it is on this that the
salvific meaning of the implementation of the Council essentially depends.

Keeping constantly in view these premises in which the
theology of faith is briefly summed up, we can consider the
prospects of its enrichment from the standpoint of the
development of the believer's consciousness and the formation of appropriate attitudes. As both Revelation and experience teach us, faith is expressed in a certain 'attitude':
this too is confirmed by the Council's statements quoted in
Chapter I. There we saw that man responds to God's self-
revelation by offering himself wholly to him (cf. DV 5). This
response is the fruit of faith, and it is thus clear that the
essence of faith consists of more than a purely intellectual
assent to the truth revealed by God, or a kind of reflection of
that truth in man's consciousness. 'Self-abandonment to God'
as a response to revelation bears witness also to the fact that
faith expresses itself through man's attitude: this attitude belongs to the very essence of faith, since it corresponds to the full
reality of revelation. This is not merely a fact or set of facts to
be accepted by the mind: it is God's action in unfolding
himself to man through Jesus Christ and becoming part of his
life and destiny. We might say, weighing our words carefully,
that revelation expresses an 'attitude' on God's part towards

men, and consequently the response to it must be expressed in man's attitude towards God.

We are not defining the term 'attitude' in any special way, but rather using it in its ordinary sense, while trying to avoid any ambiguity it may have by pointing out certain secondary meanings which are not intended. The word is usually applied analogically and denotes various relationships which are endorsed as a whole by the individual consciousness. In simple terms, we may say that an attitude is an active relationship but is not yet action. It follows upon cognition and enriched awareness, but is something new and different from these. It involves 'taking up a position' and being ready to act in accordance with it. In a sense it represents what Thomist psychology would call *habitus* and even *habitus operativus*, but the two are not identical. Leaving this enquiry to psychologists and, if need be, psychologists of religion, we wish only to note that the internal reality that we call an 'attitude' presupposes a fairly precise understanding of man's subjectivity – as does consciousness, with which we were concerned in the previous part of this study. In both cases we have to do with the human expression of the enrichment of faith, as we know it from revelation and experience.

In the Constitution on Divine Revelation (*Dei Verbum*) the Council indicates the basic character of the attitude with which man expresses his response to God's self-revelation, namely a 'free commitment of his entire self' (DV 5). This we shall therefore take as fundamental to the rest of our study. Although we shall not attempt to analyse it in detail, it will always be present to our minds in our consideration of particular attitudes to be discovered in the teaching of Vatican II, even if it is expressed and realized in different ways. The process of the enrichment of faith, which is part of the Council's plan and towards which the implementation of the Council should be directed, is in the last analysis comprised in the development and strengthening of that attitude. The enrichment and deepening of the consciousness of individuals and believing communities has as its object the development of the attitude in question, and is to be measured by the degree to which it attains that object. Faith without works is dead (cf. James 2:26): it cannot consist merely of knowledge or the content of consciousness. Essential to faith is an attitude of self-commitment to God – a continual readiness to perform the fundamental 'action' which corresponds to the reality of revelation, and all others acts which spring from it and to which it gives their proper character. In speaking of the attitude of self-commitment to God, Vatican II touches on the most vital and vivifying point relating to the whole process of the enrichment of faith.

Seeking in the Council's teaching as a whole some fuller dimension of that basic attitude, we must call attention to the reality of Mission, which is closely linked with Revelation and defines in a dynamic manner the mystery of the Church itself. God reveals himself and his plan of salvation to mankind through the mission of the Son and the Holy Spirit. Thus in the Council's teaching awareness of salvation is closely linked with the revelation of the Most Holy Trinity, as we have already seen. However, the mission of the divine Persons to mankind is not only a revelation but also a work of salvation by which mankind becomes the People of God. The Church originated and continues to originate from that divine mission: this gives a 'missionary' character to its whole existence, and at the same time basically determines the attitude of every Christian and, in a sense, of every believer, even if he has not been incorporated into the Church through Baptism and is only 'related' to it, as *Lumen Gentium* puts it (cf. LG 14–16). For everyone first of all finds himself personally, albeit only potentially, within the ambit of the salvific mission of the divine Trinity, which is accomplished by means of the Church; and everyone, or at least every Christian, shares in some manner in the mission of the Church itself.

What is meant by the Church's mission? In the first place it signifies the *status missionis* arising from the salvific mission of the Trinity, for which the Church was called into existence. In this sense the Church is always in a state of mission (*Ecclesia est in statu missionis*). As will be seen, this does not initially imply a function or institution, but defines the nature of the Church and indicates its close link with the mystery of the divine Trinity through the mission of the Persons: the Son who comes to us from the Father in the Holy Spirit and the Spirit who proceeds from the Father and the Son. In this sense, and on the basis of this reality, we can and should define the attitude of every human being in the Church.

Everyone in the Church is in a 'state of mission', as is the whole Church – by which we do not as yet mean any particular function or specific task, particularly of an institutional kind. It is a question simply, and above all, of the attitude which is the proper response to Revelation. Revelation is not identical with Mission, but is realized in it. The Christian believer who responds to God's self-revelation must find himself within the sphere of that divine mission. 'Committing his entire self to God', he must not only accept the divine mission but in some degree share in it. We can indeed to a certain extent equate the fundamental attitude of self-commitment to God with the missionary attitude: man commits himself to God by taking whole-heartedly on himself the divine mission in which Revelation becomes a reality. He accepts the mission in this way, both in himself and in the community. Thus he takes part in the 'state of mission' in which all the Church continually finds itself; and each individual is a unique, unrepeatable embodiment of the salvific 'state'.

This attitude is closely linked with that of bearing witness, and is to some extent identical with it. The human being who commits himself entirely to God accepts with his whole self the divine testimony made known in Jesus Christ, and is thus prepared to bear witness to Christ and to God. In this attitude we recognize the whole existential dynamic of faith and the profession of faith. Perhaps the traditional formula 'to accept as true whatever God has revealed and what the Church teaches us to believe' implied a rather passive and mainly receptive notion of 'acceptance', which was more or less identified as the basic element of a profession of faith. Vatican II expressly emphasizes the fact that witness consists in believing and professing the faith, that is accepting God's witness to himself and responding to it with one's own. In this conception we recognize the fundamental dynamism of the dialogue of salvation of which Paul VI wrote in the encyclical *Ecclesiam suam*. This is the essential and decisive dimension of the 'dialogue of salvation' between God and man.

In *Dei Verbum* we read:

DV 4 | Christ . . . accomplished the saving work . . . completed and perfected Revelation and confirmed it with divine guarantees . . . He revealed that God was with us, to deliver us from the darkness of sin and death, and to raise us up to eternal life.

The Constitution goes on to say:

DV 8 | Thus God, who spoke in the past, continues to converse with the spouse of his beloved Son. And the Holy Spirit, through whom the living voice of the Gospel rings out in the Church – and through her in the world – leads believers to the full truth, and makes the Word of Christ dwell in them in all its richness (cf. Col. 3:16).

DV 7 | This sacred Tradition, then, and the sacred Scripture of both Testaments, are like a mirror, in which the Church, during its pilgrim journey here on earth, contemplates God, from whom she receives everything, until such time as she is brought to see him face to face as he really is (cf. Jn. 3:2).

DV 13 | . . . the marvellous condescension of eternal wisdom is plain to be seen. Indeed the words of God, expressed in the words of men, are in every way like human language, just as the Word of the eternal Father, when he took on himself the flesh of human weakness, became like men.

DV 17 | The Word of God, which is the power of God for salvation to everyone who has faith (cf. Rom. 1:16), is set forth and displays its power in a most wonderful way in the writings of the New Testament. For when the time had fully come (cf. Gal. 4:4), the Word became flesh and dwelt among us full of grace and truth (cf. Jn. 1:14). Christ established on earth the kingdom of God, revealed his Father and himself by deeds and words; and by his death, resurrection and glorious ascension, as well as by sending the Holy Spirit, completed his work. Lifted up from the earth he draws all men to himself (cf. Jn. 10:32, Gk. text), for he alone has the words of eternal life (cf. Jn. 6:68). This mystery was not made known to other generations as it has now been revealed to his holy apostles and prophets by the Holy Spirit (cf. Eph. 3:4–6, Gk. text), that they might preach the Gospel, stir up faith in Jesus Christ and the Lord, and bring together the Church. The writings of the New Testament stand as a perpetual and divine witness to these realities.

These passages make it clear that faith consists in accepting revelation as the witness of Jesus Christ to God, and also in being ready to bear witness oneself.

In the documents of Vatican II we repeatedly encounter the

expression 'offer witness' or 'bear witness'. For example, in the Decree on Missions:

AGD 11 | All Christians by the example of their lives and the witness of the word, wherever they live, have an obligation to manifest the new man which they put on in baptism . . . so that others, seeing their good works, might glorify the Father (cf. Matt. 5:16) and more perfectly perceive the true meaning of human life and the universal solidarity of mankind. In order to bear witness to Christ fruitfully, they should establish relationships of respect and love with those [others].

Similarly Article 1 of Chapter II of the Decree on Missions is entitled 'Christian Witness'. As can be seen, mission and witness are closely linked together.

AGD 12 | The disciples of Christ, being in close contact with men through their life and work, hope to offer them an authentic Christian witness and work for their salvation, even in those places where they cannot preach Christ in full.

Speaking of the tasks of the laity in missionary activity, the Decree says:

AGD 21 | The principal duty of both men and women is to bear witness to Christ, and this they are obliged to do by their life and their words, in the family, in their social group, and in the sphere of their profession.

The Decree then explains the very essence of this witness in the words: 'In them must be seen the new man who has been created according to God in justice and holiness of truth' (AGD 21). Previously it points out that individual churches should be 'by the example of the lives of the faithful and of the whole community, a sign indicating Christ' to those who do not believe in him (AGD 20).

The duty to bear witness is, of course, particularly incumbent on all missionaries:

AGD 24 | By a truly evangelical life, with great patience and longanimity, in kindness and unfeigned love (cf. 2 Cor. 6:4 ff.) he will bear witness to his Lord, if necessary to the shedding of his blood.

All the above passages are taken from the Decree *Ad Gentes Divinitus*, which is concerned with the Church's missionary activity. However, as we have pointed out, it is not only a question of 'missions' in the stricter sense. The Church is 'missionary' by virtue of its own nature as the instrument of the divine Mission, and this fact must be expressed in the attitude of every member of the People of God whether or not he or she is connected in any way with 'missions' in the institutional sense. 'Mission' understood in this sense is so linked with bearing witness that the latter must be considered as the proper expression of mature faith. As the above passages show, this expression of faith is a testimony not in words only but in one's whole life: it is the existential 'revelation of the new man'. The fact that the Council regards witness-bearing in this way is confirmed by numerous statements elsewhere than in *Ad Gentes*. For instance, speaking of the pastoral office of bishops in the Church, the Council expresses itself as follows:

CD 11 | Bishops should devote themselves to their apostolic office as witnesses of Christ to all men. They should not limit themselves to those who already acknowledge the Prince of Pastors, but should also devote their energies wholeheartedly to those who have strayed in any way from the path of truth or who have no knowledge of the gospel of Christ and of his saving mercy.

On the subject of the training and life of priests:

PO 3 | They could not be the servants of Christ unless they were witnesses and dispensers of a life other than that of this earth. On the other hand they would be powerless to serve men if they remained aloof from their life and circumstances.

The Decree on the Renewal of Religious Life declares that:

PC 25 | All religious, therefore, with undiminished faith, with charity towards God and their neighbour, with love for the cross and with the hope of future glory, should spread the good news of Christ throughout the whole world, so that their witness will be seen by all men.

Again, the religious calling 'witnesses to the new and eternal life which we have acquired through the redemptive work of Christ' (LG 44). Elsewhere we read that 'the unity of the brethren' in the religious life 'is a symbol of the coming of Christ (cf. John 13:35; 17:21) and is a source of great apostolic power' (PC 15).

The importance of witness-bearing is emphasized several times in the Decree on the Apostolate of the Laity. For instance:

AA 16 | A special form of the individual apostolate is the witness of a whole lay life issuing from faith, hope and charity; it is a sign very much in keeping with our times, and a manifestation of Christ living in his faithful.

AA 6 | This witness of life, however, is not the sole element in the apostolate; the true apostle is on the lookout for occasions of announcing Christ by word.

In connection with marriage and family life the Council also refers several times to the need to bear witness, teaching that

Christian husbands and wives should 'strive to promote the values of marriage and the family . . . by the witness of their own lives' (GS 52).

> GS 48 | The Christian family springs from marriage, which is an image and a sharing in the partnership of love between Christ and the Church; it will show forth to all men Christ's living presence in the world and the authentic nature of the Church by the love and generous fruitfulness of the spouses, by their unity and fidelity, and by the loving way in which all members of the family cooperate with each other.

Consequently: 'Christian couples are, for each other, for their children and for their relatives, cooperators of grace and witnesses of the faith' (AA 11). This witness-bearing within the conjugal and family community also extends to the world outside, as we read:

> GS 49 | Authentic married love will be held in high esteem, and healthy public opinion will be quick to recognize it, if Christian spouses give outstanding witness to faithfulness and harmony in their love, if they are conspicuous in their concern for the education of their children, and if they play their part in a much needed cultural, psychological, and social renewal in matters of marriage and the family.

This is reflected in the task of education in which Christians, 'conscious of their vocation . . .

> GE 2 | should learn to give witness to the hope that is in them (cf. 1 Pet. 3:15) and to promote the Christian concept of the world whereby the natural values, assimilated into the full understanding of man redeemed by Christ, may contribute to the good of society as a whole.

The needs and opportunities for bearing Christian witness are manifold. *Gaudium et Spes* enumerates the various spheres – culture, economics, politics, international relations – in which Christian participation and collaboration constitute a basis for this purpose:

AA 27 | Through this dynamic, yet prudent, cooperation, which is of great importance in temporal activities, the laity bears witness to Christ the Saviour of the world, and to the unity of the human family.

GS 62 | Therefore, the faithful ought to work in close conjunction with their contemporaries and try to get to know their ways of thinking and feeling, as they find them expressed in current culture. Let the faithful incorporate the findings of new sciences and teachings and the understanding of the most recent discoveries with Christian morality and thought, so that their practice of religion and their moral behaviour may keep abreast of their acquaintance with science and of the relentless progress of technology: in this way they will succeed in evaluating and interpreting everything with an authentically Christian sense of values.

Or again, in the Decree on the Means of Social Communication:

IM 13 | Pastors of souls should be particularly zealous in this field, since it is closely linked with their task of preaching the Gospel. Laymen who work professionally in these media should endeavour to bear witness to Christ: first of all, by doing their work competently and in an apostolic spirit, secondly by collaborating directly, each one according to his ability, in the pastoral activity of the Church, making a technical, economic, cultural or artistic contribution.

As we also read in *Gaudium et Spes*:

GS 72 | Christians engaged actively in modern economic and social progress and in the struggle for justice and charity must be convinced that they have much to contribute to the prosperity of mankind and to world peace. Endowed with the skill and experience so absolutely necessary for them, let them preserve a proper sense of values in their earthly activity in loyalty to Christ and his Gospel, in order that their lives, individual as well as social, may be inspired by the spirit of the Beatitudes, and in particular by the spirit of poverty.

GS 75 | Christians must be conscious of their specific and proper role in the political community: they should be a shining example by their sense of responsibility and their dedication to the common good; they should show in practice how authority can be reconciled with freedom, personal initiative and with the solidarity and the needs of the whole social framework, and the advantages of unity with profitable diversity.

And in the Decree on the Apostolate of the Laity:

AA 29 | In this way the layman actively inserts himself deep into the very reality of the temporal order and takes his part competently in the work of the world. At the same time, as a living member and witness of the Church, he brings its presence and its action into the heart of the temporal sphere.

For, 'by preaching the truths of the Gospel and clarifying all sectors of human activity through its teaching and the witness of its members, the Church respects and encourages the political freedom and responsibility of the citizen' (GS 76).

On the basis of all these texts we can form an idea of the importance of testimony, and indirectly of the witness-bearing attitude. The importance of testimony in the teaching of Vatican II is explicitly analogical, as the Council speaks of the testimony of God and that of man which in various ways corresponds to the divine testimony and is a multiform response to revelation. In every case, however, the response is a witness and the witness is a response. The Council also speaks of bearing witness to Christ, in accordance with his command 'You shall be my witnesses' (Acts 1:8). It speaks, too, of witness borne to and by the Church. This is the objective aspect of testimony and witness-bearing. Subjectively it realizes itself by word and deed and the whole of life, based on the new man 'created after the likeness of God in true righteousness and holiness' (Eph. 4:24).

It can be seen from this that the attitude of witness-bearing has an internal dimension and profundity of its own and also an inter-human and social dimension, which as it were defines its extension and range. The content of testimony also follows from this. The internal dimension and the depth of Christian testimony are linked to the maturity with which man accepts the witness of Christ to God. The inter-human dimension and the social extension of testimony are in a sense identified with the apostolate, of which we shall speak presently. However, both dimensions must be connected: they cannot be divided. The apostolate of the hierarchy and the laity, the whole activity of the Church, and in particular its missionary activity, depend in the case of every member of the People of God on his assuming the Mission whereby the Father presents to the human family his eternal plan, actualizing it through the mission of the Word and the Spirit; thus they depend on the acceptance of the testimony of God, which in turn seeks to express itself in various ways in the testimony of man and succeeds in doing so to the extent that it cooperates with grace. The witness-bearing attitude is always a specific, unique and unrepeatable product of the encounter and dialogue in which God reveals himself and man in reply entrusts himself to him, abandoning himself completely in faith; in this abandonment he finds himself again in the ambit of the salvific mission of which he becomes an agent and participator.

In conclusion we should quote a passage from *Lumen Gentium* about the laity, which in a wider context applies to all Christians:

> LG 38 | Each individual layman must be a witness before the world to the resurrection and life of the Lord Jesus, and a sign of the living God. All together, and each one to the best of his ability, must nourish the world with spiritual fruits (cf. Gal. 5:22). They must diffuse in the world the spirit which animates those poor, meek and peacemakers whom the Lord in the Gospel proclaimed blessed (cf. Mt. 5:3–9). In a word: 'what the soul is in the body, let Christians be in the world'.

When it comes to further distinguishing and co-ordinating the attitudes which are of essential importance to the implementation of the Council in the Church, we must say at once that in spite of all distinctions these various attitudes penetrate and include one another to a great extent. In the present chapter we seem to have suggested the fertile ground in which all these attitudes develop. 'Mission and testimony' are the basis of the enrichment of faith, which is expressed in both these attitudes.

In its pastoral orientation the Council gives, as we see, a profound response to the question 'What does it mean to be a believer, a Christian in the Church and in the modern world?' The Council does not merely outline an external plan for the renewal of the Church, based on new structures that correspond more completely to the present-day demands of communal sociology; it also outlines a real plan for the enrichment of faith. The considerations in the present chapter show in what manner the Council's teaching envisages that fundamental process which tends to impart life and vigour to the faith of every Christian – a process necessary to the implementation of the Council and, through this, the self-realization of the Church. The union of this process with the attitude of witness-bearing establishes a link between us and the primitive Church, which experienced the Mission of the divine Persons at the moment it took place in history. The Christian of today is historically two thousand years away from that event, but he shares in the same manner in the Mission of the divine Persons. He must strive to cultivate within himself that attitude of testimony which is derived from the Mission of the divine Persons in such a way that, while bearing the mark of the divine *mysterium*, it also reflects the signs of his own time.

CHAPTER II

Analysis of the attitude of participation

We approach the analysis of the attitude of participation in the conviction that it will reveal to us the deeper and more universal meaning that the Council desires to give to the Christian life, in which human testimony becomes the expression of the salvific mission of God. Vatican II links this mission with the threefold power of Christ as priest, prophet and king, while also showing how participation in that power determines the reality of the Christian life. For this very reason we must define the attitude of participation more closely, not only because we believe that it is a central theme of the Conciliar doctrine concerning the People of God, but the attitude of participation explains to us in a more adequate and comprehensive manner the significance of the attitude of testimony in which the reality of faith is expressed. The Christian bears witness to Christ not 'from outside' but on the basis of participation, in him, in his mission. In this way the reality of faith takes shape, as does the Christian testimony in which it is expressed. Faith, in all the wealth of its personal and communal characteristics, is essentially and basically a participation in the testimony of Christ. This is the testimony of God himself, to which Christ has given expression and human dimensions by his triple power as priest, prophet and king.

It should be noted that by 'power' we do not mean the 'right to govern', as ordinary language and a certain association of ideas might suggest, but rather a 'task' or 'office' (cf. Latin *munus in tria munera Christi*) together with the ability to perform it. In speaking of participation in the threefold power of Christ, the Council teaches that the whole People of God and its individual members share in the priestly, prophetic and kingly offices that Christ took upon himself and fulfilled, and in the power which enabled him to do so. These offices are part of the Redeemer's mission, and participation in them derives from the fact that redemption continues to be a reality in the Church: it does so thanks to the power with which the Redeemer endowed the People of God and its individual members. The Redeemer is our Mediator with the Father.

The Conciliar teaching allows us to think of participation in Christ's threefold office not only in the ontological sense but also in that of specific attitudes. These express themselves in the attitude of testimony and give it a dimension of its own, as it were an interior form derived from Christ himself – the form of his mission and of his power. 'It was for this purpose that God sent his Son, whom he appointed heir of all things (cf. Heb. 1:2), that he might be teacher, king and priest of all' (LG 13). The whole People of God, including the laity, participate in this threefold mission, as the Council repeatedly makes clear.

LG 31 | The term 'laity' is here understood to mean all the faithful except those in Holy Orders and those who belong to a religious state approved by the Church. That is, the faithful who by Baptism are incorporated into Christ are placed in the People of God, and in their own way share the priestly, prophetic and kingly office of Christ, and to the best of their ability carry on the mission of the whole Christian people in the Church and in the world.

This threefold participation is very clearly linked with the Mission which forms the content of Christian testimony. It is right, therefore, that on the basis of the attitude of testimony we should try to define the attitudes which derive from 'sharing in the priestly, prophetic and kingly office of Christ'. It should be noted at the outset that these attitudes interpenetrate and in a certain sense determine one another. They form, so to speak, an organic complex within the fundamental attitude of testimony, creating a fertile soil for the development of that attitude while at the same time conditioning it, giving it depth and true significance. And it is undoubtedly difficult to separate and distinguish with precision the effect of the Christian's in the individual powers and offices of Christ. Nonetheless, the Council texts indicate the main lines of the distinction which we too shall try to follow, since the prospect of the enrichment of faith, as opened up by Vatican II, leads in that direction, and it is thus incumbent on us to understand and assimilate that prospect as completely as possible.

1. *The* munus sacerdotale: *sharing in Christ's priesthood*

The Council expressly distinguishes the 'common priesthood of the faithful' from the hierarchical one of priests and ministers, and this distinction enables us to understand more clearly the attitude that is proper to all Christians by reason of their participation in the priesthood of Christ.

LG 10 | Though they differ essentially and not only in degree, the common priesthood of the faithful and the ministerial or hierarchical priesthood are none the less ordered one to another; each in its own proper way shares in the one priesthood of Christ. The ministerial priest, by the sacred power that he has, forms and rules the priestly people; in the person of Christ he effects the eucharistic sacrifice and offers it to God in the name of all the people. The faithful indeed,

> by virtue of their royal priesthood, participate in the offering of the Eucharist. They exercise that priesthood, too, by the reception of the sacraments, prayer and thanksgiving, the witness of a holy life, abnegation and active charity.

This key passage not only indicates extremely clearly the relationship between the hierarchical priesthood, the fruit of a special sacrament in the Church, and the common priesthood of all Christians, but also points out that all the baptized share in the priestly office of Christ himself. This participation is at the base of every actual eucharistic community, still more the community of the whole Church.

LG 10 | The baptized, by regeneration and the anointing of the Holy Spirit, are consecrated to be a spiritual house and a holy priesthood, that through all the works of Christian men they may offer spiritual sacrifices and proclaim the perfection of him who has called them out of darkness into his marvellous light (cf. 1 Pet. 2:4-10). Therefore all the disciples of Christ, persevering in prayer and praising God (cf. Acts 2:42-7), should present themselves as a sacrifice, living, holy and pleasing to God (cf. Rom. 12:1).

PO 2 | The Lord Jesus 'whom the Father consecrated and sent into the world' (Jn. 10:36) makes his whole Mystical Body sharer in the anointing of the Spirit wherewith he has been anointed: for in that Body all the faithful are made a holy and kingly priesthood, they offer spiritual sacrifices to God through Jesus Christ, and they proclaim the virtues of him who has called them out of darkness into his admirable light.

In Chapter IV of *Lumen Gentium*, which treats of the position of the laity in the Church, we read:

LG 34 | Since he wishes to continue his witness and his service through the laity also, the supreme and eternal priest, Christ Jesus, vivifies them with his spirit and ceaselessly impels them to accomplish every good and perfect work.

To those whom he intimately joins to his life and mission he also gives a share in his priestly office, to offer spiritual worship for the glory of the Father and the salvation of man. Hence the laity, dedicated as they are to Christ and anointed by the Holy Spirit, are marvellously called and prepared so that even richer fruits of the Spirit may be produced in them. For all their works, prayers and apostolic undertakings, family and married life, daily work, relaxation of mind and body, if they are accomplished in the Spirit – indeed even the hardships of life if patiently borne – all these become spiritual sacrifices acceptable to God through Jesus Christ (cf. Pet. 2:5). In the celebration of the Eucharist these may most fittingly be offered to the Father along with the body of the Lord. And so, worshipping everywhere by their holy actions, the laity consecrate the world itself to God.

From these texts of Vatican II it can be seen that the common priesthood of the faithful and their sharing, through baptism, in the priesthood of Christ is thus linked to a particular attitude, whereby man commits himself and the world to God. This takes place through Jesus Christ: 'All the faithful . . . offer spiritual sacrifices to God through Jesus Christ' (PO 2). This also implies the analogy with Christ's sacrificial attitude, and his priesthood is reflected here in a lively fashion, as though the image of Christ the priest was imparted to the faithful. It must be emphasized that this is not merely a question of external resemblance but the fruit of internal participation and the work of the Holy Spirit, which operates in all the baptized to form the attitude which expresses their resemblance to Christ the priest. This attitude in which man, through and with Christ – 'together with the sacrifice of the Lord's body' – offers himself and the world to the Father expresses in a particularly intimate but fundamental way the existential essence of faith. For it is in faith, as the Council teaches, that man, responding to God's self-revelation, 'commits this entire self to God'. This commitment, contained in the very essence of faith, is realized most fully in the attitude which derives from sharing in the priesthood of Christ. This attitude, in fact, seems to endow the acts of Christian faith with their fullest existential dimension.

There is thus good reason to consider participation in the priesthood of Christ and the attitude that derives therefrom, before turning to the prophetic and kingly aspects. While all these aspects indicate the orientation of the Conciliar enrichment of faith in respect of the attitudes of every Christian, it is participation in the priesthood of Christ which denotes the simplest and the most complete attitude. This contains within itself the authentic Christian relationship with God and, the mystery of creation and redemption, seen in the way in which the consciousness of these mysteries is presupposed and also deepened by the Council. This attitude also expresses the vocation of the person in its existential nucleus – a vocation referred to by *Gaudium et Spes* in the words to which we must constantly return, from various points of view and in different contexts:

> GS 24   It follows, then, that if man is the only creature on earth that God has wanted for its own sake, man can fully discover his true self only in a sincere giving of himself.

When man gives himself to God in this way, he rediscovers himself most fully.

In this light, the attitude which derives from sharing in the priesthood of Christ is seen as one which contains in a special way all the richness of faith, both as regards content and as regards subjective commitment. The Conciliar teaching, which lays so much emphasis on this attitude, also shows us its proper place in the inner life of every Christian and the life of every Christian community, in which all the wealth of faith must be sought and developed. It can in a sense be said that the doctrine concerning Christ's priesthood and man's share in it is at the very centre of the teaching of Vatican II and contains in a certain manner all that the Council wished to say about the Church, mankind and the world.

Only against the background of the truth concerning Christ's priesthood, in which all the People of God share, does the Council delineate the mutual 'subordination' between the priesthood of all the faithful and the hierarchical priesthood.

PO 2 | However, the Lord also appointed certain men as ministers, in order that they might be united in one body in which 'all the members have not the same function' (Rom. 12:4). These men were to hold in the community of the faithful the sacred power of Order, that of offering sacrifice and forgiving sins, and were to exercise the priestly office publicly on behalf of men in the name of Christ. Thus Christ sent the apostles as he himself had been sent by the Father, and then through the apostles made their successors, the bishops, sharers in his consecration and mission. The function of the bishops' ministry was handed over in a subordinate degree to priests so that they might be appointed in the order of the priesthood and be co-workers of the episcopal order for the proper fulfilment of the apostolic mission that had been entrusted to it by Christ.

CD 15   It is therefore bishops who are the principal dispensers of the mysteries of God, and it is their function to control, promote and protect the entire liturgical life of the Church entrusted to them.

LG 26   The bishop, invested with the fullness of the sacrament of Orders, is 'the steward of the grace of the supreme priesthood', above all in the Eucharist, which he himself offers, or ensures that it is offered, from which the Church ever derives its life and on which it thrives.

PO 5   For in the most blessed Eucharist is contained the whole spiritual good of the Church, namely Christ himself our Pasch and the living bread which gives life to men through his flesh – that flesh which is given life and gives life through the Holy Spirit. Thus men are invited and led to offer themselves, their works and all creation with Christ.

PO 2   Through the ministry of priests the spiritual sacrifice of the faithful is completed in union with the sacrifice of Christ the only mediator, which in the Eucharist is offered through the priests' hands in the name of the whole Church in an unbloody and sacramental manner until the Lord himself come. The ministry of priests is directed to this and finds its consummation in it. For their ministration, which begins with the announcement of the Gospel, draws its

> force and power from the sacrifice of Christ and tends to this, that 'the whole redeemed city, that is, the whole assembly and community of the saints should be offered as a universal sacrifice to God through the High Priest who offered himself in his passion for us that we might be the body of so great a Head'.

In the light of these texts we can see clearly the reciprocal 'subordination' of the general and the hierarchical priesthood in the Church. Christ instituted the latter as a function of the former, and therefore it is not only hierarchical but also 'ministerial': it is there to serve (*ministrare*) so that there may be maintained and developed in the People of God everything that bears witness to their sharing in the priesthood of Christ, in other words the attitude which derives from that sharing. The attitude whereby man commits himself and the world to God is the simplest and profoundest expression of faith, the interior witness offered to the God of creation, revelation and redemption. The ministry of bishops and priests is directed towards this very attitude. Hence the priesthood of ministers and that of the faithful are closely linked with the Eucharist, in which Christ invites men 'to offer themselves, their works and all creation' with him (PO 5) and through which he leads them to offer 'spiritual sacrifices' to God (cf. PO 2). The work of our salvation is accomplished in the divine sacrifice of the Eucharist (cf. SC 2), in which priests of the hierarchy perform their principal function.

PO 2 | Because it is joined with the episcopal order the office of priests shares in the authority by which Christ himself builds up and sanctifies and rules his Body. Hence the priesthood of priests, while presupposing the sacraments of initiation, is nevertheless conferred by its own particular sacrament. Through that sacrament priests by

the anointing of the Holy Spirit are signed with
a special character and so are configured to
Christ the priest in such a way that they are able
to act in the person of Christ the head.

If the sacerdotal ministry in a sense separates bishops and
ordained priests from the members of the People of God who
only share in the general priesthood, the former should all the
more be distinguished by the attitude which derives from
sharing in the priesthood of Christ.

PO 13 | Priests as ministers of the sacred mysteries,
especially in the sacrifice of the Mass, act in a
special way in the person of Christ who gave
himself as a victim to sanctify men. And this is
why they are invited to imitate what they handle,
so that as they celebrate the mystery of the Lord's
death they may take care to mortify their
members from vices and concupiscences.

PO 14 | The fact of the matter is that Christ, in order
ceaselessly to do that same will of his Father in
the world through the Church, is working
through his ministers and therefore remains
always the principle and source of the unity of
their life. Therefore priests will achieve the
unity of their life by joining themselves with
Christ in the recognition of the Father's will
and in the gift of themselves to the flock entrusted
to them . . . the priestly soul strives to make its
own what is enacted on the altar of sacrifice.

We find an expression of this attitude in celibacy.

PO 16 | By preserving virginity or celibacy for the sake
of the kingdom of heaven priests are consecrated
in a new and excellent way to Christ. They more
readily cling to him with undivided heart and

dedicate themselves more freely in him and through him to the service of God and of men. They are less encumbered in their service of his kingdom and of the task of heavenly regeneration. In this way they become better fitted for a broader acceptance of fatherhood in Christ.

By means of celibacy, then, priests profess before men their willingness to be dedicated with undivided loyalty to the task entrusted to them, namely that of espousing the faithful to one husband and presenting them as a chaste virgin to Christ. They recall that mystical marriage, established by God and destined to be fully revealed in the future, by which the Church holds Christ as her only spouse. Moreover they are made a living sign of that world to come, already present through faith and charity, a world in which the children of the resurrection shall neither be married nor take wives.

As can be seen we are here within the area of the same matters of faith which strongly affected the mind of the Church during the Council, with particular reference to vocations and the religious state. These themes are here seen against a still broader background, which determines the participation in Christ's priesthood of those who, as ordained ministers, instruct and govern the priestly people, offering the Eucharistic sacrifice in the person of Christ (cf. LG 28). In that sacrifice, and thus in their mission, is expressed the hierarchy of values which should in a special way permeate the lives of priests, who 'can learn . . . to cultivate human values and appreciate created goods as gifts of God'.

PO 17 | While living in the world they should still realize that according to the Word of our Lord and Master they are not of the world. By using the world, then, as those who do not use it they

> will come to that liberty by which they will be freed from all inordinate anxiety and will become docile to the divine voice in their daily life. From this liberty and docility grows that spiritual insight through which is found a right attitude to the world and to earthly goods.
>
> In fact priests are invited to embrace voluntary poverty. By it they become more clearly conformed, to Christ and more ready to devote themselves to their sacred ministry.

The attitude which results from sharing in the priesthood of Christ unites all the baptized, and is thus common to the whole People of God. In this way they offer themselves and the world to God through Christ. But those who have received the sacrament of Orders and are thus called to a position of authority in the Church are required to give still clearer evidence of that attitude, and in it a stronger sense of the hierarchy of values and the eschatological outlook with which the history of salvation is continually imbued by the sacrifice and priesthood of Christ.

PO 22 | For all priests are cooperating in carrying out God's saving plan . . . Only gradually is this mystery carried into effect . . . all these truths are hidden with Christ in God it is by faith especially that they can be perceived.

Participation in the priesthood of Christ, which is common to all the baptized, and a certain common attitude which derives therefrom, is at the origin of priestly vocations in the Church.

OT 2 | The duty of fostering vocations falls on the whole Christian community, and they should discharge it principally by living full Christian lives . . .

Such active collaboration by all God's people in the task of fostering vocations is a response to the action of divine Providence.

Thus the priest can be 'chosen from among men' (Heb. 5:1) because the whole people is already 'a royal priesthood' (1 Peter 2:9).

2. The meaning of the liturgy

LG 10 | The priest . . . in the person of Christ effects the eucharistic sacrifice and offers it to God in the name of all the people. The faithful indeed, by virtue of their royal priesthood, participate in the offering of the Eucharist. They exercise that priesthood, too, by the reception of the sacraments, prayer and thanksgiving, the witness of a holy life, abnegation and active charity.

It is said elsewhere that 'The sacred nature and organic structure of the priestly community is brought into operation through the sacraments and the exercise of virtues' (LG 11). From this it can be seen that the attitude which results from sharing in the priesthood of Christ is manifested and confirmed not only by the testimony of liturgical life but also by the whole of Christian morality and the aspiration to holiness.

However, following the Council's lead we wish to devote particular attention to the liturgy. Much has been written on thus subject, and much has been done to renew the liturgy in accordance with the norms of Vatican II. We shall therefore consider only the specific relationship between renewal and real participation in the priesthood of Christ.

SC 7 | The liturgy, then, is rightly seen as an exercise of the priestly office of Jesus Christ. It involves the presentation of man's sanctification under the guise of signs perceptible by the senses and its accomplishment in ways appropriate to each of these signs. In it full public worship is performed by the Mystical Body of Jesus Christ, that is, by the Head and his members.

SC 7 | Christ, indeed, always associates the Church with himself in this great work in which God is perfectly glorified and men are sanctified. The Church is his beloved Bride who calls to her Lord, and through him offers worship to the eternal Father.

SC 7 | To accomplish so great a work Christ is always present in his Church, especially in her liturgical celebrations. He is present in the Sacrifice of the Mass not only in the person of his minister, 'the same now offering, through the ministry of priests, who formerly offered himself on the cross', but especially in the eucharistic species. By his power he is present in the sacraments so that when anybody baptizes it is really Christ himself who baptizes. He is present in his word since it is he himself who speaks when the holy scriptures are read in the Church. Lastly, he is present when the Church prays and sings, for he has promised 'where two or three are gathered together in my name there am I in the midst of them' (Mt. 18:20).

The Constitution on the Sacred Liturgy concentrates on the general principles of its renewal and development, based on the premiss that 'every liturgical celebration, because it is an action of Christ the Priest and of his Body, which is the Church, is a sacred action surpassing all others. No other action of the Church can equal its efficacy by the same title and to the same degree' (SC 7).

SC 10 | Nevertheless the liturgy is the summit toward which the activity of the Church is directed; it is

> also the fount from which all her power flows . . .
> From the liturgy, therefore, and especially from
> the Eucharist, grace is poured forth upon us as
> from a fountain, and the sanctification of men in
> Christ and the glorification of God to which all
> other activities of the Church are directed, as
> toward their end, are achieved with maximum
> effectiveness.

For this reason the Council placed in the forefront of its
plans and tasks a renewal of the liturgy in order that all might
take part in it with profit. Many pages of the Constitution
show the Council's profound concern for a conscious and
active participation in the liturgy on the part of the faithful:

SC 14 | Mother Church earnestly desires that all the
faithful should be led to that full, conscious, and
active participation in liturgical celebrations
which is demanded by the very nature of the
liturgy, and to which the Christian people, 'a
chosen race, a royal priesthood, a holy nation,
a redeemed people' (1 Pet. 2:9, 4–5) have a right
and obligation by reason of their baptism.

In the restoration and promotion of the
sacred liturgy the full and active participation
by all the people is the aim to be considered
before all else, for it is the primary and indispensable source from which the faithful are to
derive the true Christian spirit.

Clearly it is above all a question of renewal and, in a sense,
of producing a liturgical 'attitude' among pastors and layfolk.
For this purpose the Council envisaged an updating of texts
and rites, which the Church is now systematically bringing
about.

SC 21 | In this restoration both texts and rites should
be drawn up so as to express more clearly the

holy things which they signify. The Christian
people, as far as is possible, should be able to
understand them with ease and take part in
them fully, actively, and as a community.

The texts of Scripture are the source from which 'lessons
are read and afterwards explained in the homily, and psalms
are sung. It is from the scriptures that the prayers, collects
and hymns draw their inspiration and their force, and that
actions and signs derive their meaning' (SC 24).

SC 26 | Liturgical services are not private functions but
are celebrations of the Church . . . pertaining
to the whole Body of the Church. They manifest
it, and have effects upon it. But they also touch
individual members of the Church in different
ways, depending on their orders, their role in the
liturgical services, and their actual participation
in them.

The Church manifests itself in the liturgy and realizes
itself in it as a hierarchical community.

SC 27 | It must be emphasized that rites which are
meant to be celebrated in common, with the
faithful present and actively participating, should
as far as possible be celebrated in that way
rather than by an individual and quasi-privately.
This applies with special force to the celebration of Mass (even though every Mass has of
itself a public and social nature) and to the
administration of the sacraments.

Elsewhere we read:

SC 41 | The principal manifestation of the Church
consists in the full, active participation of all
God's holy people in the same liturgical celebrations, especially in the same Eucharist, in one

> prayer, at one altar, at which the bishop presides, surrounded by his college of priests and by his ministers.

We might add, following the Council's thought, that the Church then manifests itself as a 'royal priesthood', a community of the People of God which is truly sharing in the priesthood of Christ.

Thus the Council's concern for a full, conscious participation in the liturgy and the development of a 'liturgical attitude' is at the same time a sign of concern for the attitude which should be inspired by participation in Christ's priesthood, both by the celebrants and by the faithful.

SC 48 | The Church, therefore, earnestly desires that Christ's faithful, when present at this mystery of faith, should not be there as strangers or silent spectators. On the contrary, through a good understanding of the rites and prayers they should take part in the sacred action, conscious of what they are doing, with devotion and full collaboration. They should be instructed by God's word, and be nourished at the table of the Lord's Body. They should give thanks to God. Offering the immaculate victim, not only through the hands of the priest but also together with him, they should learn to offer themselves. Through Christ, the Mediator, they should be drawn day by day into ever more perfect union with God and each other, so that finally God may be all in all.

Then come prescriptions for the liturgy of the word, the homely, the 'prayer of the faithful' (SC 51-2) and the encouragement of sacramental communion: 'The more perfect form of participation in the Mass whereby the faithful, after the priest's communion, receive the Lord's Body from the same sacrifice, is warmly recommended' (SC 55). Next follow rules concerning communion under both species and concelebration (SC 55–6).

SC 19 | With zeal and patience pastors of souls must promote the liturgical instruction of the faithful and also their active participation, both internal and external, taking into account their age, condition, way of life and level of religious culture. By so doing pastors will be fulfilling one of the chief duties of a faithful dispenser of the mysteries of God, and in this matter they must lead their flock not only by word but also by example.

As *Lumen Gentium* points out in the passage already quoted several times, Christians also exercise their royal priesthood by participation in the sacraments.

SC 59 | The purpose of the sacraments is to sanctify men, to build up the Body of Christ, and, finally, to give worship to God. Because they are signs they also instruct. They not only presuppose faith, but by words and objects they also nourish, strengthen, and express it. That is why they are called 'sacraments of faith'. They do, indeed, confer grace, but, in addition, the very act of celebrating them most effectively disposes the faithful to receive this grace to their profit, to worship God duly, and to practise charity.

It is, therefore, of the greatest importance that the faithful should easily understand the sacramental signs, and should eagerly frequent those sacraments which were instituted to nourish the Christian life.

The attitude which results from participation in Christ's priesthood is expressed through participation in the sacraments, that is through sacramental life. The passage quoted includes all that testifies to the depth of this attitude and its close connection with the sanctification of man. This derives from the fact that the priesthood of Christ has realized itself in the work of redemption, so that all those who truly participate in it enjoy the fruit of that work, which is holiness. This is the purpose and effect of sharing in Christ's priesthood through the sacraments of the Church. As the Council teaches us:

LG 11 | Incorporated into the Church by Baptism, the faithful are appointed by their baptismal charac-ter to Christian religious worship; reborn as sons of God, they must profess before men the faith they have received from God through the Church. By the sacrament of Confirmation they are more perfectly bound to the Church and are endowed with the special strength of the Holy Spirit. Hence they are, as true witnesses of Christ, more strictly obliged to spread the faith by word and deed. Taking part in the eucharistic sacrifice, the source and summit of the Christian life, they offer the divine victim of God and themselves along with it. And so it is that, both in the offering and in Holy Commu-nion, each in his own way, though not of course indiscriminately, has his own part to play in the liturgical action. Then, strengthened by the body of Christ in the eucharistic communion, they manifest in a concrete way that unity of the People of God which this holy sacrament aptly signifies and admirably realizes.

Those who approach the sacrament of Penance obtain pardon from God's mercy for the offence committed against him, and are, at the same time, reconciled with the Church which they have wounded by their sins and which by charity, by example and by prayer labours for their conversion. By the sacred anointing of the sick and the prayer of the priests the whole Church commends those who are ill to the suffering and glorified Lord that he may raise them up and save them (cf. Jas. 5:14–16). And indeed she exhorts them to contribute to the good of the People of God by freely uniting themselves to the passion and death of Christ (cf. Rom. 8:17; Col. 1:24; Tim. 2:11–12; 1 Pet. 4:13). Those among the faithful who have received Holy Orders are appointed to nourish the Church with the word and grace of God in the name of Christ. Finally, in virtue of the sacrament of Matrimony by which they signify and share (cf. Eph. 5:32) the mystery of the unity and faithful love between Christ and the Church, Christian married couples help one another to attain holiness in their married life and in the rearing of their children. Hence by reason of their state in life and of their position they have their own gifts in the People of God (cf. 1 Cor. 7:7). From the marriage of Christians there comes the family in which new citizens of human society are born and, by the grace of the Holy Spirit in Baptism, those are made children of God so that the People of God may be perpetuated throughout the centuries.

The exposition of the doctrine on the sacraments in *Lumen Gentium* emphasizes their sanctifying and also their 'communal' significance, both of which derive from the sharing of all God's People in the priesthood of Christ. 'Strengthened by so many and such great means of salvation, all the faithful, whatever their condition or state – though each in his own way

– are called by the Lord to that perfection of sanctity with which the Father himself is perfect' (LG 11). The attitude which derives from participation in the priesthood of Christ is essentially the attitude of Christians striving after holiness, an endeavour which is that of the individual in the community of the Church. Thus Vatican II exhorts bishops and priests, as pastors presiding over the community, to exercise a sanctifying office (*munus sanctificandi*).

It speaks of bishops as 'spiritual guides of their flocks' (CD 15) and, turning to the priests who assist them, declares:

CD 30 | In carrying out their work of sanctification parish priests should ensure that the celebration of the Eucharistic Sacrifice is the centre and culmination of the entire life of the Christian community. It should also be their aim to ensure that the faithful receive spiritual nourishment from a frequent and devout reception of the sacraments and from an attentive and fervent participation in the liturgy. Parish priests must constantly bear in mind how much the sacrament of penance contributes to the development of the Christian life.

The Council's line with regard to liturgical renewal, with its emphasis on the full and conscious participation of the faithful, serves to stress what in the theology of the sacraments is called *opus operantis*. The sacraments not only confer grace, 'but, in addition, the very act of celebrating them most effectively disposes the faithful to receive this grace to their profit, to worship God duly, and to practise charity' (SC 59).

SC 59 | It is therefore of the greatest importance that the faithful should easily understand the sacramental signs, and should eagerly frequent those sacraments which were instituted to nourish the Christian life.

This is also the emphasis of the norms of Vatican II regarding the liturgy of particular sacraments and the need for its renewal, and the norms concerning the liturgy of sacramentals.

SC 61 | . . . the liturgy of the sacraments and sacramentals sanctifies almost every event . . . with the divine grace which flows from the paschal mystery of the Passion, Death and Resurrection of Christ. From this source all sacraments and sacramentals draw their power. There is scarcely any proper use of material things which cannot thus be directed toward the sanctification of men and the praise of God.

The Constitution also states that 'The sacramentals are to be revised, account being taken of the primary principle of enabling the faithful to participate intelligently, actively and easily. The circumstances of our times must also be considered' (SC 79). It adds that 'Provision should be made for the administration of some sacramentals, at least in special circumstances and at the discretion of the ordinary, by qualified lay persons' (SC 79). Above all 'Funeral rites should express more clearly the paschal character of Christian death' (SC 81).

The priesthood of Christ manifests itself in all its fullness in the paschal mystery. In that mystery Christ offered himself in the sacrifice of redemption, which is the inexhaustible source of the sanctification of every human being. The Christian draws upon that source through the sacraments, and through them he also realizes and expresses his own participation in the priesthood of Christ. The liturgy makes this possible inasmuch as it unites in itself the reality (*res*) and the sign (*sacramentum*). The reality and the sacramental signs penetrate Christian life and develop participation in the priesthood of Christ, which in turn should mean the development of a corresponding attitude. Thus the Constitution on the liturgy emphasizes the importance of the *opus operantis*.

SC 11 | But in order that the liturgy may be able to produce its full effects it is necessary that the faithful come to it with proper dispositions, that their minds be attuned to their voices, and that they cooperate with heavenly grace lest they receive it in vain. Pastors of souls must, therefore, realize that, when the liturgy is celebrated, something more is required than the laws governing valid and lawful celebration. It is their duty also to ensure that the faithful take part fully aware of what they are doing, actively engaged in the rite and enriched by it.

The penetration of the life of Christians by the priesthood of Christ is expressed 'in prayer and praising God' (LG 10). For:

SC 83 | Jesus Christ, High Priest of the New and Eternal Covenant, taking human nature, introduced into this earthly exile that hymn which is sung throughout all ages in the halls of heaven. He attaches to himself the entire community of mankind and has them join him in singing his divine song of praise.

For he continues his priestly work through his Church. The Church, by celebrating the Eucharist and by other means, especially the celebration of the divine office, is ceaselessly engaged in praising the Lord and interceding for the salvation of the entire world.

SC 85 | Hence all who take part in the divine office are not only performing a duty for the Church, they are also sharing in what is the greatest honour for Christ's Bride; for by offering these praises to God they are standing before God's throne in the name of the Church, their Mother.

The Constitution on the liturgy attaches particular importance to the breviary as the 'official prayer' of the Church, in which the 'sacerdotal office' is expressed; but participation in the general priesthood of Christ finds expression in any prayer uttered by the People of God. Every prayer is in some sense an offering of oneself and of the world to the Father through Christ.

SC 12 | The spiritual life, however, is not limited solely to participation in the liturgy. The Christian is indeed called to pray with others, but he must also enter into his bedroom to pray to his Father in secret; furthermore, according to the teaching of the apostle, he must pray without ceasing. We also learn from the same apostle that we must always carry around in our bodies the dying of Jesus, so that the life also of Jesus may be made manifest in our mortal flesh. That is why we beg the Lord in the Sacrifice of the Mass that 'receiving the offering of the Spiritual Victim' he may fashion us for himself 'as an eternal gift'.

While earnestly promoting the renewal of the liturgy, the Council emphasizes that this must not become an end in itself. The liturgy 'is the primary and indispensable source from which the faithful are to derive the true Christian spirit' (SC 14). This is how we are to understand its importance, and it is from this point of view that it is to be brought up to date.

SC 21 | For the liturgy is made up of unchangeable elements divinely instituted, and of elements subject to change. These latter not only may be changed but ought to be changed with the passage of time, if they have suffered from the

> intrusion of anything out of harmony with the
> inner nature of the liturgy or have become less
> suitable.

The plan for the renewal of the liturgy is so conceived as fully to achieve its end. Liturgy fulfils its purpose by means of the cycle of the liturgical year and the music and sacred art that are closely linked with it. The liturgical year enables us to live the mysteries of the redemption, which are 'in some way made present for all time; the faithful lay hold of them and are filled with saving grace' (SC 102). Vatican II lays down basic directions for this purpose, as also for art and sacred music:

SC 122 | The fine arts are rightly classed among the noblest activities of man's genius; this is especially true of religious art and of its highest manifestation, sacred art. Of their nature the arts are directed toward expressing in some way the infinite beauty of God in works made by human hands. Their dedication to the increase of God's praise and of his glory is more complete, the more exclusively they are devoted to turning men's minds devoutly toward God.

3. *The* munus propheticum: *responsibility for the Word of God*

We now turn to the attitude which, according to the teaching of Vatican II, derives from participation in the *munus propheticum* of Christ: *munus*, as already explained, signifies both an office and the power to perform it. Christ accomplished his prophetic mission: he was the incarnate Word and expressed divine truth in human language. The Church, as the People of God, participates in that mission, and the fact that it does so is of enormous importance for the enrichment of faith, not only as regards content but also as regards attitude. First and foremost here comes responsibility towards the People of God, participates in that mission, and the consciousness of this participation is of enormous importance for the enrichment of faith, not only as regards content but also as regards attitude. First and foremost here comes responsibility towards the word of God entrusted to the Church. The Council too emphasizes this attitude above all. A prophet is one who speaks in the name of the Lord, who knows the truth contained in the word of God; he bears it in himself, imparts it to others and guards it as his dearest heritage.

SC 12 | The holy People of God shares also in Christ's prophetic office: it spreads abroad a living witness to him, especially by a life of faith and love and by offering to God a sacrifice of praise, the fruit of lips praising his name (cf. Heb. 13:15). The whole body of the faithful who have an anointing that comes from the holy one (cf. 1 Jn. 2:20 and 27) cannot err in matters of belief. This characteristic is shown in the supernatural appreciation of the faith (*sensus fidei*) of the whole people, when, 'from the bishops to the last of the faithful' they manifest a universal consent in matters of faith and morals. By this appreciation of the faith, aroused and sustained by the Spirit of truth, the People of God, guided by the sacred teaching authority (*magisterium*), and obeying it, receives not the mere word of men, but truly the word of God (cf. 1 Th. 2:13), the faith once for all delivered to the saints (cf. Jude 3). The People unfailingly

> adheres to this faith, penetrates it more deeply
> with right judgment, and applies it more fully in
> daily life.

Vatican II clearly places participation in the prophetic mission of Christ and the prophetic nature of Christian testimony on a par with the attitude which derives from sharing in the priesthood of Christ. None the less it is a different nature and attitude and calls for separate analysis. The essential point seems to be that 'appreciation of the faith' (*sensus fidei*) of which Vatican II says that it is 'aroused and sustained by the Spirit of truth' (thus it is a direct and authentic fruit of grace) and manifests itself through the people's 'universal consent in matters of faith and morals' (thus it attains the dimension of the community of the Church, which it determines'. This consensus, according to the Council, is not static but dynamic. The people 'receives not the mere word of men, but truly the word of God, . . . the faith once for all delivered to the saints'; it 'unfailingly adheres to this faith, penetrates it more deeply with right judgement, and applies it more fully in daily life' (LG 12). We find here fresh confirmation of the guideline for the enrichment of faith which we have taken as basic to the implementation of the Council. Faith, which is essentially supernatural, takes into itself the whole dynamic structure of human knowledge, permeates it and expresses itself in it. The prophetic nature of the attitude of Christian testimony is centred in the sense of responsibility towards the gift of truth contained in Revelation. This is expressed through the *sensus fidei* and determines the close harmony between faith and the teaching office of the Church; and it is a manifestation of the same responsibility towards the truth of God and the same sharing in the *munus propheticum* of Christ.

We shall try to consider all these aspects in the order suggested by the text quoted from *Lumen Gentium*, beginning with the universal 'appreciation of the faith' that belongs to the whole People of God, and then considering the magisterium which presupposes and so to speak conditions that universal sense; this 'conditioning' comes from its authority, for teaching in the Church is also a specific power, received by the Apostles directly from Jesus Christ.

DV 7 | In order that the full and living Gospel might always be preserved in the Church the apostles left bishops as their successors. They gave them 'their own position of teaching authority'.

DV 8 | In this way the Church, in her doctrine, life and worship, perpetuates and transmits to every generation all that she herself is, all that she believes.

DV 10 | Sacred Tradition and sacred Scripture make up a single sacred deposit of the Word of God, which is entrusted to the Church. By adhering to it the entire holy people, united to its pastors, remains always faithful to the teaching of the apostles, to the brotherhood, to the breaking of bread and the prayers (cf. Acts 2:42, Greek). So, in maintaining, practising and professing the faith that has been handed on there should be a remarkable harmony between the bishops and the faithful.

But the task of giving an authentic interpretation of the Word of God, whether in its written form or in the form of Tradition, has been entrusted to the living teaching office of the Church alone. Its authority in this matter is exercised in the name of Jesus Christ. Yet this Magisterium is not superior to the Word of God, but is its servant. It teaches only what has been handed on to it. At the divine command and with the help of the Holy Spirit, it listens to this

> devotedly, guards it with dedication and expounds it faithfully. All that it proposes for belief as being divinely revealed is drawn from this single deposit of faith.

The unanimity of pastors and the faithful in 'maintaining, practising and professing the faith that has been handed on' is thus guaranteed and conditioned by the supernatural appreciation of the faith possessed by the whole People of God, as well as by the teaching office of the Church. The *munus propheticum* is exercised through both.

LG 35
> Christ is the great prophet who proclaimed the kingdom of the Father both by the testimony of his life and by the power of his word. Until the full manifestation of his glory he fulfils this prophetic office, not only by the hierarchy who teach in his name and by his power, but also by the laity. He accordingly both establishes them as witnesses and provides them with the appreciation of the faith (*sensus fidei*) and the grace of the word (cf. Acts 2:17–18; Apoc. 19:10) so that the power of the Gospel may shine out in daily family and social life. They show themselves to be the children of the promise if, strong in faith and hope, they make the most of the present time (Eph. 5:16; Col. 4:5), and with patience await the future glory (cf. Rom. 8:25). Let them not hide this their hope, then, in the depths of their hearts, but rather express it through the structure of their secular lives in continual conversion and in wrestling 'against the world rulers of this darkness, against the spiritual forces of iniquity' (Eph. 6:12).

LG 35
> . . . the laity become powerful heralds of the faith in things to be hoped for (cf. Heb. 11:1)

if they join unhesitating profession of faith to the life of faith. This evangelization, that is, the proclamation of Christ by word and the testimony of life, acquires a specific property and peculiar efficacy because it is accomplished in the ordinary circumstances of the world.

Lumen Gentium then emphasizes the prophetic character of matrimonial and family life.

LG 35 | The Christian family proclaims aloud both the present power of the kingdom of God and the hope of the blessed life. Hence, by example and by their testimony, they convict the world of sin and give light to those who seek the truth.

As sharers in the *munus propheticum* of Christ, the laity, 'even when occupied by temporal affairs, . . . can and must do valuable work for the evangelization of the world'. They should 'diligently apply themselves to a more profound knowledge of revealed truth and earnestly beg of God the gift of wisdom' (LG 35).

Responsibility towards divine truth, and the prophetic character of Christian witness, are particularly expressed in the religious life. 'The religious state of life, in bestowing greater freedom from the cares of earthly existence on those who follow it, simultaneously reveals more clearly to all believers the heavenly goods which are already present in this age . . . The religious state constitutes a closer imitation and an abiding re-enactment in the Church of the form of life which the Son of God made his own when he came into the world to do the will of the Father and which he propounded to the disciples who followed him' (LG 44).

In the life and ministry of priests, responsibility towards the gift of divine truth contained in Revelation is linked not only with the duty to profess the faith but, in a special way, with their particular mission of preaching.

PO 4 | The People of God is formed into one in the first place by the Word of the living God, which is quite rightly sought from the mouth of priests . . . it is the first task of priests as co-workers of the bishops to preach the Gospel of God to all men . . . For by the saving Word of God faith is aroused in the heart of unbelievers and is nourished in the heart of believers. By this faith then the congregation of the faithful begins and grows, according to the saying of the apostle: 'Faith comes from what is heard, and what is heard comes by the preaching of Christ' (Rom. 10:17).

Priests then owe it to everybody to share with them the truth of the Gospel in which they rejoice in the Lord. Therefore, whether by having their conversation heard among the gentiles they lead people to glorify God, or by openly preaching proclaim the mystery of Christ to unbelievers; or teach the Christian message or explain the Church's doctrine; or endeavour to treat of contemporary problems in the light of Christ's teaching – in every case their role is to teach not their own wisdom but the Word of God and to issue an urgent invitation to all men to conversion and to holiness.

This passage strongly emphasizes responsibility to the Word of God. If the Council laid stress on this in its statements concerning the laity, it is still more understandable that it should do so when speaking of the life and activity of those whose duty it is to proclaim the Word. Vatican II is concerned not only with the authenticity of the Word but also its efficacy through the preaching of its ministers.

PO 4 | Moreover, the priest's preaching, often very difficult in present-day conditions, if it is to become more effective in moving the minds of his hearers, must expound the Word of God not merely in a general and abstract way but by an application of the eternal truth of the Gospel to the concrete circumstances of life.

As a particular test of the authenticity and effectiveness of the Word when preached, the Council mentions participation in the Eucharist, which 'appears as the source and summit of all preaching of the Gospel; catechumens are gradually led up to participation in the Eucharist, while the faithful who have already been consecrated in baptism and confirmation are fully incorporated in the Body of Christ by the reception of the Eucharist' (PO 5). The word of God as transmitted by priests becomes fully effective when it bears fruit in heartfelt participation in the Eucharist.

The sense of responsibility to the word of God, closely linked with the sense of faith of the whole Church, is differently manifested in lay people, priests and religious, but in each form it expresses the attitude which derives from sharing in the *munus propheticum* of Christ. In each form, too, it is fundamentally based on the infallibility with which Christ endowed his Church. As to this, Vatican II recalls the doctrine of its predecessor.

LG 25 | This infallibility, however, with which the divine redeemer wished to endow his Church in defining doctrine pertaining to faith and morals, is co-extensive with the deposit of revelation, which must be religiously guarded and loyally and courageously expounded. The Roman Pontiff, head of the college of bishops, enjoys this infallibility in virtue of his office, when, as supreme pastor and teacher of all the faithful – who confirms his brethren in the faith (cf. Lk.

22:32) – he proclaims in an absolute decision a doctrine pertaining to faith or morals . . . The infallibility promised to the Church is also present in the body of bishops when, together with Peter's successor, they exercise the supreme teaching office. Now the assent of the Church can never be lacking to such definitions on account of the same Holy Spirit's influence, through which Christ's whole flock is maintained in the unity of the faith and makes progress in it.

The nature of the infallibility which belongs to the Successor of St Peter is also explained by Vatican II on the basis of the teaching of Vatican I:

LG 25 | For that reason his definitions are rightly said to be irreformable by their very nature and not by reason of the assent of the Church, inasmuch as they were made with the assistance of the Holy Spirit promised to him in the person of blessed Peter himself; and as a consequence they are in no way in need of the approval of others, and do not admit of appeal to any other tribunal. For in such a case the Roman Pontiff does not utter a pronouncement as a private person, but rather does he expound and defend the teaching of the Catholic faith as the supreme teacher of the universal Church, in whom the Church's charism of infallibility is present in a singular way.

The whole People of God has enjoyed and continues to enjoy real participation in the prophetic mission of Christ, with which must clearly be linked responsibility towards the truth that Christ as prophet proclaimed. This fact is expressed by the charisma of infallibility.

DV 10 | Yet this Magisterium is not superior to the Word of God, but is its servant.

LG 25 | Furthermore, when the Roman Pontiff, or the body of bishops together with him, define a doctrine, they make the definition in conformity with revelation itself, to which all are bound to adhere and to which they are obliged to submit; and this revelation is transmitted integrally either in written form or in oral tradition through the legitimate succession of bishops and above all through the watchful concern of the Roman Pontiff himself; and through the light of the Spirit of truth it is scrupulously preserved in the Church and unerringly explained. The Roman Pontiff and the bishops, by reason of their office and the seriousness of the matter, apply themselves with zeal to the work of enquiring by every suitable means into this revelation and of giving apt expression to its contents.

LG 25 | Although the bishops, taken individually, do not enjoy the privilege of infallibility, they do, however, proclaim infallibly the doctrine of Christ on the following conditions: namely, when, even though dispersed throughout the world but preserving for all that amongst themselves and with Peter's successor the bond of communion, in their authoritative teaching concerning matters of faith and morals, they are in agreement that a particular teaching is to be held definitively and absolutely. This is still more clearly the case when, assembled in an ecumenical council, they are, for the universal Church, teachers of and judges in matters of

> faith and morals, whose decisions must be
> adhered to with the loyal and obedient assent
> of faith.

Vatican II enables us to understand more fully the 'doctrine
of infallibility' and also the 'institution' of infallibility in the
Church, against the background of universal participation in
the *munus propheticum* of Christ and the 'appreciation of the
faith' that it involves. This participation is here primary and
fundamental: Christ, as Prophet, desires his Church to be
'devoted to the Apostles' teaching' (Acts 2:42) and to enjoy
without possibility of error the gift of truth contained in
Revelation: therefore he has bestowed the charisma of infallible teaching on the College of Bishops with the Successor of
St Peter at its head, and more particularly on that Successor
himself. The obedience of each and every disciple of Christ to
the supreme magisterium of the Church is the expression of
responsibility to the word of God and to the gift of truth
embodied in Revelation. The element of responsibility gives
to this obedience in faith the character of an active and committed attitude. It is significant that the Council at no point
repeats the traditional distinction between the *Ecclesia docens*
and the *Ecclesia discens*: this is evidently because it wished to
avoid an insufficient consciousness of universal sharing in the
munus propheticum of Christ.

LG 25 | Among the more important duties of bishops that
> of preaching the Gospel has pride of place. For
> the bishops are heralds of the faith, who draw
> new disciples to Christ; they are authentic
> teachers, that is, teachers endowed with the
> authority of Christ, who preach the faith to the
> people assigned to them, the faith which is
> destined to inform their thinking and direct their
> conduct; and under the light of the Holy Spirit

they make that faith shine forth, drawing from the storehouse of revelation new things and old (cf. Mt. 13:52); they make it bear fruit, and with watchfulness they ward off whatever errors threaten their flock (cf. 2 Tim. 4:14). Bishops who teach in communion with the Roman Pontiff are to be revered by all as witnesses of divine and Catholic truth; the faithful, for their part, are obliged to submit to their bishops' decision, made in the name of Christ, in matters of faith and morals, and to adhere to it with a ready and respectful allegiance of mind. This loyal submission of the will and intellect must be given, in a special way, to the authentic teaching authority of the Roman Pontiff, even when he does not speak *ex cathedra*.

Responsibility towards the truth of God as given to the Church in Revelation is expressed not only in the solicitous protection of the Church from error but also in the rich and vital process whereby the word of God lives in the Church. This is brought out in several passages of the Constitution *Dei Verbum*:

DV 23 | The spouse of the incarnate Word, which is the Church, is taught by the Holy Spirit. She strives to reach day by day a more profound understanding of the sacred Scriptures, in order to provide her children with food from the divine words.

DV 21 | And such is the force and power of the Word of God that it can serve the Church as her support and vigour, and the children of the Church as strength for their faith, food for the soul, and a pure and lasting fount of spiritual life.

And therefore

> DV 21 | The Church has always venerated the divine Scriptures as she venerated the Body of the Lord, in so far as she never ceases, particularly in the sacred liturgy, to partake of the bread of life and to offer it to the faithful from the one table of the Word of God and the Body of Christ.

> DV 26 | Just as from constant attendance at the eucharistic mystery the life of the Church draws increase, so a new impulse of spiritual life may be expected from increased veneration of the Word of God, which 'stands for ever' (Is. 40:8; cf. 1 Pet. 1:23–5).

The Council points out that 'In the sacred books the Father who is in heaven comes lovingly to meet his children, and talks with them' (DV 21).

> DV 25 | Let them remember, however, that prayer should accompany the reading of sacred Scripture, so that a dialogue takes place between God and man. For, 'we speak to him when we pray; we listen to him when we read the divine oracles'.

In these passages the Council shows how much importance it attaches to the dialogue of salvation through which the word of God lives in men's hearts, and how 'the treasure of Revelation entrusted to the Church should more and more fill the hearts of men' (DV 26).

A lively echo of these statements is found in the Constitution on the Sacred Liturgy.

> SC 51 | The treasures of the Bible are to be opened up more lavishly so that a richer fare may be provided for the faithful at the table of God's word. In this way a more representative part

of the sacred scriptures will be read to the
people in the course of a prescribed number of
years.

The whole subject of the liturgical renewal, of which we have
already spoken, must be seen not only from the point of view
of participation in the priesthood of Christ but also from
that of the prophetic aspect emphasized by the Constitution
on the Liturgy, when it associates the 'table of the Lord's
Body' with the 'table of God's word' – as was done by witnesses
of the most ancient tradition.

SC 33 | Although the sacred liturgy is principally the
worship of the divine majesty it likewise contains
much instruction for the faithful. For in the
liturgy God speaks to his people, and Christ is
still proclaiming his Gospel. And the people reply
to God both by song and prayer . . . Thus not
only when things are read 'which were written
for our instruction' (Rom. 15:4), but also when
the Church prays or sings or acts, the faith of
those taking part is nourished, and their minds
are raised to God so that they may offer him
their spiritual homage and receive his grace
more abundantly.

The word of God lives in the Church, as we have already
seen, through the preaching office of bishops and the priests
who are their helpers. By proclaiming the word of God, the
Church performs its mission internally as well as externally.

AGD 13 | Wherever God opens a door for the word in
order to declare the mystery of Christ, then the
living God, and he whom he has sent for the
salvation of all, Jesus Christ, are confidently
and perseveringly proclaimed to all men. And
this is in order that non-Christians, whose heart
is being opened by the Holy Spirit, might, while

believing, freely turn to the Lord who, since he
is the 'way, the truth and the life' (Jn. 14:6),
will satisfy all their inner hopes, or rather
infinitely surpass them.

Such are the words of the Decree on the Church's Missionary Activity. The proclamation of the Gospel serves
towards conversion, and conversion is always a kind of
extension of the Church, as the Decree teaches us, whether
ad extra or *ad intra*.

Responsibility towards the word of God and revealed truth
has always permeated and given form to the advance of
knowledge in the Church, including theology, philosophy
and other sciences. This broad stream of cognitive activity
plays a special part in the training of priests; the Council has
devoted a decree to this subject, in which we read:

OT 14 | In the revision of ecclesiastical studies the main
object to be kept in mind is a more effective
coordination of philosophy and theology so
that they supplement one another in revealing
to the minds of the students with ever increasing
clarity the Mystery of Christ, which affects the
whole course of human history, exercises an
unceasing influence on the Church, and operates
mainly through the ministry of the priest.

The Decree on the Training of Priests gives a number of
indications regarding the study of various branches of
ecclesiastical science, while at the same time emphasizing the
subjective aspect of education.

OT 15 | The teaching method adopted should stimulate
in the students a love of rigorous investigation,
observation and demonstration of the truth, as
well as an honest recognition of the limits of
human knowledge. Careful attention should be
paid to the bearing of philosophy on the real

problems of life, as well as to the questions which engage the minds of the students. The students themselves should be helped to perceive the connection between philosophical arguments and the mysteries of salvation which theology considers in the higher light of faith.

Participation in the *munus propheticum* of Christ, and the prophetic nature of Christian witness expressed in responsibility towards revealed truth, correspond profoundly to that responsibility towards truth that is proper to the human mind as such. Hence the prophetic vocation of every Christian presupposes and requires adequate education and training. The Council has devoted a separate Declaration to Christian education, in which we read:

GE 10   The Church likewise devotes considerable care to higher-level education, especially in universities and faculties. Indeed, in the institutions under its control the Church endeavours systematically to ensure that the treatment of the individual disciplines is consonant with their own principles, their own methods, and with a true liberty of scientific enquiry. Its object is that a progressively deeper understanding of them may be achieved, and, by a careful attention to the current problems of these changing times and to the research being undertaken, the convergence of faith and reason in the one truth may be seen more clearly.

'The Christian outlook should acquire, as it were, a public, stable and universal influence in the whole process of the promotion of higher culture.' Its representatives 'should be outstanding in learning, ready to undertake the more responsible duties of society, and to be witnesses in the world to the true faith' (GE 10), i.e. mature participants in the *munus propheticum.* With this in view:

> GE 4 | In the exercise of its functions in education the Church is appreciative of every means that may be of service, but it relies especially on those which are essentially its own. Chief among these is catechetical instruction.

As will be seen, there is a wide range of methods of instruction in the faith, from catechetics to Catholic universities, of which the Christian should take advantage in so far as he is called to participate in the *munus propheticum* of Christ.

The same prophetic aspect of Christian vocation and witness-bearing directs our attention and that of the Council to those media 'which directly touch man's spirit and have opened up new avenues of easy communication of all kinds of news, ideas and orientations.' They are called 'means of social communication' because they can 'of their nature reach and influence not merely single individuals but . . . the whole of human society: the press, the cinema, radio, television' and other similar media (IM 1).

> IM 3 | The Catholic Church was founded by Christ our Lord to bring salvation to all men. It feels obliged, therefore, to preach the gospel. In the same way, it believes that its task involves employing the means of social communication to announce the good news of salvation and to teach men how to use them properly.

In this field too we see clearly the part played by responsibility towards the truth on the part of those who share in the *munus propheticum* of Christ, whether in transmitting ideas or receiving them.

> IM 4 | If the media are to be correctly employed, it is essential that all who use them know the principles of the moral order and apply them faithfully in this domain.

IM 11 | A special responsibility for the proper use of the means of social communication rests on journalists, writers, actors, designers, producers, exhibitors, distributors, operators, sellers, critics – all those, in a word, who are involved in the making and transmission of communications in any way whatever. It is clear that a very great responsibility rests on all of these people in today's world: they have power to direct mankind along a good path or an evil path by the information they impart and the pressure they exert.

The Church is fully aware of the great importance of this field of information for the spiritual lives of men.

IM 5 | There exists therefore in human society a right to information on the subjects that are of concern to men either as individuals or as members of society, according to each man's circumstances. The proper exercise of this right demands that the content of the communication be true and – within the limits set by justice and charity – complete. Further, it should be communicated honestly and properly. This means that in the gathering and in the publication of news the moral law and the legitimate rights and dignity of man should be upheld. All knowledge is not profitable, but on the other hand 'love builds' (1 Cor. 8:1).

The Decree then considers the problem of 'the relation between the rights of art – to use a current expression – and the moral law' (IM 6). The media serve to form public opinion, which today 'exercises enormous influence over the lives, private or public, of all citizens, no matter what their walk in life. It is therefore necessary that all members of society meet the demands of justice and charity in this domain' (IM 8).

In this sphere of modern life too there is a definite place for the attitude which derives from participation in the *munus propheticum*, not only because the means of social communication can serve to proclaim the word of God, but also because in the preparation and transmission of information attention must be paid to the right to truth and thus the duty to give correct information. The Decree rightly emphasizes the Christian moral order before all else, since this order clearly has a prophetic significance of its own.

4. *The* munus regale *as the basis of Christian morality*

Although morality, in its Christian significance and spiritual character, also falls within the *munus propheticum*, its closest link is with the *munus regale* of Christ. Let us first briefly recall that the kingly mission of Our Lord finds expression in the Church through the pastoral ministry entrusted to the Apostles and their successors.

LG 27 | The bishops, as vicars and legates of Christ, govern the particular Churches assigned to them by their counsels, exhortations and example, but over and above that also by the authority and sacred power which indeed they exercise exclusively for the spiritual development of their flock in truth and holiness, keeping in mind that he who is greater should become as the lesser, and he who is the leader as the servant (cf. Lk. 22:26–7).

Elsewhere we find the following passage concerning the way in which the pastoral ministry should be exercised.

LG 28 | As to the faithful, they (the priests) should bestow their paternal attention and solicitude on them, whom they have begotten spiritually through baptism and instruction (cf. 1 Cor. 4:15; 1 Pet. 1:23). Gladly constituting themselves models of the flock (cf. 1 Pet. 5:3), they should preside over and serve their local community in such a way that it may deserve to be called by the name which is given to the unique People of God in its entirety, that is to say, the Church of God (cf. Cor. 1:2; 2 Cor. 1:1, and *passim*). They should be mindful that by their daily conduct and solicitude they display the reality of a truly priestly and pastoral ministry both to believers and unbelievers alike, to Catholics and non-Catholics; that they are bound to bear witness before all men of the truth and of the life, and as good shepherds seek after those too (cf. Lk. 15:4–7) who, whilst having been baptized in the Catholic Church, have given up the practice of the sacraments, or even fallen away from the faith.

However, in expounding the *munus regale* and human participation in it, the Council's teaching emphasizes a new approach.

LG 36 | Christ, made obedient unto death and because of this exalted by the Father (cf. Ph. 2:8–9), has entered into the glory of his kingdom. All things are subjected to him until he subjects himself and all created things to the Father, so that God may be all in all (cf. 1 Cor. 15:27–8). He communicated this power to the disciples that they be constituted in royal liberty and, by self-abnegation of a holy life, overcome the reign of sin in themselves (cf. Rom. 6:12) – that indeed by

> serving Christ in others they may in humility and
> patience bring their brethren to that king, to serve
> whom is to reign.

The text of *Lumen Gentium* clearly connects the kingly
mission of Christ with the vocation of his disciples and
confessors to the state of 'royal freedom'. This, we read,
consists in leading the kind of life in which a Christian
conquers the 'rule of sin' in himself by means of self-denial.

It is thus clearly a question of sanctity in the moral sense, of
dominion over evil, in which, in a sense, man's own kingliness
is displayed. Man is called to realize in himself this form
of kingly self-rule. The Council's teaching attributes a
strictly evangelical significance to the perennial truth of the
human ethos. In the first place we learn from the text quoted
that man's aspiration towards 'royal freedom' through
dominion over sin makes him similar to Christ, who was
glorified and exalted for his obedience to the Father even
unto death. Every Christian who conquers sin by imitating
Christ achieves the royal self-dominion that is proper to
human beings; by so doing he shares in the *munus regale* of
Christ and helps to bring about Christ's kingdom. This
sharing is not merely subjective but objective, historical and
eschatological: for, when all things are subjected to Christ,
'then the Son himself will also be subjected to him who put
all things under him, that God may be everything to everyone'
(1 Cor. 15:27–8).

This Christian vision – which is at the same time a full,
eschatological prospect of the kingship of man in the Kingdom
of Christ – is closely linked with the interpersonal and social
aspect of the Gospel morality. This consists of 'serving Christ
in others', so that Christians 'may in humility and patience
bring their brethren to that king (LG 36). Participation in
Christ's *munus regale* is closely linked to the apostolate, of
which we shall speak later. At this point we wish to emphasize
especially the attitude of Christian morality which is character-

istic of participation in Christ's *munus regale*. Only Christ is 'that king to serve whom is to reign' (LG 36; cf. 1 Kings 3:7). The teaching of Vatican II emphasizes the kingliness of service as it first emphasized the kingliness of dominion over sin. Here too subjective participation in the *munus regale* of Christ is linked to the objective increase of his kingdom. What the passage of *Lumen Gentium* says about the laity also applies to all Christ's disciples.

> LG 36 | The Lord also desires that his kingdom be spread by the lay faithful: the kingdom of truth and life, the kingdom of holiness and grace, the kingdom of justice, love and peace. In this kingdom creation itself will be delivered from the slavery of corruption into the freedom of the glory of the sons of God (cf. Rom. 8:21). Clearly, a great promise, a great commission is given to the disciples: 'all things are yours, you are Christ's, and Christ is God's' (1 Cor. 3:23).

The attitude which derives from participation in the *munus regale* of Christ becomes, in the light of the Council's teaching, a specific determinant of the whole of Christian morality in its natural relation to Christ as the most perfect model. Christian morality is characterized by this relationship and hence by the profound, significant theme of the 'kingship' of man as well as the objective process of the increase of the kingdom of God towards its ultimate fulfilment.

This kingship, and the development of the kingdom of Christ that goes with it, is expressed in turn in the Christian's relationship with the world.

> LG 36 | The faithful must, then, recognize the inner nature, the value and the ordering of the whole of creation to the praise of God. Even by their secular activity they must aid one another to greater holiness of life, so that the world may be

filled with the spirit of Christ and may the more
effectively attain its destiny in justice, in love and
in peace.

This passage is from Chapter IV of *Lumen Gentium*, which
deals with the role of the laity in the Church. Although what
it says applies to all disciples of Christ, it rightly states that
'The laity enjoy a principal role in the universal fulfilment of
this task' (LG 36).

LG 36 | Therefore, by their competence in secular
disciplines and by their activity, interiorly raised
up by grace, let them work earnestly in order
that created goods through human labour,
technical skill and civil culture may serve the
utility of all men according to the plan of the
creator and the light of his word. May these
goods be more suitably distributed among all
men and in their own way may they be conducive
to universal progress in human and Christian
liberty. Thus, through the members of the
Church, will Christ increasingly illuminate the
whole of human society with his saving light.

This aspect of participation in the *munus regale* of Christ is
closely linked with God's original command to man to
'subdue the earth' (Gen. 1:28), a command and a destiny
on which light is thrown by the revelation of Christ. Christians
will measure up to that eternal plan only when they have come
to understand 'the inner nature . . . of the whole of creation'
and, as a result, are able to 'bring created goods to perfection';
this is the task and purpose of human labour, which will then
reflect the kingly mission of Christ. The whole work of trans-
forming the world and bringing it to man's level by means of
science, technology and civilization – all this bears the imprint
of man's kingship and his sharing in the *munus regale* of
Christ. Vatican II sees one aspect of that participation in the

skill and activity of the laity, 'interiorly raised up by grace'. The activity resulting from 'competence in secular disciplines' must not only express itself in works of technology and civilization but must also serve to strengthen justice, love and peace among men. *Lumen Gentium* subordinates material to moral progress. Men must see that the goods of creation are 'more suitably distributed among all men' because this is 'conducive to universal progress in human and Christian liberty'. Thus in the sphere of dominion over the world and material progress, proper participation in the *munus regale* of Christ is linked with the moral aspect of that progress. Material progress in itself cannot express and fulfil the kingship of man in all its completeness.

> LG 36 | Moreover, by uniting their forces, let the laity so remedy the institutions and conditions of the world when the latter are an inducement to sin, that these may be conformed to the norms of justice, favouring rather than hindering the practice of virtue. By so doing they will impregnate culture and human works with a moral value.

By 'impregnating culture and human works with a moral value' (as Part 2 of *Gaudium et Spes* expounds in more detail), Christians act on themselves and others to bring about that kingship of man which is essentially realized through moral values. In this way they also labour for the increase of Christ's kingdom in the world, because when all areas of human life are imbued with moral value, 'the field of the World is better prepared for the seed of the divine word and the doors of the Church are opened more widely so that the message of peace may enter the world' (LG 36).

Morals and moral values are presented by the Council as an integral part of the Christian mission. To imbue the various aspects of life with moral values is to fill them with the spirit of Christ. At the same time these values are the basic good

of every person and human society. Christians must be aware
of both these aspects of morality and of both the distinctions
between them and also their close connection.

LG 36 | Because of the very economy of salvation the
faithful should learn to distinguish carefully
between the rights and the duties which they
have as belonging to the Church and those which
fall to them as members of the human society.
They will strive to unite the two harmoniously,
remembering that in every temporal affair they
are to be guided by a Christian conscience, since
not even in temporal business may any human
activity be withdrawn from God's dominion.
In our times it is most necessary that this distinction and harmony should shine forth as clearly
as possible in the manner in which the faithful
act, in order that the mission of the Church may
correspond more fully with the special circumstances of the world today. It must be recognized
that the terrestrial city, rightly concerned with
secular affairs, is governed by its own principles.

The last words of this passage are related to the principle of
the autonomy of earthly things, the Church's recognition of
which is confirmed by *Gaudium et Spes* (GS 36). In this field
too, Christian morality becomes the source of the attitudes
which express participation in the *munus regale* of Christ. The
Christian is aware that morality contributes essentially to the
shaping of human life on the temporal plane, and also to the
increase of the kingdom of God. In the moral attitude and the
maturity of his conscience and activity he recognizes not only
the nature of man's 'royalty' but also that of participation in
the kingly mission of Christ himself. This awareness most not
divert him from the duty of imbuing the various fields of
human life with moral values, but should impel him to do so
more and more, as Vatican II makes clear.

GS 43 | Let there, then, be no such pernicious opposition between professional and social activity on the one hand and religious life on the other. The Christian who shirks his temporal duties shirks his duties towards his neighbour, neglects God himself, and endangers his eternal salvation. Let Christians follow the example of Christ who worked as a craftsman; let them be proud of the opportunity to carry out their earthly activity in such a way as to integrate human, domestic, professional, scientific and technical enterprises with religious values, under whose supreme direction all things are ordered to the glory of God.

The fact that Christian morality is based on the very reality of the *munus regale* of Christ throws a different light on what *Gaudium et Spes* says of modern atheism.

GS 20 | Modern atheism often takes on a systematic form also which, in addition to other causes, so insists on man's desire for autonomy as to object to any dependence on God at all. Those who profess this kind of atheism maintain that freedom consists in this, that man is an end to himself, and the sole maker, with supreme control, of his own history (*propriae suae historae solus artifex et demiurgus*). They claim that this outlook cannot be reconciled with the assertion of a Lord who is author and end of all things, or that at least it makes such an affirmation altogether unnecessary. The sense of power which modern technical progress begets in man may encourage this outlook.

Among the various kinds of present-day atheism, that one should not go unnoticed which looks for man's autonomy through his economic and social emancipation. It holds that religion, of its very nature, thwarts such emancipation by raising man's hopes in a future life, thus both deceiving him and discouraging him from working for a better form of life on earth.

As the same document goes on to say, 'The Church, as given over to the service of both God and man, cannot cease from reproving with the utmost firmness' . . . those ideologies 'which cast man down from the noble state to which he is born' (GS 21). This is a corollary of the Christian conviction of the kingliness of man and his participation in the *munus regale* of Christ.

GS 35 | Human activity proceeds from man: it is also ordered to him. When he works, not only does he transform matter and society, but he fulfils himself. He learns, he develops his faculties, and he emerges from and transcends himself. Rightly understood, this kind of growth is more precious than any kind of wealth that can be amassed. It is what a man is, rather than what he has, that counts.

Our analysis of the attitude of participation has emphasized everything that, according to the Council's doctrine, is of fundamental importance to the enrichment of Christian faith. If faith is the attitude in which man responds to God's self-revelation by abandoning himself completely to him, man must seek in Christ the reasons for his own attitude and his own response. Christ is not only he who has revealed God and through whom God has revealed himself; Christ is also he who determines man's response in faith. He does so not only as regards the contents of faith but also with reference to the very existence of the one who believes, who professes the faith and desires to 'bear witness'. The sphere of the content of faith and that of man's whole existence in faith interpenetrate and form each other.

All that the Council says of the threefold mission of Christ as priest, prophet and king, and of his threefold power constituting the inner physiognomy of the whole People of God – all this forms the content of faith, serves to enrich the believer's consciousness, determines his existence in faith and shapes his inward attitude. The attitude which derives from sharing in the threefold power of Christ is the expression not only of a conscious faith ripening in man's inmost heart, but also of Christ guiding the development of the faith of the whole People and each one of its members. Christ and the Christian encounter each other intimately in the priestly, prophetic and kingly mission, and it is this participation which forms the essential characteristics of the Christian.

The features in which the Christian resembles Christ are interior ones but are also 'missionary', since it is thanks to them that the mission of Christ lives on in mankind and in human individuals. These features constitute the reality of the People of God in and through every man and woman. They do not constitute this reality in its profoundest ontological depth, however, since this is effected solely by the grace of 'adoption as sons of God'. This grace is the most essential, interior and mysterious feature of resemblance to the incarnate Son of God, but after it come the features which reflect the mission of Christ. They, and the whole mission itself, belong to the human dimension of the history of salvation; in a sense, too, they determine it and operate in its favour. The Son of God, as man, was priest, prophet and king. The natural development of the characteristics and attitudes which derive from participation in the mission of Christ as priest, prophet and king cannot take place independently of the profound basis of the resemblance of every man to the Son of God, which is the grace of adoption. Thus the formation of these attitudes should be seen as both a touchstone and an expression of man's supernatural maturity 'in Christ', which is of essential significance to the life and mission of the People of God.

This is confirmed by the following passage from the Declaration on Christian Education:

GE 2 | All Christians – that is, all those who having been reborn in water and the Holy Spirit are called and in fact are children of God – have a right to a Christian education. Such an education not only develops the maturity of the human person in the way we have described, but is especially directed towards ensuring that those who have been baptized, as they are gradually introduced to a knowledge of the mystery of salvation, become daily more appreciative of the gift of faith which they have received. They should learn to adore God the Father in spirit and in truth (Jn. 4:23), especially through the liturgy. They should be trained to live their own lives in the new self, justified and sanctified through the truth (Eph. 4:22–4). Thus they should come to true manhood, which is proportioned to the completed growth of Christ (cf. Eph. 4:13), and make their contribution to the growth of the Mystical Body.

Christian education must help Christians to 'become daily more appreciative of the gift of faith': that is, it must enrich their faith. This enrichment must follow the line of participation as described by the Council, thanks to which the Christian in a certain sense rediscovers himself in Christ so that he may recognize Christ and Christ's mission in himself and in the dimensions of his own life and his own vocation.

CHAPTER III

The attitude of human identity and Christian responsibility

The foregoing analysis of the attitude of participation has brought out the basic aspects of the Christian's self-identification with the mission of Christ, which serve profoundly to enrich his faith and inner life. Linked with them is the Christian's search for his own proper place in the vast and varied community of the People of God. This place is, so to speak, indicated and assigned to each human being by Christ, the sole mediator, who orients the whole of humanity and every member of it towards God, imprinting on his inmost being the reality of this orientation.

Along with this, Vatican II identifies and describes the attitude of 'human identity' as the proper one for a Christian life enriched by Christ. A close study of the Council documents confirms the existence of this attitude at the profoundest level of the Council's thought and intentions, in the sphere of that fundamental plan within which we discern the pastoral tasks incumbent on us. It would seem that most of the elements which characterize the attitude of 'human identity' are to be found in the Constitution *Gaudium et Spes*: in this respect as in others, this document complements *Lumen Gentium*, which deals above all with the attitude of participation. Other Council documents to some extent, but above all *Gaudium et Spes* teaches that the Christian's proper attitude of participation in the threefold mission of Christ is and should be permeated by all that is authentically human.

The discernment of this attitude in the Conciliar teaching,

and a close study of it, mean that we must overcome or rather oppose what contemporary thought defines as 'alienation'. This concept has become, as it were, the root and epitome of the arguments against religion in general and Christianity in particular. A close study of the teaching of Vatican II, and *Gaudium et Spes* especially, shows to what extent and in what sense man is at the centre of religion, and above all of Christianity. We discover him in all his reality and with all his specific problems, in the reality of creation and of the redemption that the Church proclaims and by which it lives. These divine realities in their essence do not lead man away from himself: they rather enable him to enter into himself more profoundly, to discover the whole truth of his own humanity and personality, which is the contrary of 'alienation'. We thus note once again that the attitude of 'human identity', inwardly permeates the attitude of participation whereby the Christian identifies himself with the mission of Christ himself. A study of the Council's teaching leads us to define this attitude as one of the essential determinants of the implementation of the Council.

It is clear from what we have so far said that the attitude of human identity is closely linked to that of participation. A further analysis will confirm that these attitudes converge particularly in the sphere of morality. This means that 'identification with man' is not static in character, but dynamic and normative. It is a question of the attitude of human identity which is pervaded by the aspiration and effort towards creating human dignity and that of the human community. With this, it seems, are related the chief normative elements and the most evident ethical tendencies in the Council's teaching as a whole. 'Technical progress is of less value than advances towards greater justice, wider brotherhood, and a more human social environment' (GS 35).

1. *Identity and solidarity*

This aspect of the Council's teaching is touched on in the very first words of *Gaudium et Spes*, where we read:

> GS 1 | The joy and hope, the grief and anguish of the men of our time, especially of those who are poor or afflicted in any way, are the joy and hope, the grief and anguish of the followers of Christ as well. Nothing that is genuinely human fails to find an echo in their hearts. For theirs is a community composed of men, of men who, united in Christ and guided by the holy Spirit, press onwards towards the kingdom of the Father and are bearers of a message of salvation intended for all men. That is why Christians cherish a feeling of deep solidarity with the human race and its history.

This passage is concerned with union in the widest possible context of human existence, a union which basically determines the attitude of 'human identity'.

> GS 3 | The Council, as witness and guide to the faith of the whole people of God, gathered together by Christ, can find no more eloquent expression of its solidarity and respectful affection for the whole human family, to which it belongs, than to enter into dialogue with it about all these different problems. The Council will clarify these problems in the light of the Gospel and will furnish mankind with the saving resources which the Church has received from its founder under the promptings of the Holy Spirit. It is man himself who must be saved: it is mankind

that must be renewed. It is man, therefore, who is the key to this discussion, man considered whole and entire, with body and soul, heart and conscience, mind and will.

This is the reason why this sacred Synod, in proclaiming the noble destiny of man and affirming an element of the divine in him, offers to co-operate unreservedly with mankind in fostering a sense of brotherhood to correspond to this destiny of theirs.

From the Preface onwards, this pastoral Constitution maps out the identity and solidarity which should become the content of the life and attitude of every Christian.

GS 11 | . . . the people of God, and the human race which is its setting, render service to each other; and the mission of the Church will show itself to be supremely human by the very fact of being religious.

GS 12 | Believers and unbelievers agree almost unanimously that all things on earth should be ordained to man as to their centre and summit.

Of great importance in analysing the attitude of human identity is an understanding of the condition of man in the modern world, such as that contained in the introductory exposition of *Gaudium et Spes*. This is not a mere description, but takes full account of the fact that in all that constitutes the situation of man in the modern world, his 'condition' in the widest sense of the term, the Christian recognizes himself and perceives a basic dimension of his own existence. It is not possible to quote the whole exposition here or to analyse it fully, but it is worth while reading it in full to understand the manifold changes which determine that condition and are the basis of the Christian's 'human identity'.

GS 4 | A transformation of this kind brings with it the serious problems associated with any crisis of growth. Increase in power is not always accompanied by control of that power for the benefit of man. In probing the recesses of his own mind man often seems more uncertain than ever of himself: in the gradual and precise unfolding of the laws of social living, he is perplexed by uncertainty about how to plot its course . . .

Small wonder then that many of our contemporaries are prevented by this complex situation from recognizing permanent values and duly applying them to recent discoveries. As a result they hover between hope and anxiety and wonder uneasily about the present course of events. It is a situation that challenges men to reply; they cannot escape.

The attitude of human identity formulated by Vatican II consists primarily in the fact that the Christian accepts as his own the different elements of the condition of man in the modern world and follows attentively the trend of the questions that man and humanity pose to themselves in their various environments and relationships, in view of that condition.

GS 7 | A change in attitudes and structures frequently calls accepted values into question. This is true above all of young people who have grown impatient at times and, indeed, rebellious in their distress. Conscious of their own importance in the life of society, they aspire to play their part in it all the sooner. Consequently, it frequently happens that parents and teachers face increasing difficulties in the performance of their tasks.

Traditional institutions, laws and modes of

> thought and emotion do not always appear to be in harmony with today's world. This has given rise to a serious disruption of patterns and even of norms of behaviour.

GS 6
> On the whole, the bonds uniting man to his fellows multiply without ceasing, and 'socialization' creates yet other bonds, without, however, a corresponding personal development, and truly personal relationships 'personaliza-ever, a corresponding personal development and truly personal relationships ('personalization').

The changes spoken of in the Preface of *Gaudium et Spes* are marked by the tensions we find 'on the level of race and social class between the affluent and the underdeveloped nations; we find them between international bodies set up in the interests of peace and the ambitions of ideological indoctrination along with national or bloc expansionism. In the midst of it all stands man, at once the author and the victim of mutual distrust, animosity, conflict and woe'. (GS 8).

This may be called the external and 'macroscopic' dimension of the condition of man in the modern world. *Gaudium et Spes* links it with the internal dimension that belongs to each separate individual.

GS 8
> The headlong development of the world and a keener awareness of existing inequalities make for the creation and aggravation of differences and imbalances. On the personal level there often arises an imbalance between an outlook which is practical and modern and a way of thinking which fails to master and synthesize the sum total of its ideas. Another imbalance occurs between concern for practicality and the demands of moral conscience, not to mention

that between the claims of group living and the needs of individual reflection and contemplation. A third imbalance takes the form of conflict between specialization and an overall view of reality.

GS 7 | As regards religion there is a completely new atmosphere that conditions its practice. On the one hand people are taking a hard look at all magical world-views and prevailing superstitions and demanding a more personal and active commitment of faith, so that not a few have achieved a lively sense of the divine. On the other hand greater numbers are falling away from the practice of religion. In the past it was the exception to repudiate God and religion to the point of abandoning them, and then only in individual cases; but nowadays it seems a matter of course to reject them as incompatible with scientific progress and a new kind of humanism. In many places it is not only in philosophical terms that such trends are expressed, but there are signs of them in literature, art, the humanities, the interpretation of history and even civil law: all of which is very disturbing to many people.

This picture of the condition of man in the modern world also contains a certain testimony of the identity of every Christian which lies at the root of the attitude of 'human identity' that is part of the Council's teaching. It is doubtless not without a profound reason that the pastoral document takes as its starting point in this direction the fact that:

GS 9 | These claims are but the sign of a deeper and more widespread aspiration. Man as an individual and as a member of society craves a life

> that is full, autonomous, and worthy of his
> nature as a human being; he longs to harness
> for his own welfare the immense resources of the
> modern world. Among nations there is a
> growing movement to set up a worldwide
> community.

If the attitude of human identity begins with keeping in mind and in a sense appropriating all the 'situational' elements which make up the reality of human existence in the modern world, it develops, however, when one starts to display the two principal aspirations referred to in the last quoted passage, viz. that for the dignity of the human person and that for communion among mankind. Both these are linked to the evangelical order of values and the whole Christian ethos. It is significant that Part 1 of *Gaudium et Spes* is entitled 'The Church and Man's Vocation' and that its first chapter is on 'The Dignity of the Human Person'.

We have already quoted several passages from this Chapter. Christian doctrine embodies the profound concept of the 'humanization' of all that man comes into contact with in his existence and activity on earth.

GS 15 | Our age, more than any of the past, needs such
       | wisdom if all that man discovers is to be ennobled
       | through human effort.

This thought recurs several times in various Conciliar texts. To 'make human life more human' is the Council's fundamental objective, closely linked to the desire to share in the divine life and in the mission of Christ. This connection reveals still more plainly the dignity of the whole person of man, both body and spirit.

GS 14 | For this reason man may not despise his bodily
       | life. Rather he is obliged to regard his body as
       | good and to hold it in honour, since God has
       | created it and will raise it up on the last day.

Nevertheless man has been wounded by sin. He finds by experience that his body is in revolt. His very dignity therefore requires that he should glorify God in his body, and not allow it to serve the evil inclinations of his heart.

Thus it is clear that the formation of what we call the attitude of 'human identity' consists not only in accepting the situation of man in the modern world but in sharing fully in the aspirations which have as their end the true dignity of man. In this way we must discover conscience and the objective moral order to which the human conscience is subordinate.

GS 16 | Deep within his conscience man discovers a law which he has not laid upon himself but which he must obey. Its voice, ever calling him to love and to do what is good and to avoid evil, tells him inwardly at the right moment: do this, shun that. For man has in his heart a law inscribed by God. His dignity lies in observing this law, and by it he will be judged. His conscience is man's most secret core, and his sanctuary. There he is alone with God whose voice echoes in his depths. By conscience, in a wonderful way, that law is made known which is fulfilled in the love of God and of one's neighbour.

IM 6 | The Council proclaims that all must accept the absolute primacy of the objective moral order. It alone is superior to and is capable of harmonizing all forms of human activity . . . Only the moral order touches man in the totality of his being as God's rational creature, called to a supernatural destiny. If the moral order is fully and faithfully observed, it leads man to full perfection and happiness.

For this reason the Declaration on Christian Education

teaches that:

> GE 1 | Children and young people have the right to be stimulated to make sound moral judgements based on a well-formed conscience and to put them into practice with a sense of personal commitment.

A right conscience and the objective moral order correspond to each other and together constitute the dignity of man.

> GS 16 | Through loyalty to conscience Christians are joined to other men in the search for truth and for the right solution to so many moral problems which arise both in the life of individuals and from social relationships. Hence, the more a correct conscience prevails, the more do persons and groups turn aside from blind choice and try to be guided by the objective standards of moral conduct. Yet it often happens that conscience goes astray through ignorance which it is unable to avoid, without thereby losing its dignity. This cannot be said of the man who takes little trouble to find out what is true and good, or when conscience is by degrees almost blinded through the habit of committing sin.

At the base of the moral order, a right human conscience perceives and accepts 'that law which is fulfilled in the love of God and of one's neighbour' (GS 16). In the Decree on the Apostolate of the Laity we find a passage dealing expressly with the evangelical precept of charity.

> AA 8 | The greatest commandment of the law is to love God with one's whole heart and one's neighbour as oneself (cf. Mt. 22:37–40). Christ has made this love of the neighbour his personal commandment and enriched it with a new meaning when

he willed himself, along with his brothers, to be the object of this charity, saying: 'When you showed it to one of the least of my brothers here, you showed it to me' (Mt. 25:40). In assuming human nature he has united to himself all humanity in a supernatural solidarity which makes of it one single family. He has made charity the distinguishing mark of his disciples, in the words: 'By this will all men know you for my disciples, by the love you bear one another' (Jn. 13:35).

The precept of charity is at the root of the whole moral order. It also contains the principle of action thanks to which human life can become more and more human, as the Council repeatedly puts it. This principle has a decisive effect in forming the attitude of human identity by which the Christian should be characterized. The Gospel shows that this attitude finds its model in the 'identification' of Christ, the Son of God, with men as his brothers, for whom he constitutes a supernatural centre of human solidarity in the widest possible sphere.

AA 14 | Among the signs of our times, particularly worthy of note is the ever growing and inescapable sense of the solidarity of all peoples. It is the task of the lay apostolate to take pains in developing this sense and transforming it into a really sincere desire for brotherly union.

Chapter II of Part 1 of *Gaudium et Spes* shows in what way we should understand and realize the attitude of human identity, of profound solidarity with men and mankind in the various situations of life.

GS 27 | Today there is an inescapable duty to make ourselves the neighbour of every man, no matter who he is, and if we meet him, to come to his aid

> in a positive way, whether he is an aged person
> abandoned by all, a foreign worker despised
> without reason, a refugee, an illegitimate child
> wrongly suffering for a sin he did not commit, or
> a starving human being who awakens our
> conscience by calling to mind the words of
> Christ: 'As you did it to one of the least of these
> my brethren, you did it to me' (Mt. 25:40).

The Constitution speaks here in concrete terms, as in the passage quoted from St Matthew's Gospel. It also refers to 'awareness of the sublime dignity of the human person, who stands above all things and whose rights and duties are universal and inviolable' (GS 26). This growing awareness means that 'The social order and its development must constantly yield to the good of the person' (GS 26).

GS 29 | All men are endowed with a rational soul and are
> created in God's image; they have the same
> nature and origin and, being redeemed by Christ,
> they enjoy the same divine calling and destiny;
> there is here a basic inequality between all men
> and it must be given ever greater recognition.
>
> Undoubtedly not all men are alike as regards
> physical capacity and intellectual and moral
> powers. But forms of social or cultural discrimi-
> nation in basic personal rights on the grounds of
> sex, race, colour, social conditions, language or
> religion, must be curbed and eradicated as
> incompatible with God's design.

Revealed truth concerning man, as the Council often points out, constitutes the most solid basis of the attitude of identity and human solidarity.

GS 29 | It is up to public and private organizations to
> be at the service of the dignity and destiny of
> man; let them spare no effort to banish every

vestige of social and political slavery and to safeguard basic human rights under every political system. And even if it takes a considerable time to arrive at the desired goal, these organizations should gradually be brought into harmony with spiritual realities, which are the most sublime of all.

The Council emphasizes the primacy of the spirit in human morality. Charity is the force of the spirit and the realization of the spiritual order in interpersonal relations. This is the truth of the Gospel which Vatican II recalls to the modern world.

AA 8 | If this exercise of charity is to be above all criticism, and seen to be so, one should see in one's neighbour the image of God in which he has been created, and Christ the Lord to whom is really offered all that is given to the needy. The liberty and dignity of the person helped must be respected with the greatest sensitivity. Purity of intention should not be stained by any self-seeking or desire to dominate. The demands of justice must first of all be satisfied; that which is already due in justice is not to be offered as a gift of charity. The cause of evils, and not merely their effects, ought to disappear. The aid contributed should be organized in such a way that beneficiaries are gradually freed from their dependence on others and become self-supporting.

These words from the Decree on the lay apostolate explain how works of charity should be performed towards our neighbour, whether individually or socially. The primacy of the spirit is expressed in charity, and from St Paul's epistle to the Corinthians (1 Cor. 13) we learn what charity should be.

The Conciliar text brings out the fundamental criterion for distinguishing between the duties of social morality which derive from justice and those based on charity. Charity is directed towards the individual: it respects his true dignity, which is closely linked with the attribute of freedom. Thus charity respects the person above any for as of calculation or thought of profit. It does not make use of man, but serves his humanity. The text just quoted helps us to see how charity conditions the attitude of human identity and how that attitude is to be understood.

Gaudium et Spes indicates in a brief summary all the features of modern life which are radically contrary to justice towards human beings and still more contrary to charity towards the human person. These words recall some texts of St Paul.

GS 27 | The varieties of crime are numerous: all offences against life itself, such as murder, genocide, abortion, euthanasia and wilful suicide; all violations of the integrity of the human person, such as mutilation, physical and mental torture, undue psychological pressures; all offences against human dignity, such as subhuman living conditions, arbitrary imprisonment, deportation, slavery, prostitution, the selling of women and children, degrading working conditions where men are treated as mere tools for profit rather than free and responsible persons: all these and the like are criminal: they poison civilization; they debase the perpetrators more than the victims, and militate against the honour of the creator.

The living man is the Creator's glory: this thought from St Irenaeus is also reflected in the Conciliar text. The Christian attitude of human identity is firmly rooted in awareness of the creation and redemption.

From this point of view Vatican II examines the processes of the so-called 'socialization' that are peculiar to the present age.

GS 25 | Nowadays for various reasons mutual relation-
ships and interdependence increase from day to
day and give rise to a variety of associations and
organizations, both public and private. This
socialization, as it is called, is not without
dangers, but it brings with it many advantages
for the strengthening and betterment of human
qualities and for the protection of human rights.

A little earlier we read:

GS 23 | One of the most striking features of today's
world is the intense development of interpersonal
relationships due in no small measure to modern
technical advances. Nevertheless genuine fraternal dialogue is advanced not so much on this
level as at the deeper level of personal fellowship,
and this calls for mutual respect for the full
spiritual dignity of men as persons. Christian
revelation greatly fosters the establishment of
such fellowship and at the same time promotes
deeper understanding of the laws of social living
with which the creator has endowed man's
spiritual and moral nature.

The Council, following the whole tradition of the social
doctrine of the Church, notes that 'there is an interdependence
between personal betterment and the improvement of society'
(GS 25). From this it draws the moral of solidarity.

GS 30 | Let everyone consider it his sacred duty to count
social obligations among man's chief duties
today and observe them as such. For the more
closely the world comes together, the more
widely do men's obligations transcend particular
groups and gradually extend to the whole world.

> This will be realized only if individuals and groups practice moral and social virtues and foster them in social living. Then, under the necessary help of divine grace, there will arise a generation of new men, the moulders of a new humanity.

The passages quoted show how Vatican II understands the scope of human solidarity, which it considers a 'sacred thing'. This solidarity in the broadest sense is arrived at by way of solidarity in the more limited groups to which human beings belong. This means that the moral attitude of every man, his 'moral and social virtues' are the basis of solidarity on every plane including the widest.

The formation of this attitude, according to the Christian view of morals, is the fruit of constant cooperation with divine grace, which leads to but also springs from an authentic spiritual maturity.

GS 31 | To achieve a greater fulfilment of their duties of conscience as individuals towards themselves and towards the various groups to which they belong, men have to be carefully educated to a higher degree of culture through the employment of the immense resources available today to the human race.

This is above all a matter of 'training youth from all social backgrounds . . . to produce the kind of men and women so desperately needed by our age – men and women not only of high culture but of great personality as well' (GS 31).

GE 1 | All men of whatever race, condition or age, in virtue of their dignity as human persons, have an inalienable right to education. This education should be suitable to the particular destiny of the individuals, adapted to their ability, sex and national cultural traditions, and should be conducive to fraternal relations with other nations in order to promote true unity and peace in the world.

The necessity and the profound importance of such education – the fruit and the pledge of an attitude of human identity and genuine solidarity – are made clear by the social realities of our time.

GS 25 | Without doubt frequent upheavals in the social order are in part the result of economic, political, and social tensions. But at a deeper level they come from selfishness and pride, two things which contaminate the atmosphere of society as well. As it is, man is prone to evil, but whenever he meets a situation where the effects of sin are to be found, he is exposed to further inducements of sin, which can only be overcome by unflinching effort under the help of grace.

The Council's analysis of social reality, a reality which must be transformed by means of proper education, is not only 'sociological' but 'evangelical', in terms of the categories of that truth concerning man which we derive from its unique source in the Gospel. However, the Christian vision of the truth concerning man, who is called on to live and work in society, does not lose sight of socio-economic conditions.

GS 31 | For freedom is often crippled by extreme destitution just as it can wither in an ivory-tower isolation brought on by overindulgence in the good things of life. It can, however, be strengthened by accepting the inevitable constraints of social life, by undertaking the manifold demands of human fellowship, and by service to the community at large.

These words sum up the significance and value of the

attitude of the human identity and genuine solidarity, consisting in the correct orientation of individual liberty towards the common good.

> GS 31 | It is necessary then to foster among all the will to play a role in common undertakings. One must pay tribute to those nations whose systems permit the largest possible number of the citizens to take part in public life in a climate of genuine freedom.

The verdict of *Gaudium et Spes* corresponds to that of the Church's whole doctrinal tradition concerning individualism and totalitarianism in life and the social order.

Within the framework of human social life the precept of love as the foundation of social morality sometimes finds situations which entail opposition as well as those which provide opportunities for solidarity.

> GS 28 | Those also have a claim on our respect and charity who think and act differently from us in social, political, and religious matters. In fact the more deeply we come to understand their ways of thinking through kindness and love, the more easily will we be able to enter into dialogue with them.
>
> Love and courtesy of this kind should not, of course, make us indifferent to truth and goodness. Love, in fact, impels the followers of Christ to proclaim to all men the truth which saves. But we must distinguish between the error (which must always be rejected) and the person in error, who never loses his dignity as a person even though he flounders amid false or inadequate religious ideas. God alone is the judge and the searcher of hearts: he forbids us to pass judgement on the inner guilt of others.

Hence in the paragraphs concerning the Church's relations with atheism we read:

GS 21 | Although the Church altogether rejects atheism, she nevertheless sincerely proclaims that all men, those who believe as well as those who do not, should help to establish right order in this world where all live together. This certainly cannot be done without a dialogue that is sincere and prudent. The Church therefore deplores the discrimination between believers and unbelievers which some civil authorities unjustly practice in defiance of the fundamental rights of the human person. She demands effective freedom for the faithful to be allowed to build up God's temple in this world also. She courteously invites atheists to weigh the merits of the Gospel of Christ with an open mind.

2.   *The main spheres of Christian responsibility*

DH 1 | Contemporary man is becoming increasingly conscious of the dignity of the human person; more and more people are demanding that men should exercise fully their own judgement and a responsible freedom in their actions and should not be subject to the pressure of coercion but be inspired by a sense of duty.

These are the opening words of the Declaration on Religious Liberty, and they enable us to understand the essence of Christian responsibility as conceived by Vatican II. It is expressed through a firm awareness of duty springing from a rightly formed conscience. Responsibility is closely associated with the dignity of the individual, for it expresses the self-determination – the reverse of wilfulness – in which man makes proper use of his freedom by allowing himself to be guided by genuine values and a law of righteousness.

It is not surprising that the attitude of responsibility, thus understood, is close to the doctrine of Vatican II: it is in fact one of the chief elements of the Council's plan for the enrichment of faith which is a basic feature of its teaching.

> DH 9 | The Declaration of this Vatican Council on man's right to religious freedom is based on the dignity of the person, the demands of which have become more fully known to human reason through centuries of experience. Furthermore, this doctrine of freedom is rooted in divine revelation.

The Council emphasizes the close connection between responsibility and the natural freedom of the human person.

> DH 7 | In availing themselves of any freedom men must respect the moral principle of personal and social responsibility: in exercising their rights individual men and social groups are bound by the moral law to have regard for the rights of others, their own duties to others and the common good of all. All men must be treated with justice and humanity.

The attitude of mature responsibility is certainly the element which, on the part of every man and woman, 'makes human life more human'. The Council thus expects this attitude from every man and above all from every Christian, and it calls on legislators and the organizers and guardians of social life to act in such a way as to encourage the attitude of social responsibility.

DH 8 | For this reason this Vatican Council urges everyone, especially those responsible for educating others, to try to form men with a respect for the moral order who will obey lawful authority and be lovers of true freedom – men, that is, who will form their own judgements in the light of truth, direct their activities with a sense of responsibility, and strive for what is true and just in willing cooperation with others.

DH 7 | For the rest, the principle of the integrity of freedom in society should continue to be upheld. According to this principle man's freedom should be given the fullest possible recognition and should not be curtailed except when and in so far as is necessary.

In this context we can and should speak of interdependence and mutual influence between responsibility and liberty. The Council emphasizes that the attitude of responsibility is conditioned by the 'integral freedom' of man in society, while experience constantly teaches that internal and external liberty is essential to the development of a responsible attitude. But we must also note that only mature responsibility conditions freedom of either kind. In other words, only the responsible man derives true profit from inner freedom. There is, moreover, no good reason to limit his external freedom; any such limitation is contrary to social morality and to the fundamental 'economy of human values' which is both the purpose and the essential condition of the true development of society.

The aim of education is to fortify man's attitude of responsibility.

GE 1 | True education is directed towards the formation of the human person in view of his final end and the good of that society to which he belongs and in the duties of which he will, as an adult, have a share.

GS 35 | Here then is the norm for human activity – to harmonize with the authentic interests of the human race, in accordance with God's will and design, and to enable men as individuals and as members of society to pursue and fulfil their total vocation.

The attitude of Christian responsibility is like that of human responsibility, but it also presupposes the reality of creation and redemption with which is associated the dimension of values that form the Christian ethos in all its fullness. Vatican II places before our eyes some spheres of Christian responsibility and singles out some 'more urgent problems', especially in the pastoral Constitution *Gaudium et Spes*. In all these spheres the Council's teaching establishes the fundamental postulate of responsibility for every human being.

This postulate, which applies to every human being and especially to every Christian, emphasizes the dignity and vocation of the human person. This is seen particularly in the conception of man's relationship with God that is presented by the Constitution on Divine Revelation and the Declaration on Religious Liberty, and also in the conception of man's relationship with the world – a relationship which, according to the Church's teaching, forms part of the Council's consciousness as it is constituted in the final analysis by ultimately constituted by the truth concerning creation and redemption.

It may be said without exaggeration that the whole work of Vatican II sprang from a particular sense of responsibility towards man and his fate in this world and the next. It is here that we must seek the basic measure of all Christian responsibility: man is, so to speak, the central value to which that responsibility is referred in every sphere.

GS 34 | With an increase in human power comes a broadening of responsibility on the part of individuals and communities: there is no question, then, of the Christian message inhibiting men from building up the world or making them disinterested in the good of their fellows: on the contrary it is an incentive to do these very things.

AA 14 | Catholics are to be keen on collaborating with all men of good will in the promotion of all that is true, just, holy, all that is worthy of love (cf. Phil. 4:8). They are to enter into dialogue with them, approaching them with understanding and courtesy; and are to search for means of improving social and public institutions along the lines of the Gospel.

Vatican II does not enumerate all the fields of Christian responsibility, but draws attention only to some. In our account of the attitude of Christian responsibility we shall follow its example.

The first important sphere in which this attitude should be displayed is that of marriage and the family. As the title of Chapter I of Part 2 of *Gaudium et Spes* suggests, it is a question of enhancing the dignity of family life, a task and vocation which is above all that of married couples themselves.

GS 47 | It is for these reasons that the Council intends to present certain key points of the Church's teaching in a clearer light; and it hopes to guide and encourage Christians and all men who are trying to preserve and to foster the dignity and supremely sacred value of the married state.

It is worth re-reading the whole of this Chapter of the pastoral Constitution, which, in the light of its introductory note on marriage and the family in the modern world, emphasizes the sanctity of marriage and the family, their place in the divine plan of salvation, and the true meaning of married love and of its relation to procreation. It is impossible to quote here the whole of the relevant text, but a few passages may serve,

GS 48 | Authentic married love is caught up into divine love and is directed and enriched by the redemptive power of Christ and the salvific action of the Church, with the result that the spouses are effectively led to God and are helped and strengthened in their lofty role as fathers and mothers. Spouses, therefore, are fortified and, as it were, consecrated for the duties and dignity of their state by a special sacrament.

AA 11 | The mission of being the primary vital cell of society has been given to the family by God himself. This mission will be accomplished if the family, by the mutual affection of its members and by family prayer, presents itself as a domestic sanctuary of the Church.

Gaudium et Spes expresses full comprehension and respect for married love and all that pertains to it. It stresses that parents should 'give suitable and timely instruction to young people . . . about the dignity of married love, its role and its exercise,' so that, 'having learnt to reverence chastity, they will at a suitable age be able to engage in honourable courtship and enter upon marriage of their own' (GS 49). As regards the relation between conjugal love and procreation, the Council points out that 'there can be no conflict between the divine laws governing the transmission of life and the fostering of married love' (GS 51).

GS 50 | Married couples should regard it as their proper mission to transmit human life and to educate their children; they should realize that they are thereby cooperating with the love of God the

Creator and are, in a certain sense, its interpreters. This involves the fulfilment of their role with a sense of human and Christian responsibility and the formation of correct judgements through docile respect for God and common reflection and effort; it also involves a consideration of their own good and the good of their children already born or yet to come, an ability to read the signs of the times and of their own situation on the material and spiritual level, and, finally, an estimation of the good of the family, of society, and of the Church. It is the married couple themselves who must in the last analysis arrive at these judgements before God. Married people should realize that in their behaviour they may not simply follow their own fancy but must be ruled by conscience – and conscience ought to be conformed to the law of God in the light of the teaching authority of the Church, which is the authentic interpreter of divine law. For the divine law throws light on the meaning of married love, protects it and leads it to truly human fulfilment.

The attitude of responsibility typical of the vital area of marriage and the family is seen by the Council as incumbent not only on married couples: all Christians are bound to foster the development of the essential values of marriage and the family.

GS 52   Christians should actively strive to promote the values of marriage and the family; it can be done by the witness of their own lives and by concerted action along with all men of good will. To this end the Christian instincts of the faithful, the right moral conscience of man, and the wisdom and skill of persons versed in the sacred sciences will have much to contribute.

The Constitution here appeals specifically to members of particular professions: firstly experts in biology, medicine, social science and psychology, who 'can be of service to the welfare of marriage and the family and the peace of mind of people if, by pooling their findings, they try to clarify thoroughly the different conditions favouring the proper regulation of births' (GS 52). It then speaks of the role of priests as pastors of married couples and families, and goes on to consider the part that can be played by 'family associations'. Against this wide background it illustrates the tasks of couples themselves.

> GS 52 | Let married people themselves, who are created in the image of the living God and constituted in an authentic personal dignity, be united together in equal affection, agreement of mind, and mutual holiness. Thus, in the footsteps of Christ, the principle of life, they will bear witness by their faithful love in the joys and sacrifices of their calling, to that mystery of love which the Lord revealed to the world by his death and resurrection.

The second sphere in which the Council emphasizes the attitude of Christian responsibility is the 'Proper Development of Culture', the subject of Chapter II of Part 2 of *Gaudium et Spes*. We cannot, of course, reproduce here all the wealth of ideas contained in that Chapter, but will quote some passages throwing light on Christian responsibility in the field of culture.

> GS 55 | In each nation and social group there is a growing number of men and women who are conscious that they themselves are the craftsmen and moulders of their community's culture. All over the world the sense of autonomy and responsibility increases with effects of the greatest importance for the spiritual and moral maturity

of mankind. This will become clearer to us if we place before our eyes the unification of the world and the duty imposed on us to build up a better world in truth and justice. We are witnessing, then, the birth of a new humanism, where man is defined before all else by his responsibility to his brothers and at the court of history.

GS 56 | In circumstances such as these it is no wonder that man feels responsible for the progress of culture and nourishes high hopes for it, but anxiously foresees numerous conflicting elements which it is up to him to resolve.

The Constitution proceeds to enumerate some of the chief contradictions and dilemmas in contemporary culture: the progress of science and technology and its relationship with culture centred on spiritual values; the increase of specialization and the need for synthesis; progress versus tradition; the development of knowledge and the need for wisdom; universalizing tendencies and national culture; the disproportion between the share of a small élite in the benefits of civilization and that of the great majority. Finally the question is raised:

GS 56 | . . . how are we to acknowledge as lawful the claims of autonomy, which culture makes for itself, without falling into a humanism which is purely earthbound and even hostile to religion?

In spite of these conflicting issues human culture must evolve today in such a way that it will develop the whole human person harmoniously and integrally, and will help all men to fulfil the tasks to which they are called, especially Christians who are fraternally united at the heart of the human family.

GS 57 | In their pilgrimage to the heavenly city Christians are to seek and relish the things that are above:

> this involves not a lesser, but rather a greater commitment to working with all men towards the establishment of a world that is more human. Indeed the mystery of the Christian faith provides them with an outstanding incentive and encouragement to fulfil their role even more eagerly and to discover the full sense of the commitment by which human culture becomes important in man's total vocation.

This refers both to civilization considered as a transformation of the material world into 'a dwelling-place fit for all mankind', and also to culture understood as a perfection of man himself. *Gaudium et Spes* emphasizes the contribution of science and the arts towards

GS 57 | ... bringing the human race to a higher understanding of truth, goodness, and beauty, to points of view having universal value; thus man will be more clearly enlightened by the wondrous Wisdom, which was with God from eternity, working beside him like a master craftsman, rejoicing in his inhabited world, and delighting in the sons of men. As a consequence the human spirit, freed from the bondage of material things, can be more easily drawn to the worship and contemplation of the creator. Moreover, man is disposed to acknowledge, under the impulse of grace, the Word of God ...

It can be seen how deeply the attitude of Christian responsibility has plunged its roots into culture and tends constantly to raise it to a higher level. Thanks to this attitude the Christian shares in the mission of the Church, which, while 'not tied exclusively and indissolubly' to any particular culture, can 'enter into communion with different forms of culture, thereby enriching both itself and the cultures themselves' (GS 58). For:

GS 58 | The good news of Christ never ceases to purify and elevate the morality of peoples. It takes the spiritual qualities and endowments of every age and nation, and with supernatural riches it causes them to blossom, as it were, from within; it fortifies, completes and restores them in Christ. In this way the Church carries out its mission and in that very act it stimulates and advances human and civil culture . . .

GS 59 | For the reasons given above the Church recalls to mind that culture must be subordinated to the integral development of the human person, to the good of the community and of the whole of mankind. Therefore one must aim at encouraging the human spirit to develop its faculties of wonder, of understanding, of contemplation, for forming personal judgements and cultivating a religious, moral and social sense.

Among the 'more urgent duties of Christians in regard to culture' are, first of all, those connected with spreading it throughout the world. The right to enjoy the benefits of culture must be conceded to all and made into a reality (cf. GS 60). Next come the tasks connected with educating man into a state of cultural integration (cf. GS 61). All this presupposes the necessity of a proper harmony between culture, whether personal or social, and Christian teaching (cf. GS 62).

The third major field of Christian responsibility is in socio-economic life.

GS 63 | In the sphere of economics and social life, too, the dignity and entire vocation of the human person as well as the welfare of society as a whole have to be respected and fostered; for man is the source, the focus and the end of all economic and social life.

> Like all other areas of social life, the economy of today is marked by man's growing dominion over nature, by closer and keener relationships between individuals, groups and peoples, and by the frequency of state intervention. At the same time increased efficiency in production and improved methods of distribution, of productivity and services have rendered the economy an instrument capable of meeting the growing needs of the human family.
>
> But the picture is not without its disturbing elements.

Here too, as in the introduction entitled 'The Situation of Man in the World Today', the Council document describes the various causes of the 'economic and social imbalances' and points out the disparities that exist in this area.

GS 63
> . . . much reform in economic and social life is required along with a change of mentality and of attitude by all men. It was for this reason that the Church in the course of centuries has worked out, in the light of the Gospel, principles of justice and equity demanded by right reason for individual and social life and also for international relations.

The pastoral Constitution refers to Catholic social ethics, as a whole cites some of its essential principles which are suitable for developing Christian responsibility in this wide and difficult area.

In the first place it points out that economic development must remain basically at the service of man, and that he should therefore strive to eliminate huge economic disparities (cf. GS 66).

GS 64
> Today more than ever before there is an increase in the production of agricultural and industrial

goods and in the number of services available, and this is as it should be in view of the population expansion and growing human aspirations. Therefore we must encourage technical progress and the spirit of enterprise, we must foster the eagerness for creativity and improvement, and we must promote adaptation of production methods and all serious efforts of people engaged in production – in other words of all elements which contribute to economic progress. The ultimate and basic purpose of economic production does not consist merely in the increase of goods produced, nor in profit nor prestige; it is directed to the service of man, of man, that is, in his totality, taking into account his material needs and the requirements of his intellectual, moral, spiritual, and religious life; of all men whomsoever and of every group of men of whatever race or from whatever part of the world. Therefore, economic activity is to be carried out in accordance with techniques and methods belonging to the moral order, so that God's design for man may be fulfilled.

The fundamental premiss of the Church's social doctrine is the primacy of ethics over economics, as expressed in the foregoing text. The Constitution also recalls 'Some Principles Governing Economic and Social Life as a Whole', beginning with human labour. This, it points out, 'surpasses in value all other elements of economic life, for the latter are only means to an end' (GS 67).

GS 67 | Human work, whether exercised independently or in subordination to another, proceeds from the human person, who as it were impresses his seal on the things of nature and reduces them to his will. By his work a man ordinarily provides

> for himself and his family, associates with others as his brothers, and renders them service; he can exercise genuine charity and be a partner in the work of bringing divine creation to perfection ... Through the homage of work offered to God man is associated with the redemptive work of Jesus Christ, whose labour with his hands at Nazareth greatly ennobled the dignity of work. This is the source of every man's duty to work loyally as well as his right to work.

Corresponding to this right, society has the duty to provide work and reward it equitably. The Constitution speaks out against the fact that 'it frequently happens, even today, that workers are almost enslaved by the work they do'. Instead, 'the entire process of productive work must be accommodated to the needs of the human person and the nature of his life, with special attention to domestic life and particularly that of mothers of families, taking sex and age always into account' (GS 67). As well as the right to a fair wage, there is also a right to rest and recreation.

In the following paragraphs the Constitution speaks of the participation of workers in enterprises and in planning the economy in general, and gives concise suggestions for the resolution of socio-economic conflicts (cf. GS 68). It explains briefly in what way the Church has always understood, as it still does today, the fundamental principle that the fruits of the earth are intended for all men (cf. GS 69). A separate paragraph (GS 70) deals with investment and money. The next section, on the question of ownership, explains the nature of the legitimacy of private property, and also touches on the problem of large estates (GS 71). All the elements of Catholic social ethics are touched on in Chapter III of *Gaudium et Spes* from the point of view of Christians 'engaged actively in modern economic and social progress and in the struggle for justice and charity' (GS 72).

The attitude of Christian responsibility is emphasized by Vatican II not only in socio-economic matters but also in politics, which is another field in which such responsibility is exercised.

GS 75 | Christians must be conscious of their specific and proper role in the political community: they should be a shining example by their sense of responsibility and their dedication to the common good.

AA 14 | In their patriotism and in their fidelity to their civic duties Catholics will feel themselves bound to promote the true common good; they will make the weight of their convictions so influential that as a result civil authority will be justly exercised and laws will accord with moral precepts and the common good. Catholics versed in politics and, as should be the case, firm in the faith and Christian teaching should not decline to enter public life; for by a worthy discharge of their functions they can work for the common good and at the same time prepare the way for the Gospel.

The Constitution shows, at least in broad lines, what we should understand by 'preparing the way for the Gospel' in political life. This is largely the province of Catholic social ethics, the basic principles of which are emphasized in the pastoral Constitution. Chapter IV of Part 2 of *Gaudium et Spes* surveys modern public life in general terms, recalls the nature and purpose of the political community (cf. GS 74), and examines the necessity and conditions of the collaboration of all members of that community in its various tasks.

GS 73 | There is no better way to establish political life on a truly human basis than by encouraging an inward sense of justice, of good will, and of service to the common good, and by consolidating the basic convictions of men as to the true nature of the political community and the aim, proper exercise, and limits of public authority.

GS 73 | A keener awareness of human dignity has given rise in various parts of the world to an eagerness to establish a politico-juridical order in which the rights of the human person in public life will be better protected – for example, the right of free assembly and association, the right to express one's opinions and to profess one's religion privately and publicly. The guarantee of the rights of the person is, indeed, a necessary condition for citizens, individually and collectively, to play an active part in public life and administration.

The Council regards this participation in public life as a right and a duty for Christians, and devotes a separate Chapter to the subject. Analysing the problem of a just relationship between the political community and the Church, it emphasizes that a clear distinction should be made 'between the activities of Christians acting individually or collectively in their own name, as citizens guided by the dictates of a Christian conscience, and their activity acting along with their pastors in the name of the Church' (GS 76). We shall return to this question of relations between Church and State.

The last important problem of the Church in the modern world, and perhaps the widest sphere of Christian responsibility, is dealt with in Part 2, Chapter V of *Gaudium et Spes*, which is entitled, 'The Fostering of Peace and Establishment of Community of Nations'. The urgency of this problem lies in the fact that 'the whole human race faces a moment of supreme crisis in its advance towards maturity' and that mankind 'will not succeed in accomplishing the task awaiting it, that is the establishment of a truly human world for all men over the entire earth, unless everyone devotes himself to the cause of true peace with renewed vigour' (GS 77). After explaining the nature of peace in the light of natural law and the truth of the Gospel (GS 78), the document analyses in detail the moral problem of presentday warfare and 'reminds men that the natural law of peoples and its universal principles still retain their binding force (GS 79). The conscience of the human race requires that we should eliminate the horrors of war and especially of total war; the arms race must be ended, and war should be 'completely outlawed by international agreement' (cf. GS 80–2). Accordingly the Constitution goes on to emphasize strongly the need to create an international community whose fundamental task would be to discern the true causes of conflicts and seek remedies for them (cf. GS 83–90). Realizing that conflicts are deeply rooted in economic inequality, the Council regards economic cooperation as a basic task of national communities and international institutions. It also formulates more detailed norms for international cooperation in view of the situation of underdeveloped or developing nations and of richer societies (cf. GS 86), and gives particular attention to demographic problems (cf. GS 87).

The tasks confronting Christians are outlined against this wide background.

GS 88 | Christians should willingly and wholeheartedly support the establishment of an international order that includes a genuine respect for legitimate freedom and friendly sentiments of brotherhood towards all men. It is all the more urgent now that the greater part of the world is in a state of such poverty that it is as if Christ himself were crying out in the mouths of these poor people to the charity of his disciples. Let us not be guilty of the scandal of having some nations, most of whose citizens bear the name of Chris-

> tians, enjoying an abundance of riches, while others lack the necessities of life and are tortured by hunger, disease, and all kinds of misery. For the spirit of poverty and charity is the glory and witness of the Church of Christ.
>
> We must praise and assist those Christians, especially those young Christians, who volunteer their services to help other men and other peoples. Indeed it is a duty for the whole people of God, under the teaching and example of the bishops, to alleviate the hardships of our times within the limits of its means, giving generously, as was the ancient custom of the Church, not merely out of what is superfluous, but also out of what is necessary.

The Council emphasizes the value of the constructive presence of the Church in the international community, helping to strengthen peace throughout the world and to lay a solid foundation for the construction of fraternal union among all men by proclaiming the divine and natural law. 'Motivated by the sole desire of serving all men,' the Church makes this contribution 'both by means of its official channels and through the full and sincere collaboration of all Christians' (GS 89). The Constitution emphasizes the participation of Catholic Christians and the separated brethren in international institutions devoted to collaboration in the cause of justice and peace (cf. GS 90). *Justitia et Pax* is indeed the title of the central organ of the post-Conciliar Church, set up as a result of the inspiration and exhortation of the pastoral Constitution. Its primary object is to educate men to make a reality of the Christian mission of peace.

GS 82 | State leaders' peace-making efforts will be in vain as long as men are divided and warring among themselves through hostility, contempt, and distrust, as well as through racial hatred and uncompromising ideologies. Hence there is a very urgent need of re-education and a new orientation of public opinion. Those engaged in the work of education, especially youth education, and the people who mould public opinion, should regard it as their most important task to educate the minds of men to renewed sentiments of peace. Every one of us needs a change of heart; we must set our gaze on the whole world and look to those tasks we can all perform together in order to bring about the betterment of our race.

The Council did not treat ethical problems in a detailed and specific way as had been proposed in the first drafts of its discussion papers. Nevertheless, the whole range of problems in Christian ethics determined the basic orientation of the Council and is in evidence in both the central documents of Vatican II: it appears in the Council's teaching concerning the People of God and its mission, which constitutes the concrete form of the Church's presence in the modern world. The attitude of 'human identity' and 'Christian responsibility' is the integrating element of the mission of the People of God, without which one cannot speak of its authentic realization. The Council chose to envisage and expound ethical matters in a pastoral rather than a doctrinal manner, but of course the two aspects complement each other. It will be the task of moral theologians to expound the doctrinal foundations of the attitudes which the Council's teaching seeks to inculcate. Although the Council left to one side many problems that are the subject of discussion and study in the field of ethics and moral theology, nevertheless it revealed once again in broad lines the personal yet universal character of the morality which has its roots in the Gospel and meets the demands of our own time.

Thus the attitude we have tried to delineate in this Chapter is of great importance for the implementation of the Council. In defining it as an attitude of 'human identity' we are, it would seem, touching on a particularly sensitive point from the standpoint of modern man, and we have shown how that identity is the basis not only of the solidarity so often emphasized by the Council, but above all of authentic Christian responsibility. The Christian attains his human identity by remaining faithful to the law of charity in the various spheres of his life and activity. At that point the Christian's human identity coincides with his participation in the mystery of Christ and in his mission, and the two attitudes merge into one. Vatican II says of Christ that he 'reveals man to himself' (GS 22): he does not diminish the human identity of any of those who share in his Mystery, but on the contrary deepens and enriches it. Thus the attitude of human identity is, to the Christian, the essential characteristic of his living faith.

GS 91 | Drawn from the treasures of the teaching of the Church, the proposals of this Council are intended for all men, whether they believe in God or whether they do not explicitly acknowledge him; they are intended to help them to a keener awareness of their own destiny, to make the world conform better to the surpassing dignity of man, to strive for a more deeply rooted sense of universal brotherhood, and to meet the pressing appeals of our times with a generous and common effort of love.

CHAPTER IV

The ecumenical attitude

The ecumenical attitude not only finds expression in the teaching of Vatican II but is given a profound and articulate motivation in the doctrine concerning the Church as the universal People of God. By giving the Church this conception of itself, the Council at the same time imparts to it an ecumenical attitude in the broadest sense. Although, strictly speaking, this attitude is concerned with Christians who are separated from the Church, to some extent it also has a bearing on relations with non-Christian religions, as the relevant Declaration confirms.

> NA 1 | In this age of ours, when men are drawing more closely together and the bonds of friendship between different peoples are being strengthened, the Church examines with greater care the relation which she has to non-Christian religions. Ever aware of her duty to foster unity and charity among individuals, and even among nations, she reflects at the outset on what men have in common and what tends to promote fellowship among them.

These words may be said to express the humanistic background of ecumenism in the broadest sense. We also find in them a confirmation of the attitude of human identity and solidarity of which we have already spoken.

However, in the teaching of Vatican II this attitude has above all a profound religious sense.

NA 1 | All men form but one community. This is so because all stem from the one stock which God created to people the entire earth and also because all share a common destiny, namely God. His providence, evident goodness, and saving designs extend to all men against the day when the elect are gathered together in the holy city which is illuminated by the glory of God, and in whose splendour all peoples will walk.

Men look to their different religions for an answer to the unsolved riddles of human existence. The problems that weigh heavily on the hearts of men are the same today as in the ages past. What is man? What is the meaning and purpose of life? What is upright behaviour, and what is sinful? Where does suffering originate, and what end does it serve? How can genuine happiness be found? What happens at death? What is judgement? What reward follows death? And finally, what is the ultimate mystery, beyond human explanation, which embraces our entire existence, from which we take our origin and towards which we tend?

The awareness of what links together the followers of various religions, including non-Christian ones, gives a sense of unity and a disposition to overcome resistance on both sides, as the Declaration indicates. For instance:

NA 3 | The Church has also a high regard for the Muslims . . .

Over the centuries many quarrels and dissensions have arisen between Christians and Muslims. The sacred Council now pleads with all to forget the past, and urges that a sincere effort be made to achieve mutual understanding;

for the benefit of all men, let them together preserve and promote peace, liberty, social justice and moral values.

The Council also recognizes the importance of ecumenism in a broad sense in the field of temporal responsibility, which Christians wish to share with the whole human race.

As regards the followers of the religion of the Old Testament, the Council, 'sounding the depths of the mystery which is the Church, remembers the spiritual ties which link the people of the New Covenant to the stock of Abraham' (NA 4).

NA 4 | Since Christians and Jews have such a common spiritual heritage, this sacred Council wishes to encourage and further mutual understanding and appreciation. This can be obtained, especially, by way of biblical and theological enquiry and through friendly discussions.

NA 5 | We cannot truly pray to God the Father of all if we treat any people in other than brotherly fashion, for all men are created in God's image. Man's relation to God the Father and man's relation to his fellow-men are so dependent on each other that the Scripture says 'he who does not love, does not know God' (1 Jn. 4:8).

There is no basis therefore, either in theory or in practice, for any discrimination between individual and individual, or between people and people, in respect of human dignity or the rights which flow from it.

Therefore, the Church reproves, as foreign to the mind of Christ, any discrimination against people or any harassment of them on the basis of their race, colour, condition in life or religion.

NA 4 | The Church always held and continues to hold that Christ out of infinite love freely underwent suffering and death because of the sins of all men, so that all might attain salvation. It is the duty of the Church, therefore, in her preaching to proclaim the cross of Christ as the sign of God's universal love and the source of all grace.

Thus the ecumenical attitude is rooted in faith in the fatherhood of God embracing the universe and in the redemption of Christ, which is offered to all men without exception. The true ecumenical attitude is an expression of that faith: it springs from it and testifies to its enrichment. At the same time it is the expression of a profound love for man and respect for his inner liberty – that 'responsible liberty' which corresponds to an inward conviction concerning truth, 'especially in the religious sphere', as the Council states in its Declaration on Religious Liberty.

DH 2 | The Vatican Council declares that the human person has a right to religious freedom . . . The Council further declares that the right to religious freedom is based on the very dignity of the human person as known through the revealed word of God and by reason itself.

DH 3 | Therefore [man] must not be forced to act contrary to his conscience. Nor must he be prevented from acting according to his conscience, especially in religious matters.

DH 2 | Therefore the right to religious freedom has its foundation not in the subjective attitude of the individual but in his very nature.

DH 10 | It is therefore fully in accordance with the nature of faith that in religious matters every form of coercion by men should be excluded.

DH 12 | The Church, therefore, faithful to the truth of the Gospel, is following in the path of Christ and the apostles when she recognizes the principle that religious liberty is in keeping with the dignity of man and divine revelation and gives it her support . . . Although in the life of the people of God in its pilgrimage through the vicissitudes of human history there has at times appeared a form of behaviour which was hardly in keeping with the spirit of the Gospel and was even opposed to it, it has always remained the teaching of the Church that no one is to be coerced into believing.

Since the love of men demands respect for 'responsible liberty' in the religious sphere, it must also seek ways of approaching them more closely and bringing about real unity, especially with followers of Christ. Accordingly:

UR 1 | The restoration of unity among all Christians is one of the principal concerns of the Second Vatican Council. Christ the Lord founded one Church and one Church only. However, many Christian communions present themselves to men as the true inheritors of Jesus Christ; all indeed profess to be followers of the Lord but they differ in mind and go their different ways, as if Christ himself were divided. Certainly such division openly contradicts the will of Christ, scandalizes the world, and damages that most holy cause, the preaching of the Gospel to every creature.

The Decree on Ecumenism, after noting in the Introduction the historical fact of schism, remarks that in our day there is a growing desire for unity among Christians.

UR 1 | The Lord of Ages nevertheless wisely and patiently follows out the plan of his grace on our behalf, sinners that we are. In recent times he has

> begun to bestow more generously upon divided Christians remorse over their divisions and longing for unity. Taking part in this movement, which is called ecumenical, are those who invoke the Triune God and confess Jesus as Lord and Saviour. They do this not merely as individuals but also as members of the corporate groups in which they have heard the Gospel, and which each regards as his Church and indeed, God's. And yet, almost everyone, though in different ways, longs for the one visible Church of God, a Church truly universal and sent forth to the whole world that the world may be converted to the Gospel and so be saved, to the glory of God.

In Chapter I the Decree formulates the 'Catholic principles of ecumenism'. Chapter II speaks of the introduction of ecumenism into everyday life, which is of fundamental importance for the formation of an ecumenical attitude in the Church. After referring to the schisms that took place even in Apostolic times, the document goes on to speak of later events as a result of which 'large communities became separated from full communion with the Catholic Church – for which, often enough, men on both sides were to blame' (UR 3). We should point out at once that these separated Christian communities, in the East and in the West, are spoken of at length in Chapter III of the Decree. For the present we may note the statement that 'one cannot charge with the sin of the separation those who at present are born into these communities and in them are brought up in the faith of Christ, and the Catholic Church accepts them with respect and affection as brothers' (UR 3); and again, 'They are with good reason accepted as brothers by the children of the Catholic Church' (UR 3). This statement is fully in line with the Declaration on Religious Liberty, already quoted.

Emphasizing the sense of special brotherhood with separated

Christians, Vatican II points out the objective basis of the unity between them. Admittedly 'the differences that exist in varying degrees – whether in doctrine and sometimes in discipline, or concerning the structure of the Church – do indeed create many obstacles, sometimes serious ones, to full ecclesiastical communion.' However, 'the ecumenical movement is striving to overcome these obstacles' (UR 3), and it is based on elements of genuine unity.

UR 3 | Some even very many, of the most significant elements and endowments which together go to build up and give life to the Church itself, can exist outside the visible boundaries of the Catholic Church: the written Word of God; the life of grace; faith, hope and charity, with the other interior gifts of the Holy Spirit, as well as visible elements. All of these, which come from Christ and lead back to him, belong by right to the one Church of Christ.

UR 3 | The brethren divided from us also perform many liturgical actions of the Christian religion. In ways that vary according to the condition of each Church or community, these liturgical actions most certainly can truly engender a life of grace, and, one must say, can aptly give access to the communion of salvation.

It follows that the separated Churches and communities as such, though we believe they suffer from the defects already mentioned, have been by no means deprived of significance and importance in the mystery of salvation. For the Spirit of Christ has not refrained from using them as means of salvation which derive their efficacy from the very fullness of grace and truth entrusted to the Catholic Church.

UR 3 | Nevertheless, our separated brethren, whether considered as individuals or as communities and Churches, are not blessed with that unity which Jesus Christ wished to bestow on all those to whom he has given new birth into one body, and whom he has quickened to newness of life – that unity which the Holy Scriptures and the ancient Tradition of the Church proclaim. For it is through Christ's Catholic Church alone, which is the universal help towards salvation, that the fullness of the means of salvation can be obtained. It was to the apostolic college alone, of which Peter is the head, that we believe that Our Lord entrusted all the blessings of the New Covenant, in order to establish on earth the one Body of Christ into which all those should be fully incorporated who belong in any way to the people of God.

Faith in the Apostolic Church, guided by the Holy Spirit, is the basis on which ecumenical action should be founded: 'The sacred Council exhorts all the Catholic faithful to recognize the signs of the times and to take an active and intelligent part in the work of ecumenism' (UR 4). Thus the Council not only endorses the ecumenical movement but urges the faithful to press on with it.

The basic principle of ecumenism, which speaks of the necessity of this work, is then set out in more detail, which is of essential importance for defining the ecumenical attitude.

UR 4 | The term 'ecumenical movement' indicates the initiatives and activities encouraged and organized, according to the various needs of the Church and as opportunities offer, to promote Christian unity. These are: first, every effort to avoid expression, judgements and actions which

> do not represent the condition of our separated brethren with truth and fairness and so make mutual relations with them more difficult. Then, 'dialogue' between competent experts from different Churches and communities; in their meetings, which are organized in a religious spirit, each explains the teaching of his communion in greater depth and brings out clearly its distinctive features.

Thus the ecumenical attitude must be marked in the first place by full respect for human beings, by readiness to meet and cooperate with them, and by a 'dialogue' or exchange of opinions on doctrinal matters, which of course presupposes adequate theological preparation. This exchange of opinions, the object of which is to enable the parties to know one another, must above all be prayerful.

> UR 4 | In ecumenical work, Catholics must assuredly be concerned for their separated brethren, praying for them, keeping them informed about the Church, making the first approaches towards them.

It is not only a question of praying for the separated brethren but also of praying with them so that the Church may become one.

> UR 8 | It is a recognized custom for Catholics to meet for frequent recourse to that prayer for the unity of the Church with which the Saviour himself on the eve of his death so fervently appealed to his father: 'That they may all be one' (Jn. 17:20).
>
> In certain circumstances, such as in prayer services 'for unity' and during ecumenical gatherings, it is allowable, indeed desirable that

> Catholics should join in prayer with their separated brethren. Such prayers in common are certainly a very effective means of petitioning for the grace of unity, and they are a genuine expression of the ties which still bind Catholics to their separated brethren. 'For where two or three are gathered together in my name, there am I in the midst of them' (Mt. 18:20).

It may be said that in the whole of its ecumenical action the Council clearly underlines the primacy of prayer.

UR 24 | This Council declares that it realizes that this holy objective – the reconciliation of all Christians in the unity of the one and only Church of Christ – transcends human powers and gifts. It therefore places its hope entirely in the prayer of Christ for the Church, in the love of the Father for us, and in the power of the Holy Spirit. 'And hope does not disappoint, because God's love has been poured forth in our hearts through the Holy Spirit who has been given to us' (Rom. 5:5).

This shows most clearly the connection between the ecumenical attitude and the whole process of the enrichment of faith which should lead from Vatican II to the future of the Church as the People of God. The Council is well aware that the schisms that have taken place through history have left a deep mark on human souls and the organization of the separated communities. Humanly speaking they appear irreversible and insurmountable; but it must be remembered that ecumenical action and a truly ecumenical attitude can be born only of the hope, based on faith, that, although the Church is divided by men, in the mind and will of Christ it is one and undivided. With the help of grace, and notwithstanding present and past divisions, men must hope that they will one day restore the Church to that single and undivided state.

UR 7 | Thus, in humble prayer we beg pardon of God and of our separated brethren, just as we forgive them that offend us.

The primacy of faith, hope and prayer is linked with the necessity of spiritual renewal and profound conversion. Hence the Decree speaks to Catholics as follows.

UR 4 | Their primary duty is to make a careful and honest appraisal of whatever needs to be renewed and done in the Catholic household itself, in order that its life may bear witness more clearly and faithfully to the teachings and institutions which have been handed down from Christ through the apostles.

It goes on to say:

UR 4 | For although the Catholic Church has been endowed with all divinely revealed truth and with all means of grace, yet its members fail to live by them with all the fervour that they should. As a result the radiance of the Church's face shines less brightly in the eyes of our separated brethren and of the world at large, and the growth of God's kingdom is retarded.

And elsewhere we read:

UR 7 | There can be no ecumenism worthy of the name without interior conversion. For it is from newness of attitudes of mind, from self-denial and unstinted love, that desires of unity take their rise and develop in a mature way. We should therefore pray to the Holy Spirit for the grace to be genuinely self-denying, humble, gentle in the service of others and to have an attitude of brotherly generosity towards them.

The faithful should remember that they promote union among Christians better, that indeed they live it better, when they try to live holier lives according to the Gospel. For the closer their union with the Father, the Word, and the Spirit, the more deeply and easily will they be able to grow in mutual brotherly love.

UR 8 | This change of heart and holiness of life, along with public and private prayer for the unity of Christians, should be regarded as the soul of the whole ecumenical movement, and merits the name 'spiritual ecumenism'.

Since we are speaking here of the ecumenical attitude as an element in the implementation of Vatican II, we must lay stress on this aspect of 'spiritual ecumenism', which provides a solid basis for the renewal of the Church and the union of Christians. Of course it is not possible for everybody to take part in the ecumenical dialogue, but all members of the Church can share in 'spiritual ecumenism'. It should be observed, with reference to the distinction, often discussed in the Council, between the vertical and the horizontal orientation, that Vatican II assigns primary importance to the former and derives from it the function of the 'ecumenical dialogue'. The union of Christians can only be the fruit of grace, a sign of God's forgiveness which we must first implore and deserve. Only from God can all our efforts on the 'horizontal' plane receive the necessary strength and authentic 'ecumenical' meaning.

This does not mean that the Council underestimates the universal need for action and dialogue. On the contrary:

UR 4 | This sacred Council is gratified to note that the participation by the Catholic faithful in ecumenical work is growing daily. It commends this work to the bishops everywhere in the world for their diligent promotion and prudent guidance.

UR 5 | The concern for restoring unity involves the whole Church, faithful and clergy alike. It extends to everyone, according to the talent of each, whether it be exercised in daily Christian living or in theological and historical studies. This concern itself already reveals to some extent the bond of brotherhood existing among all Christians, and it leads towards full and perfect unity, in accordance with what God in his kindness wills.

UR 9 | We must become familiar with the outlook of our separated brethren. Study is absolutely required for this, and it should be pursued in fidelity to the truth and with a spirit of good will.

Clearly we cannot come closer together except by first knowing each other.

UR 9 | Catholics who already have a proper grounding need to acquire a more adequate understanding of the respective doctrines of our separated brethren, their history, their spiritual and liturgical life, their religious psychology and cultural background. Most valuable for this purpose are meetings of the two sides – especially for discussion of theological problems – where each can treat with the other on an equal footing, provided that those who take part in them under the guidance of the authorities are truly competent. From such dialogue will emerge still more

clearly what the situation of the Catholic Church
really is. In this way, too, we will better understand the outlook of our separated brethren and
more aptly present our own belief.

After warning against the 'false irenicism' which is foreign
to the spirit of ecumenism (UR 11), the Council formulates the
positive principles on which the ecumenical dialogue should
be based, especially as far as Catholic theologians are concerned.

UR 11 | Furthermore, in ecumenical dialogue, Catholic
theologians, standing fast by the teaching of the
Church yet searching together with separated
brethren into the divine mysteries, should do so
with love for the truth, with charity, and with
humility. When comparing doctrines with one
another, they should remember that in Catholic
doctrine there exists an order or 'hierarchy' of
truths, since they vary in their relation to the
foundation of the Christian faith. Thus the way
will be opened whereby this kind of 'fraternal
rivalry' will incite all to a deeper realization and
a clearer expression of the unfathomable riches
of Christ.

These words prescribe a methodology of ecumenical studies
which is of great importance for the theological dialogue. It
must not be forgotten that 'many Christians do not understand
the Gospel in the same way as Catholics, and do not admit the
same solutions for the more difficult problems of modern
society' (UR 23). This confirms the necessity of avoiding that
false irenicism which gives the impression that practically
nothing divides us. At the same time we must realize that, like
us, the separated brethren 'want to cling to Christ's word as the
source of Christian virtue and to obey the command of the
Apostle: "Whatever you do in word or in work, do all in the

name of the Lord Jesus, giving thanks to God the Father through him" (Col. 3:17)' (UR 23). And the Decree concludes:

UR 23 | Hence, the ecumenical dialogue could start with the moral application of the Gospel.

Despite the differences, referred to in the passage quoted above, as regards the interpretation of the Gospel in its 'moral application', Vatican II sees ample opportunity for ecumenical cooperation in this field. Indeed, the faith by which all believe in Christ.

UR 23 | The faith by which they believe in Christ bears fruit in praise and thanksgiving for the benefits received from the hands of God. Joined to it is a lively sense of justice and a true charity towards others. This active faith has been responsible for many organizations for the relief of spiritual and material distress, the furtherance of education of youth, the improvement of social conditions of life, and the promotion of peace throughout the world.

GS 40 | Furthermore, the Catholic Church gladly values what other Christian Churches and ecclesial communities have contributed and are contributing cooperatively to the realization of this aim.

This common task comes down to 'humanizing the family of man and its history' (GS 40). As the Decree on Ecumenism says:

UR 12 | Cooperation among Christians vividly expresses that bond which already unites them, and it sets in clearer relief the features of Christ the Servant. Such cooperation, which has already begun in many countries, should be developed more and more, particularly in regions where social and technological evolution is taking place. It should contribute to a just appreciation of the dignity of the human person, to the promotion of the blessings of peace, the application of Gospel principles to social life, and the advancement of the arts and sciences in a truly Christian spirit. It should use every possible means to relieve the afflictions of our times, such as famine and natural disasters, illiteracy and poverty, lack of housing, and the unequal distribution of wealth. Through such cooperation, all believers in Christ are able to learn easily how they can understand each other better and esteem each other more, and how the road to the unity of Christians may be made smooth.

The way to the 'moral application of the Gospel' as indicated by Vatican II must, as we see, be of service to the modern world and also promote the unity of Christians. The path of ecumenical cooperation seems closer and more accessible than that of theological dialogue; but, while proceeding on this path, we must be careful not to lose sight of truth and not to fall into 'false irenicism' and practical indifferentism. Thus, while the Council 'firmly hopes that the initiatives of the sons of the Catholic Church, joined with those of the separated brethren, will go forward without obstructing the ways of divine Providence, and without prejudging the future inspirations of the Holy Spirit' (UR 24), at the same time it urges the faithful.

UR 24 | to abstain from any frivolous or imprudent zeal, for these can cause harm to true progress towards unity. Their ecumenical activity cannot be other than fully and sincerely Catholic, that is, loyal to the truth we have received from the Apostles and the Fathers, and in harmony with the faith

which the Catholic Church has always professed,
and at the same time tending towards that fullness in which our Lord wants his Body to grow
in the course of time.

Fidelity to Apostolic truth and conformity to the faith 'that
the Church has always professed' requires us to approach with
great care the question of *communicatio in sacris*.

UR 8 | Yet worship in common (*communicatio in sacris*)
is not to be considered as a means to be used
indiscriminately for the restoration of unity
among Christians. There are two main principles
upon which the practice of such common
worship depends: first, that of the unity of the
Church which ought to be expressed; and second,
that of the sharing in the means of grace. The
expression of unity very generally forbids common worship. Grace to be obtained sometimes
commends it.

The passage perhaps brings out most clearly of all a certain
duality in the authentic ecumenical attitude. It involves the
aspiration to unity and a tendency to claim that that unity is
already stronger than any division; but we must not forget to
respect the discipline of faith and obedience to the truth already
possessed by various communities. Without such recognition
we may do a disservice to the true progress of unity, as the
Decree points out. The discipline of faith and loyalty to
professed truth does not conflict with the Augustinian
principle: *in necessariis unitas, in dubiis libertas, in omnibus
caritas*.

UR 4 | While preserving unity in essentials, let everyone
in the Church, according to the office entrusted
to him, preserve a proper freedom in the various
forms of spiritual life and discipline, in the
variety of liturgical rites, and even in the

theological elaborations of revealed truth. In all things let charity prevail. If they are true to this course of action, they will be giving ever richer expression to the authentic catholicity and apostolicity of the Church.

The Decree also observes that 'the divisions among Christians prevent the Church from realizing the fullness of catholicity proper to her' (UR 4).

The true ecumenical attitude tends to emphasize that fullness in spite of existing difficulties and, as it were, through them. Thus the Council's teaching on ecumenism lays stress on charity as a force making for unity in the truth, while respecting the significance of the truth professed by every Christian and every Christian community.

UR 4 | However, it is evident that the work of preparing and reconciling those individuals who wish for full Catholic communion is of its nature distinct from ecumenical action. But there is no opposition between the two, since both proceed from the marvellous ways of God.

The Council sees the ecumenical road towards the union of Christians in its own proper nature, and recognizes that the Holy Spirit is working in that direction. We owe fidelity to the Holy Spirit, and this we express by the attitude of ecumenism.

Much has been done since Vatican II to foster the ecumenical movement, and existing groups and institutions have helped to clarify many questions affecting relations with the separated brethren. Here, however, we will confine ourselves to the teaching of the Council itself. Guided by the Holy Spirit, the Council outlines that essential form of the ecumenical attitude to be developed as part of the general enrichment of faith which is incumbent on all in their various degrees.

UR 4 | Such actions, when they are carried out by the Catholic faithful with prudent patience and under the attentive guidance of their bishops, promote justice and truth, concord and collaboration, as well as the spirit of brotherly love and unity. The result will be that, little by little, as the obstacles to perfect ecclesiastical communion are overcome, all Christians will be gathered, in a common celebration of the Eucharist, into the unity of the one and only Church, which Christ bestowed on his Church from the beginning. This unity, we believe, subsists in the Catholic Church as something she can never lose, and we hope that it will continue to increase until the end of time.

The emergence of the ecumenical attitude and its orderly development in accordance with the Council's teaching is one of the chief indices and proofs of the renewal of the Church.

UR 6 | Every renewal of the Church essentially consists in an increase of fidelity to her own calling. Undoubtedly this explains the dynamism of the movement towards unity.

Christ summons the Church, as she goes her pilgrim way, to that continual reformation of which she always has need, in so far as she is an institution of men here on earth. Consequently, if, in various times and circumstances, there have been deficiencies in moral conduct or in Church discipline, or even in the way that Church teaching has been formulated – to be carefully distinguished from the deposit of faith itself – these should be set right at the opportune moment and in the proper way.

Church renewal therefore has notable ecumenical importance.

At the end of *Gaudium et Spes* the Council states that 'the unity of Christians is today awaited and longed for by many non-believers. For the more this unity is realized in truth and charity under the powerful impulse of the Holy Spirit, the more it will be a harbinger of unity and peace throughout the world' (GS 92). Hence the appeal to all our brethren in Christ to 'work together in a spirit of brotherhood to serve the human family which has been called to become in Christ Jesus the family of the sons of God' (ibid.).

CHAPTER V

The apostolic attitude

In our analysis of the process of the enrichment and deepening of faith, the attitude which we wish to define and identify as apostolic is, to some extent, a more precise version of what we described in the previous chapter which was entitled 'mission and witness'. We saw in that chapter the real basis of the apostolic attitude. If, in accordance with the teaching of Vatican II, we agree that faith, as man's response to the God who reveals himself, is expressed as readiness to accept and assume the salvific mission, then in so doing we point to the apostolic attitude and the very root of apostolicity in the life of the Christian as it is formed by faith. This matter deserves a more detailed exposition, however, as it was treated in detail by the Council. We shall attempt here to develop it in two sections, one on the apostolate in a broad sense and the other on related problems of the training which is indispensable for the apostolate.

1. *The apostolate*

LG 17 | As he had been sent by the Father, the Son himself sent the apostles (cf. Jn. 20:21) saying, 'go, therefore, and make disciples of all nations, baptizing them in the name of the Father, and of the Son, and of the Holy Spirit, teaching them to observe all that I have commanded you; and behold I am with you all days even unto the consummation of the world' (Mt. 28:18–20). The Church has received this solemn command of Christ from the apostles, and she must fulfil it to the very ends of the earth (cf. Acts 1:8). Therefore, she makes the words of the apostle her own, 'Woe to me if I do not preach the Gospel' (1 Cor. 9:16), and accordingly never ceases to send heralds of the Gospel until each time as the infant Churches are fully established, and can themselves continue the work of evangelization. For the Church is driven by the Holy Spirit to do her part for the full realization of the plan of God, who has constituted Christ as the source of salvation for the whole world.

As this passage from *Lumen Gentium* points out, Christ transmitted to the Apostles the salvific mission he had received from the Father, and the Apostles transmitted it to the Church so that she might bring it to fulfilment under the guidance of those who are the Apostles' authorized successors. 'Christ, whom the Father hallowed and sent into the world (John 10:36), has, through his Apostles, made their successors, the bishops namely, sharers in his consecration and mission; and these, in their turn, have duly entrusted in varying degrees various members of the Church with the office of their ministry' (LG 28). This refers directly to priests and deacons; but the salvific mission has been transmitted to the whole Church and, within it, to all members of the People of God without exception, although in different modes and degrees.

AA 2 | The Church was founded to spread the kingdom of Christ over all the earth for the glory of God the Father, to make all men partakers in redemption and salvation, and through them to establish the right relationship of the entire world to Christ. Every activity of the Mystical

Body with this in view goes by the name of 'apostolate'; the Church exercises it through all its members, though in various ways. In fact, the Christian vocation is, of its nature, a vocation to the apostolate as well.

This text is of great importance, as it explains the essence of the apostolate and its close connection with the Christian vocation. The apostolate of the Church, which consists in orienting the whole world towards Christ, constitutes as it were the true reality of 'being a Christian' and is essentially defined by this reality while also determining it in a decisive manner. The Council here invokes the analogy of the Mystical Body.

AA 2 | In the organism of a living body no member plays a purely passive part; sharing in the life of the body it shares at the same time in its activity. The same is true for the Body of Christ, the Church: 'the whole Body achieves full growth in dependence on the full functioning of each part' (Eph. 4:16). Between the members of this body there exists, further, such a unity and solidarity (cf. Eph. 4:16) that a member who does not work at the growth of the body to the extent of his possibilities must be considered useless both to the Church and to himself.

According to this theological premiss the apostolate of the Church is identified with apostolate in the broad sense of the mission and vocation of all baptized persons.

AA 3 | On all Christians, accordingly, rests the noble obligation of working to bring all men throughout the whole world to hear and accept the divine message of salvation.

AA 6 | The apostolate of the Church therefore, and of each of its members, aims primarily at announcing to the world by word and action the message of Christ and communicating to it the grace of Christ.

AA 25 | The right and duty of exercising the apostolate are common to all the faithful, whether clerics or lay.

PO 2 | Therefore there is no such thing as a member that has not a share in the mission of the whole Body. Rather, every single member ought to reverence Jesus in his heart and by the spirit of prophecy give testimony of Jesus.

The link between the apostolate and 'being a Christian', i.e. the very essence of the Christian vocation, means that we must consider the apostolic attitude both in its essence and in its multiplicity. The whole People of God shares in the apostolic inheritance: while the hierarchy guarantees in a particular way the 'apostolicity' of the Church, all are called on to build up the Church through their apostolate so as to 'direct the whole world towards Christ'. This means that we must define the order according to which the Church is built up and clarify the manner in which all should work together: and we shall devote a chapter to this in accordance with the Council's teaching. For the present, however, we shall consider the apostolate itself in order to draw attention to the characteristics of particular vocations among the People of God according to the thought of the Council.

As regards the relationship between the apostolate of the laity and that of the hierarchy, and hence the apostolic attitude, it must be emphasized that the two complement each other partly because the priestly vocation presupposes the apostolate of the whole People of God and in particular that of the Christian family, especially parents.

AA 11 | They are the first to pass on the faith to their children and to educate them in it. By word and example they form them to a Christian and apostolic life; they offer them wise guidance in the choice of vocation, and if they discover in them a sacred vocation they encourage it with all care.

In the present chapter we shall try to follow the thought of Vatican II by showing first in what way the apostolate is linked with the priestly and religious vocation, and then how it is linked with the vocation of the laity in the Church. These different forms of the apostolate have their common origin in the Christian vocation from which they derive and which they are aimed at finally realizing. As regards priests the Council says that 'even though by reason of the sacrament of order they fulfil the pre-eminent and essential function of father and teacher among the People of God and on their behalf, still they are disciples of the Lord along with all the faithful and have been made partakers of his kingdom by God, who has called them by his grace. Priests . . . are brothers among brothers' (PO 9).

The apostolate of priests, in its form and scope, is closely linked with the sacrament of holy orders.

PO 10 | For the priesthood of Christ, of which priests have been really made sharers, is necessarily directed to all peoples and all times, and is not confined by any bounds of blood, race, or age, as was already typified in a mysterious way by the figure of Melchizedek.

Priests, therefore, should recall that the solicitude of all the churches ought to be their intimate concern.

AGD 23 | Although the obligation of spreading the faith falls individually on every disciple of Christ, still the Lord Christ has always called from the number of his disciples those whom he has chosen that they might be with him so that he might send them to preach to the nations.

AGD 24 | When God calls, a man must reply without taking counsel with flesh and blood (cf. Gal. 1:16) and give himself fully to the work of the Gospel. However, such an answer can only be given with the encouragement and help of the Holy Spirit.

The apostolic attitude of those members of the People of God who have received the sacrament of orders has a specific characteristic whose basis is to be found in that sacrament.

PO 10 | The spiritual gift which priests have received in ordination does not prepare them merely for a limited and circumscribed mission, but for the fullest, in fact the universal mission of salvation 'to the end of the earth' (Acts 1:8). The reason is that every priestly ministry shares in the fullness of the mission entrusted by Christ to the apostles.

PO 2 | Since they share in the function of the apostles in their own degree, priests are given the grace by God to be the ministers of Jesus Christ among the nations, fulfilling the sacred task of the Gospel, that the oblation of the gentiles may be made acceptable and sanctified in the Holy Spirit. For it is by the apostolic herald of the Gospel that the People of God is called together and gathered so that all who belong to this people, sanctified as they are by the Holy Spirit, may offer themselves 'a living sacrifice, holy and acceptable to God' (Rom. 12:1).

The nature of the priestly apostolate as shown in these texts must be reflected in their training, of which we shall speak separately. By 'training' we mean that ordering of life which corresponds to different vocations in relation to various tasks within the Church. The passages quoted throw sufficient light on the nature of the mission of priests, i.e. those who have received the sacrament of holy orders.

The Council brings out on similar lines the apostolic significance of the religious vocation.

PC 1 | Amid such a great variety of gifts, however, all those who are called by God to the practice of the evangelical counsels, and who make faithful profession of them, bind themselves to the Lord in a special way. They follow Christ, who, virginal and poor (cf. Mt. 8:20; Lk. 9:58), redeemed and sanctified men by obedience unto death on the cross (cf. Phil. 2:8). Under the impulse of love, which the Holy Spirit pours into their hearts (cf. Rom. 5:5), they live more and more for Christ and for his Body, the Church (cf. Col. 1:24). The more fervently, therefore, they join themselves to Christ by this gift of their whole life, the fuller does the Church's life become and the more vigorous and fruitful its apostolate.

This passage shows the close connection between the religious vocation and the apostolate of the Church. The religious vocation shares in a special way in the salvific mission of the Church, and it too is therefore a most important form of the apostolate.

LG 44 | All the members of the Church should unflaggingly fulfil the duties of their Christian calling.

The profession of the evangelical counsels shines before them as a sign which can and should effectively inspire them to do so.

AGD 18 | Right from the planting of the Church the religious life should be carefully fostered, because not only does it provide valuable and absolutely necessary help for missionary activity, but through the deeper consecration made to God in the Church it clearly shows and signifies the intimate nature of the Christian vocation.

PC 5 | Since this gift of themselves has been accepted by the Church, they should be aware that they are dedicated to its service also. This service of God should stimulate and foster the exercise of the virtues by them, especially the virtues of humility and obedience, fortitude and chastity, by which they share in Christ's emptying of himself (cf. Phil. 2:7–8) and at the same time in his life in the spirit (cf. Rom. 8:1–13).

Religious, therefore, faithful to their profession and leaving all things for Christ's sake (cf. Mk. 10:28), should follow him, regarding this as the one thing that is necessary (cf. Lk. 10:39) and should be solicitous for all that is his (cf. Cor. 7:32).

The members of each institute, therefore, ought to seek God before all else, and solely; they should join contemplation, by which they cleave to God by mind and heart, to apostolic love, by which they endeavour to be associated with the work of redemption and to spread the kingdom of God. Since the disciples must always imitate this love and humility of Christ and bear witness of it, Mother Church rejoices that she has within herself many men and women who pursue more closely the Saviour's self-emptying and show it forth more clearly, by undertaking poverty with the freedom of God's sons, and renouncing their own will: they subject themselves to man for the love of God, thus going beyond what is of precept in the matter of perfection, so as to conform themselves more fully to the obedient Christ.

The Council teaches that the Christian vocation is by its nature a vocation to the apostolate, and in due measure it teaches this also with regard to the religious vocation.

PC 8 | The entire religious life of the members should be imbued with an apostolic spirit, and all their apostolic activity with a religious spirit. In order, therefore, that the members may first answer their call to follow Christ and to serve Christ himself in his members, their apostolic activity must needs have its source in intimate union with him. It is thus that their very love for God and their neighbour is fostered.

The Apostolate is not something external to the religious life, added on to it, but is grafted into it through the deep inner nature of the religious vocation itself.

PC 8 | Consequently, these institutes should adjust their observances and customs to the needs of their particular apostolate. Since however the active religious life takes many forms, this diversity should be taken into account when its up-to-date renewal is being undertaken, and in the various institutes the members' life in the service of Christ should be sustained by means which are proper and suitable to each institute.

PC 16 | Nuns who are engaged in the external apostolate by virtue of their own rule are to be exempted from papal cloister so that they can the better fulfil their apostolic tasks. The cloister prescribed by the constitutions must be maintained, however.

The Council gives most attention to the lay apostolate, and in this we must certainly see a 'sign of the times'. It must be recognized, moreover, that for too long the Church's teaching devoted too little attention to this problem, and that it was time to fill the gap. Now the Council has devoted a rich body of teaching to the role of the laity and their apostolate, so that it may with reason be called 'the Council of the laity'. At the same time the problem of the lay apostolate has given the opportunity for a fuller and deeper elaboration of the theme of the apostolate within Conciliar teaching as a whole, as the following text also shows:

AA 1 | The Church can never be without the lay apostolate; it is something that derives from the layman's very vocation as a Christian. Scripture clearly shows how spontaneous and fruitful was this activity in the Church's early days (cf. Acts 11:19–21; 18:26; Rom. 16:1–16; Phil. 4:3).
No less fervent a zeal on the part of lay people is called for today; present circumstances, in fact, demand from them an apostolate infinitely broader and more intense.

AA 1 | the manifest action of the Holy Spirit moving laymen today to a deeper and deeper awareness of their responsibility and urging them on everywhere to the service of Christ and the Church.

The problem of the lay apostolate is treated especially in *Lumen Gentium*, the central document of Vatican II. The Decree on the Apostolate of the Laity, while it contains a considerable wealth of doctrine, is chiefly a complementary and practical document. The laity form the widest circle of the People of God and are its social foundation. Vatican II has profoundly studied the structure of this foundation and laid stress on its dynamism.

LG 31 | Their secular character is proper and peculiar to the laity. Although those in Holy Orders may sometimes be engaged in secular activities, or even practice a secular profession, yet by reason of their particular vocation they are principally and expressly ordained to the sacred ministry. At the same time, religious give outstanding and striking testimony that the world cannot be transfigured and offered to God without the spirit of the beatitudes. But by reason of their special vocation it belongs to the laity to seek the kingdom of God by engaging in temporal affairs and directing them according to God's will. They live in the world, that is, they are engaged in each and every work and business of the earth and in the ordinary circumstances of social and family life which, as it were, constitute their very existence. There they are called by God that, being led by the spirit of the Gospel, they may contribute to the sanctification of the world, as from within like leaven, by fulfilling their own particular duties. Thus, especially by the witness of their life, resplendent in faith, hope and charity they must manifest Christ to others. It pertains to them in a special way so to illuminate and order all temporal things with which they are so closely associated that these may be effected and grow according to Christ and may be to the glory of the Creator and Redeemer.

Especially in view of the length of this passage we can hardly call it a definition of the laity, but we can say that it contains the essential truth concerning the laity's vocation and mission in the Church. By its nature 'laity' implies connection with the world, and the vocation of lay people is thus different from that of priests and religious, on whom Christ and the Church have enjoined a certain detachment from the world. Furthermore, this link with the world, this 'lay character' which is proper to the laity, is the basis of their specific apostolate, whereby they are called by God to contribute to the santification of the world. Thus the lay condition is at the service of sanctity and is therfore far from being a denial of it: it is rooted in the very essence of the Christian vocation of the laity and is a characteristic feature and expression of their specific apostolate.

AA 2 | In the Church there is diversity of ministry but unity of mission. To the apostles and their successors Christ has entrusted the office of teaching, sanctifying and governing in his name and by his power. But the laity are made to share in the priestly, prophetical and kingly office of Christ; they have therefore, in the Church and in the world, their own assignment in the mission of the whole People of God.

LG 33 | The apostolate of the laity is a sharing in the salvific mission of the Church. Through Baptism and Confirmation all are appointed to this apostolate by the Lord himself.

AA 3 | From the fact of their union with Christ the head flows the laymen's right and duty to be apostles. Inserted as they are in the Mystical Body of Christ by baptism and strengthened by the power of the Holy Spirit in confirmation, it is by the Lord himself that they are assigned to the apostolate.

LG 33 | By the sacraments, and especially by the Eucharist, that love of God and man which is the soul of the apostolate is communicated and nourished.

In the present study we set out to analyse those attitudes, the formation of which proceeds in parallel with the enrichment and deepening of faith. The formation of the apostolic attitude is rooted in the attitude of participation, as is clear from the lengthy analysis we have devoted to it. In this field, the Council has greatly enriched our understanding.

While the principal source of a Christian's participation in the mission of Christ consists in the word of God and the sacraments, we must remember that these are also permeated by the inward action of the Holy Spirit, which through various vocations is of fundamental significance to the apostolate and the building up of the Church.

LG 12 | It is not only through the sacraments and the ministrations of the Church that the Holy Spirit makes holy the People, leads them and enriches them with his virtues. Allotting his gifts according as he wills (cf. Cor. 12:11), he also distributes special graces among the faithful of every rank. By these gifts he makes them fit and ready to undertake various tasks and offices for the renewal and building up of the Church, as it is written, 'the manifestation of the Spirit is given to everyone for profit' (1 Cor. 12:7). Whether these charisms be very remarkable or more simple and widely diffused, they are to be received with thanksgiving and consolation since they are fitting and useful for the needs of the Church.

The epistles of St Paul, among other sources, tell us of charisms in the early Church. Vatican II recalls this teaching of the Apostle and applies it to the Church's daily life. In the People of God, both the hierarchy and the laity share in charismatic gifts that enable them to perform 'different works and offices' for the good of mankind and of all Christians. These gifts give life to every apostolate including that of the laity, so that they become 'good stewards of God's varied grace' (1 Peter 4:10), building up the whole Body of Christ in charity (cf. Eph. 4:16). 'From the reception of these charisms, even the most ordinary ones, there arises for each of the faithful the right and duty of exercising them in the Church and in the world for the good of men and the development of the Church' (AA 3). Rediscovering the vocation of the laity in the community of the People of God, the Council directs attention once again to the charisms inherent in their vocation and, as it were, reasserts their true importance and proper place in the life of the Church.

We should note that the charisms of the laity go together with their whole vocation.

> AA 2 | In the concrete, their apostolate is exercised when they work at the evangelization and sanctification of men; it is exercised too when they endeavour to have the Gospel spirit permeate and improve the temporal order, going about it in a way that bears clear witness to Christ and helps forward the salvation of men. The characteristic of the lay state being a life led in the midst of the world and of secular affairs, laymen are called by God to make of their apostolate, through the vigour of their Christian spirit, a leaven in the world.

This permeation by the evangelical spirit, perfecting the whole order of temporal things, seems to constitute the specific nature of the lay apostolate. It is along these lines that they should seek their apostolic tasks and cultivate the apostolic attitude. 'The mission of the Church is not only to bring men the message and grace of Christ (this is chiefly the task of the hierarchy), but also to permeate and improve the whole range of the temporal with the evangelical spirit.'

AA 5 | The work of Christ's redemption concerns essentially the salvation of men; it takes in also, however, the renewal of the whole temporal order. The mission of the Church, consequently, is not only to bring men the message and grace of Christ but also to permeate and improve the whole range of the temporal. The laity, carrying out this mission of the Church, exercise their apostolate therefore in the world as well as in the Church, in the temporal order as well as in the spiritual. These orders are distinct; they are nevertheless so closely linked that God's plan is, in Christ, to take the whole world up again and make of it a new creation, in an initial way here on earth, in full realization at the end of time. The layman, at one and the same time a believer and a citizen of the world, has only a single conscience, a Christian conscience; it is by this that he must be guided continually in both domains.

This calls to mind all the Council's teaching concerning the relationship between the temporal evolution of the world and the 'increase of the Kingdom'. This truth is particularly important to the laity in forming their mentality, conscience and apostolate. This is related to all we have said about the attitude of Christian responsibility, which is an integral part of the apostolate and especially the lay apostolate. The Decree on this subject is based on the teaching in the principal documents of Vatican II, which establish the specific mission and apostolate of the laity.

AA 7 | That men, working in harmony, should renew the temporal order and make it increasingly more perfect: such is God's design for the world.

All that goes to make up the temporal order: personal and family values, culture, economic interests, the trades and professions, institutions of the political community, international relations, and so on, as well as their gradual development – all these are not merely helps to man's last end; they possess a value of their own, placed in them by God, whether considered individually or as parts of the integral temporal structure: 'And God saw all that he had made and found it very good' (Gen. 1:31). This natural goodness of theirs receives an added dignity from their relation with the human person, for whose use they have been created. And then, too, God has willed to gather together all that was natural, all that was supernatural, into a single whole in Christ, 'so that in everything he would have the primacy' (Col. 1:18). Far from depriving the temporal order of its autonomy, of its specific ends, of its own laws and resources, or its importance for human well-being, this design, on the contrary, increases its energy and excellence, raising it at the same time to the level of man's integral vocation here below.

This last passage does not only indicate the temporal order and its various spheres as being proper to the apostolate of the laity. The Conciliar document also enables us to understand better why and in what sense the improvement of the temporal order is itself an apostolic work. This clearly illustrates the relationship of the value of temporal things to the human person, in which the dimension of nature encounters

346 Sources of Renewal

that of grace, while both attain their summit in Christ. Consequently

AA 7 | It is the work of the entire Church to fashion men able to establish the proper scale of values on the temporal order and direct it towards God through Christ . . .

Layment ought to take on themselves as their distinctive task this renewal of the temporal order. Guided by the light of the Gospel and the mind of the Church, prompted by Christian love, they should act in this domain in a direct way and in their own specific manner.

Linked to these tasks are the precepts of *Lumen Gentium* to the laity.

LG 36 | The faithful must, then, recognize the inner nature, the value and the ordering of the whole of creation to the praise of God. Even by their secular activity they must aid one another to greater holiness of life, so that the world may be filled with the spirit of Christ and may the more effectively attain its destiny in justice, in love and in peace.

Moreover, by uniting their forces, let the laity so remedy the institutions and conditions of the world when the latter are an inducement to sin, that these may be conformed to the norms of justice, favouring rather than hindering the practice of virtue. By so doing they will impregnate culture and human works with a moral value.

Here the Council's teaching explicitly connects the lay apostolate and the apostolic attitude with participation in the *munus regale* of Christ, of which we have already spoken.

Following the Council's thinking, we have thus endeavoured

to clarify the essential characteristic of the lay apostolate. The Council stresses that it is exercised above all by the presence of Christians in the world, among men, in their various walks of life. The Decree on the Missionary Activity of the Church speaks particularly of this in the section entitled 'Christian Witness'. The mere presence of the laity is not enough: they must also bear witness. Indeed the apostolic attitude can only be identified with the attitude of testimony, of which we have already spoken.

AGD 12 | The presence of Christians among these human groups should be one that is animated by that love with which we are loved by God, who desires that we should love each other with that self-same love (cf. 1 Jn. 4:11). Christian charity is extended to all without distinction of race, social condition, or religion, and seeks neither gain nor gratitude. Just as God loves us with a gratuitous love, so too the faithful, in their charity, should be concerned for mankind, loving it with that same love with which God sought man.

Love is the essential content of Christian witness and the apostolic attitude.

The apostolate of presence in the world is described by the Council in the following way.

AGD 11 | Christians should acknowledge themselves as members of the group in which they live, and through the various undertakings and affairs of human life they should share in their social and cultural life. They should be familiar with their national and religious traditions and uncover with gladness and respect those seeds of the Word which lie hidden among them. They must look to the profound transformation which is

taking place among nations and work hard so
that modern man is not turned away from the
things of God by an excessive preoccupation
with modern science and technology, but rather
aroused to desire, even more intensely, that love
and truth which have been revealed by God.
Just as Christ penetrated to the hearts of men
and by a truly human dialogue led them to the
divine light, so too his disciples, profoundly
pervaded by the Spirit of Christ, should know
and converse with those among whom they
live, that through sincere and patient dialogue
these men might learn of the riches which a
generous God has distributed among the nations.
They must at the same time endeavour to illuminate these riches with the light of the Gospel, set
them free, and bring them once more under the
dominion of God the saviour.

Thus the apostolic attitude involves creative participation
in the life, culture and activity of one's own society, nation
and time.

AGD 12   Christians ought to interest themselves, and
collaborate with others, in the right ordering of
social and economic affairs . . . They should,
furthermore, share in the efforts of those
people who, in fighting against famine, ignorance and disease, are striving to bring about
better living conditions and bring about peace
in the world.

[They] are not working for the merely material
progress or prosperity of men; but in teaching
the religious and moral truths, which Christ
illumined with his light, they seek to enhance the

dignity of men and promote fraternal unity, and, in this way, are gradually opening a wider approach to God.

LG 31 | It pertains to them in a special way so to illuminate and order all temporal things with which they are so closely associated that these may be effected and grow according to Christ and may be to the glory of the Creator and Redeemer.

AA 13 | The laity accomplish the Church's mission in the world principally by that blending of conduct and faith which makes them the light of the world; by that uprightness in all their dealings which is for every man such an incentive to love the true and the good and which is capable of inducing him at last to go to Christ and the Church; by that fraternal charity that makes them share the living conditions and labours, the suffering and yearnings of their brothers, and thereby prepare all hearts, gently, imperceptibly, for the action of saving grace; by that full awareness of their personal responsibility in the development of society, which drives them on to perform their family, social and professional duties with Christian generosity. In this way their conduct makes itself gradually felt in the surroundings where they live and work.

This apostolate should reach out to every single person in that environment; and it must not exclude any good, spiritual or temporal, that can be done for them.

AA 27 | Not seldom also do human values common to all mankind require of Christians working for

> apostolic ends that they collaborate with those who do not profess Christianity but acknowledge these values.

The preceding passage seems especially to sum up the essence and specific character of the apostolic attitude among the laity. The Council also declares that

AA 13 | Genuine apostles are not content, however, with just this; they are earnest also about revealing Christ by word to those around them. It is a fact that many men cannot hear the Gospel and come to acknowledge Christ except through the laymen they associate with.

AA 16 | Then, by the apostolate of the word, which in certain circumstances is absolutely necessary, the laity proclaim Christ, explain and spread his teachings, each one according to his condition and competence, and profess those teachings with fidelity.

Thus the apostolate of the laity which derives from the presence of Christians in the world – since the Christian vocation is apostolic by its nature – is essentially based on harmony between life and faith. This is the fundamental condition as regards the personality of every Christian, not only the laity. It is essential to the lay apostolate in its basic form and still more so when the laity, guided by the apostolic spirit, exercise the apostolate of the word. Vatican II, as we have pointed out, also sees this apostolate as viable and necessary.

AGD 15 | However, it is not sufficient for the Christian people to be present or established in a particular nation, nor sufficient that it should merely exercise the apostolate of good example; it has been established and it is present so that it might by word and deed proclaim Christ to non-Christian fellow countrymen and help them towards a full reception of Christ.

2. Training

As already mentioned, by 'training' we mean that ordering of life which corresponds to a particular vocation in the Church and is at the service of the apostolate. We therefore deal with it in the present chapter, which is concerned with the apostolic attitude. Clearly the way of living the Christian life as it is expressed in the priestly, religious or lay vocation must be diligently and carefully worked out, and hence the object of training is to produce the maturity that is proper and necessary to every vocation in the Church. The apostolate, as can be inferred from the texts quoted, is the fruit of that maturity. Thus the question of training is at the root of every authentic apostolic attitude, whether in priests, religious or lay people.

'All the faithful are invited and obliged to holiness and the perfection of their own state of life' (LG 42). The basic reason for the importance of training in the Christian life and the apostolate is to be found in the Council's teaching on the universal vocation to holiness – universal but also individualized since it is both communal. We must thus have in mind above all what Vatican II teaches in the Decree on the Apostolate of the Laity:

> AA 4 | Christ, sent by the Father, is the source of the Church's whole apostolate. Clearly then, the fruitfulness of the apostolate of lay people depends on their living union with Christ; as the Lord said himself: 'Whoever dwells in me and I in him bears much fruit, for separated from me you can do nothing' (Jn. 15:5).

Clearly this principle applies to all forms of the apostolate.

As regards training for the priestly vocation, a separate Decree is devoted to this subject. Those parts of it which deal directly with the training of priests and the role of ecclesiastical seminaries in the Church should be read together with what the Council has to say about the training of priests in the Decree on their life and ministry:

PO 12 | While it is possible for God's grace to carry out the work of salvation through unworthy ministers, yet God ordinarily prefers to show his wonders through those men who are more submissive to the impulse and guidance of the Holy Spirit and who, because of their intimate union with Christ and their holiness of life, are able to say with St Paul: 'It is no longer I who live, but Christ who lives in me' (Gal. 2:20).

For this reason this sacred Council, in the hope of attaining its pastoral objectives of interior renewal, of worldwide diffusion of the Gospel, and of dialogue with the modern world, issues the strongest exhortation to all priests to strive always by the use of all suitable means commended by the Church towards that greater holiness that will make them daily more effective instruments for the service of all God's people.

The Council recalls the well-tried means for the santification of priests.

PO 13 | In the mystery of the eucharistic sacrifice, in which priests fulfil their principal function, the work of our redemption is continually carried out. For this reason the daily celebration of it is earnestly recommended. This celebration is an act of Christ and the Church even if it is impossible for the faithful to be present. So when priests unite themselves with the act of Christ the Priest they daily offer themselves completely to God, and by being nourished with Christ's Body they share in the charity of him who gives himself as food to the faithful.

In the same way they are united with the intention and the charity of Christ when they administer the sacraments. They do this in a special way when they show themselves to be always available to administer the sacrament of Penance whenever it is reasonably requested by the faithful. In reciting the Divine Office they lend their voice to the Church which perseveres in prayer in the name of the whole human race, in union with Christ who 'always lives to make intercession for them' (Heb. 7:25).

After enumerating these methods of training, the Council document refers to the problem constituted by the situation of priests in the modern world.

PO 14 | Priests who are perplexed and distracted by the very many obligations of their position may be anxiously enquiring how they can reduce to unity their interior life and their programme of external activity.

This problem, which seems to raise a question in the minds of many priests in our time, is not left unanswered by the Council.

PO 14 | Priests will find unity of life in the unity of the Church's own mission. In this way they will be united with their Lord and through him with the Father in the Holy Spirit, and can be filled with consolation and exceedingly abound with joy.

PO 14 | In this way, by adopting the role of the good shepherd they will find in the practice of pastoral charity itself the bond of priestly perfection which will reduce to unity their life and activity. Now this pastoral charity flows especially from the eucharistic sacrifice. This sacrifice is therefore the centre and root of the whole life of the priest, so that the priestly soul strives to make its own what is enacted on the altar of sacrifice. But this cannot be achieved except through priests themselves penetrating ever more intimately through prayer into the mystery of Christ.

The priestly training, thus understood, is linked with celibacy, of which we have also treated here.

PO 16　There are many ways in which celibacy is in harmony with the priesthood. For the whole mission of the priest is dedicated to the service of the new humanity which Christ, the victor over death, raises up in the world through his Spirit and which is born 'not of blood nor of the will of the flesh nor of the will of man, but of God' (Jn 1:13).

Another aspect of priestly training is 'a right attitude to the world and to earthly goods'.

PO 17　This attitude is of great importance for priests for this reason, that the Church's mission is carried out in the midst of the world and that created goods are absolutely necessary for man's personal progress. Let priests be thankful then for everything that the heavenly Father has given them towards a proper standard of living. However, they ought to judge everything they meet in the light of faith, so that they will be guided towards the right use of things in accordance with God's will and will reject anything that is prejudicial to their mission.

Next the Decree, following the example of Christ our Lord, the Apostles and the primitive Church, reminds us that:

PO 17 | Priests and bishops alike are to avoid everything that might in any way antagonize the poor. More than the rest of Christ's disciples they are to put aside all appearance of vanity in their surroundings. They are to arrange their house in such a way that it never appears unapproachable to anyone and that nobody, even the humblest, is ever afraid to visit it.

A special Decree of the Council is concerned with training for the priesthood and with the work of ecclesiastical seminaries which, as it says, are necessary for that purpose (OT 4). 'Because of the unity of the Catholic priesthood, this priestly formation is required for all priests, secular, religious and of every rite' (OT, Introduction). Preparation for the priesthood is a matter of spiritual formation as well as intellectual and pastoral training; such spiritual formation 'with the assistance of the spritual director in particular, should be conducted in such a way that the students may learn to live in intimate and unceasing union with God the Father through his Son Jesus Christ, in the Holy Spirit' (PO 8), so as to 'follow Christ the Redeemer with generous souls and pure hearts' (PO 3).

OT 8 | Those who are to take on the likeness of Christ the priest by sacred ordination should form the habit of drawing close to him as friends in every detail of their lives. They should live his Paschal Mystery in such a way that they will know how to initiate into it the people committed to their charge. They should be taught to seek Christ in faithful meditation on the Word of God and in active participation in the sacred mysteries of the Church, especially the Eucharist and the Divine Office, to seek him in the bishop by whom they are sent and in the people to whom they are sent, especially the poor, little children, the weak, sinners and unbelievers. With the confidence of sons they should love and reverence the most blessed virgin Mary, who was given as a mother to the disciples by Jesus Christ as he was dying on the cross.

As regards exercises of piety recommended by the tradition of the Church, the Decree teaches that

OT 8 | The exercises of piety which are commended by the venerable practice of the Church should be strongly encouraged, but care must be taken that spiritual formation does not consist in these alone, nor develop religious sentiment merely. The students should learn, rather, to live according to the standard of the Gospel, to be firmly established in faith, hope and charity, so that the practice of these virtues may develop in them a spirit of prayer, may strengthen and protect their vocation and invigorate their other virtues, intensifying their zeal for winning all men to Christ.

OT 9 | The students should be thoroughly penetrated with a sense of the Mystery of the Church, which this holy Council has set particularly in relief . . . They should learn to participate with enthusiasm in the life of the Church as a whole, keeping in mind the words of St Augustine: 'A man possesses the Holy Spirit in the measure in which he loves the Church'.

The Council lays down several guidelines for training in the evangelical attitude.

OT 9 | Students must clearly understand that it is not their lot in life to lord it over others and enjoy honours, but to devote themselves completely to the service of God and the pastoral ministry. With special care they should be so trained in priestly obedience, poverty and a spirit of self-denial, that they may accustom themselves to living in conformity with the crucified Christ.

OT 11 | The students should learn self-control, develop strength of character, and in general value those good qualities which are esteemed by men and made Christ's minister acceptable. Such qualities are sincerity, a constant love of justice, fidelity to one's promises, courtesy in deed, modesty and charity in speech.

Their training should be directed towards 'the constant exercise of that perfect charity by which they can become all things to all men in their priestly ministry.' (OT 10). The reform of studies must also aim at producing a deeper spiritual formation

OT 16 | In like manner the other theological subjects should be renewed through a more vivid contact with the Mystery of Christ and the history of salvation.

As regards training in and for mission territories, the Council underlines the need to 'face up to the . . . way of thinking and acting' (AGD 16) of the peoples among whom future priests are to carry on pastoral activity.

AGD 16 | They should be formed in the spirit of ecumenism and properly prepared for fraternal dialogue with non-Christians.

AGD 24 | The one who is sent enters upon the life and mission of him 'who emptied himself, taking the nature of a slave' (Phil. 2:7). Therefore, he must be prepared to remain faithful to his vocation for life, to renounce himself and everything that up to this he possessed as his own, and 'to make himself all things to all men' (1 Cor. 9:22).

In preaching the Gospel to the nations he will proclaim with confidence the mystery of Christ whose legate he is, so that in him he will dare to speak as he ought, not being ashamed of the scandal of the Cross. Meek and humble, following in the footsteps of his master, he will show that his yoke is sweet and his burden light . . . By a truly evangelical life, with great patience and longanimity, in kindness and unfeigned love he will bear witness to his Lord, if necessary to the shedding of his blood. He will ask God for strength and courage and in the midst of great affliction and abject poverty he will know abundance of joy. Let him be convinced that obedience is the special virtue of a minister of Christ who by his obedience redeemed the human race.

Training for the religious life is a problem in itself, with which the Council deals both in *Lumen Gentium* and also in a special Decree.

PC 5 | The members of each institute should recall, first of all, that when they made profession of the evangelical counsels they were responding to a divine call, to the end that, not merely being dead to sin (cf. Rom. 6:11) but renouncing the world also, they might live for God alone. They have dedicated their whole lives to his service.

This constitutes a special consecration, which is deeply rooted in their baptismal consecration and is a fuller expression of it.

The Council recalls that 'love, as the bond of perfection and fullness of the law (cf. Col. 3:14; Rom. 13:10), gives meaning to and perfects all the means of sanctification' (LG 42), and points out that 'the Church's holiness is fostered in a special way by the manifold counsels which the Lord proposes to his disciples in the Gospel for them to observe' (LG 42). These are the counsels which show the proper orientation of the religious life and inspire the training of religious of both sexes.

LG 43 | The teaching and example of Christ provide the foundation for the evangelical counsels of chaste self-dedication to God, of poverty and of obedience. The Apostles and Fathers of the Church commend them as an ideal of life, and so do her doctors and pastors. They therefore constitute a gift of God which the Church has received from her Lord and which by his grace she always safeguards.

Guided by the Holy Spirit, Church authority has been at pains to give a right interpretation of the counsels, to regulate their practice, and also to set up stable forms of living embodying them.

LG 44 | The Christian who pledges himself to this kind of life binds himself to the practice of the three evangelical counsels by vows or by other sacred ties of a similar nature. He consecrates himself wholly to God, his supreme love. In a new and special way he makes himself over to God, to serve and honour him. True, as a baptized Christian he is dead to sin and dedicated to God; but he desires to derive still more abundant fruit from the grace of his baptism. For this purpose he makes profession in the Church of the evangelical counsels. He does so for two reasons: first, in order to be set free from hindrances that could hold him back from living God ardently and worshipping him perfectly, and secondly, in order to consecrate himself in a more thoroughgoing way to the service of God. The bonds by which he pledges himself to the practice of the counsels show forth the unbreakable bond of union that exists between Christ and his bride the Church.

Religious profession, which is rooted in the reality of baptism, strengthens the bonds by which those called to it are united with the Church. 'Finally this state manifests in a special way the transcendence of the kingdom of God and its requirements over all earthly things, bringing home to all men the immeasurable greatness of the power of Christ in his sovereignty and the infinite might of the Holy Spirit which works so marvellously in the Church' (LG 44). Thus the religious state and the training connected with it have a particular eschatological significance.

The Decree on the Renewal of Religious Life speaks similarly of the meaning of the vows whereby religious of both sexes bind themselves to keep the evangelical counsels.

PC 12 | Chastity . . . uniquely frees the heart of man (cf. 1 Cor. 7:32–5). It is a special symbol of heavenly benefits. Thus Christ's faithful religious recall that wonderful marriage made by God, which will be fully manifested in the future age, and in which the Church has Christ for her only spouse.

By the profession of obedience, 'religious . . . are united more permanently and securely with God's saving will' (PC 14).

PC 14 | [They] Subject themselves in faith to those who hold God's place, their superiors. Through them they are led to serve all their brothers in Christ, just as Christ ministered to his brothers in submission to the Father and laid down his life for the redemption of many (cf. Mt. 20:28; Jn. 10:14–18).

PC 15 | Religious, as members of Christ, should live together as brothers and should give pride of place to one another in esteem (cf. Rom. 12:10), carrying one another's burdens (cf. Gal. 6:12). A community gathered together as a true family in the Lord's name enjoys his presence (cf. Mt. 18:20) through the love of God which is poured into their hearts by the Holy Spirit (cf. Rom. 5:5).

As regards the training of layfolk, we should first recall what has been said about their state in the Church and the apostolate which is part of their Christian calling.

AA 29 | Since the laity participate in the Church's mission in a way that is their own, their apostolic training acquires a special character precisely from the secularity proper to the lay state and from its particular type of spirituality.

The Council goes on to say that

AA 29 | Education for the apostolate presupposes an integral human education suited to each one's abilities and conditions. For the layman ought to be, through an intimate knowledge of the contemporary world, a member well integrated into his own society and its culture.

This thought recurs constantly in various ways in the Council's teaching. Naturally human culture does not yet reflect the full expression of Christian life. Hence the Council goes on to say:

AA 29 | In the first place he should learn to accomplish the mission of Christ and the Church, living by faith in the divine mystery of creation and redemption, moved by the Holy Spirit who gives life to the People of God and urges all men to love God the Father, and in him to love the world of men. This education must be considered the foundation and condition of any fruitful apostolate . . .

Training for the apostolate cannot consist in theoretical teaching alone; on that account there is need, right from the start of training, to learn gradually and prudently to see all things in the light of faith, to judge and act always in its light, to improve and perfect oneself by working with others, and in this manner to enter actively into the service of the Church.

These words sum up the modern idea of the lay apostolate (*voir, juger, agir*) associated first and foremost with the Jeunesse Ouvrière Chrétienne (JOC) under the guidance of the famous Fr J. Cardijn, who was raised to the Cardinalate during the period of the Council. Training for the apostolate must form the whole Christian personality. 'Inasmuch as the human person is continuously developing and new problems are forever arising, training for the apostolate should be steadily perfected: it requires an ever more thorough knowledge and a continual adaptation of action. While meeting all its demands, concern for the unity and integrity of the human person must be kept always in the foreground, in order to preserve and intensify its harmony and equilibrium' (AA 29).

The Council also points out the necessity for the Christian education of the laity, beginning with children and young people.

AA 12 | Young people exert a very important influence in modern society . . . The growth of their social importance demands from them a corresponding apostolic activity; and indeed their natural character inclines them in this direction. Carried along by their natural ardour and exuberant energy, when awareness of their own personality ripens in them they shoulder responsibilities that are theirs and are eager to take their place in social and cultural life. If this enthusiasm is penetrated with the spirit of Christ, animated by a sense of obedience and love towards the pastors of the Church, a very rich harvest can be expected from it. The young should become the first apostles of the young.

The Council declares in several places that 'the whole family and its community life should become a kind of apprenticeship to the apostolate' (AA 30). 'Priests, for their part, should not lose sight of this question when catechizing, preaching and directing souls, and in other functions of the pastoral ministry' (ibid.). 'Children too have an apostolate of their own. In their own measure they are true living witnesses of Christ among their companions' (AA 12). Thus the Council attaches the highest importance to the whole process of education and training which takes place through the lively transmission of values from one generation to another.

AA 12 | Adults should be anxious to enter into friendly dialogue with the young, where, despite the difference in age, they could get to know one another and share with one another their own personal riches. It is by example first of all and, on occasion, by sound advice and practical help that adults should persuade the young to undertake the apostolate. The young, on their side, will treat their elders with respect and confidence; and though by nature inclined to favour what is new, they will have due esteem for praiseworthy traditions.

Thus the Council points clearly to the process of apostolic formation which is both fundamental and organic. It is a process of education and self-education, corresponding to the successive phases of development of the human personality.

AA 30 | Every single lay person should himself actively undertake his own preparation for the apostolate. Especially for adults does this hold true; for as the years pass, self-awareness expands and so allows each one to get a clearer view of the talents with which God has enriched his life, and to bring in better results from the exercise of the charisms given him by the Holy Spirit for the good of his brothers.

These are the charisms to which we have referred in the present chapter: they are of great importance to the apostolate and should be used to form the apostolic attitude.

LG 41 | Christian married couples and parents, following their own way, should support one another in grace all through life with faithful love, and should train their children (lovingly received from God) in Christian doctrine and evangelical virtues. In this way . . . they stand as witnesses and cooperators of the fruitfulness of mother Church, as a sign of, and a share in that love with which Christ loved his bride and gave himself for her. In a different way, a similar example is given by widows and single people. And those who engage in human work, often of a heavy kind, should perfect themselves through it, help their fellow-citizens, and promote the betterment of the whole of human society and the whole of creation; indeed, with their active charity, rejoicing in hope and bearing one another's burdens, they should imitate Christ who plied his hands with carpenter's tools.

As regards the laity whose apostolate is devoted to 'the Christian renewal of the temporal order', the Council emphasizes the necessity to instruct them 'in the true meaning and value of temporal goods, both in themselves and in their relation to all the aims of the human person' (AA 31). It adds that:

AA 31 | The laity should gain experience in the right use of goods and in the organization of institutions, paying heed always to the common good in the light of the principles of the Church's moral and social teaching.

AA 29 | If good human relations are to be cultivated, then it is necessary for genuine human values to stand at a premium, especially the art of living and working on friendly terms with others and entering into dialogue with them.

AA 31 | Works of charity and mercy bear a most striking testimony to Christian life; therefore, an apostolic training which has as its object the performance of these works should enable the faithful to learn from very childhood how to sympathize with their brothers, and help them generously when in need.

The apostolic attitude is expressed in relations with human beings, and is expressed in love. 'While rejoicing at initiatives taken elsewhere, the Church claims charitable works as its own mission and right.' This concerns 'mercy to the poor and the sick, charitable works and works of mutual aid for the alleviation of all kinds of human needs' (AA 8).

AA 8 | Wherever men are to be found who are in want of food and drink, of clothing, housing, medicine, work, education, the means necessary for leading a truly human life, wherever there are men racked by misfortune or illness, men suffering exile or imprisonment, Christian charity should go in search of them and find them out, comfort them with devoted care and give them the helps that will relieve their needs.

The Council presents the lay apostolate as something urged by Christ himself:

AA 33 | It is the Lord himself, by this Council, who is once more inviting all the laity to unite themselves to him ever more intimately, to consider his interests as their own (cf. Phil. 2:5), and to join in his mission as Saviour . . . He sends them as his cooperators on the Church's apostolate, an apostolate that is one yet has different forms and methods, an apostolate that must all the the time be adapting itself to the needs of the moment.'

CHAPTER VI

Building up the Church as
a community

In our study of the attitudes which should be fostered on the basis of the Council's teaching, and which in a sense form a picture of the faith of Christians at the present day, we stressed that they coincide in various respects, being in some ways identical and in many ways complementary to one another. This is abundantly confirmed at the point which our study of these attitudes has now reached. The title of the present chapter denotes an attitude or rather a complex of attitudes which the Council's teaching shows to be of specific importance to the Church and to the Christian of Vatican II. When we speak of 'building up the Church as a community' we are thinking not so much of the process of building or the actual structures envisaged by Vatican II, but rather of the attitude without which these structures and that process would be suspended in the void.

The nature of this 'community attitude', as it may be called, can be perceived from a study of Council texts which show its essence and clarify its relation to the building-up of the Church as the community of the People of God and the Body of Christ.

LG 7 | As all the members of the human body, though they are many, form one body, so also are the faithful in Christ (cf. 1 Cor. 12:12). Also, in the building up of Christ's body there is engaged a diversity of members and functions. There is only one Spirit who, according to his own richness and the needs of the ministries, gives his different gifts for the welfare of the Church (cf. 1 Cor. 12:1–11). Among these gifts the primacy belongs to the grace of the apostles, to whose authority the Spirit himself subjects even those who are endowed with charisms (cf. 1 Cor. 14). Giving the body unity through himself, both by his own power and by the interior union of the members, this same Spirit produces and stimulates love among the faithful. From this it follows that if one member suffers anything, all the members suffer with him, and if one member is honoured, all the members together rejoice (cf. 1 Cor. 12:26).

The unity of the Church as the Body of Christ is a fruit of the Holy Spirit, whose action produces multiplicity but leads to unity: a multiplicity of gifts, vocations and ministries, and the unity of the Mystical Body. Since this Body is also the People of God, we can see that the action of the Holy Spirit bears fruit in that attitude on the part of every one of its members which contributes to their union, that is to the formation of the community of the Church through the bond of the spiritual communion that is distinctive of it. In the formation of the community attitude we may thus rightly perceive an expression of that enrichment of faith for which Vatican II provides a fresh historical background and doctrinal inspiration. In the Council documents we do indeed find many texts which enable us to understand and clarify this attitude in its various aspects and spheres of action.

With the help of these texts, therefore, we shall attempt to describe the building-up of the Church community as a synthesis of structures and attitudes, while emphasizing the latter as we have done in the remainder of this study. Much has already been said about structures in the context of Vatican II renewal, and it seems to us appropriate to bring out the importance of attitudes as their indispensable counterpart.

1. *Synthesis of structures and attitudes*

Vatican II teaches in several places that the Eucharist is the foundation on which the community of the Church is to be built up.

LG 7 | Really sharing in the body of the Lord in the breaking of the eucharistic bread, we are taken up into communion with him and with one another. 'Because the bread is one, we, though many, are one body, all of us who partake of the one bread' (1 Cor. 10:17). In this way all of us are made members of his body (cf. 1 Cor. 12:27), 'but severally members one of another' (Rom. 12:4).

LG 17 | Each disciple of Christ has the obligation of spreading the faith to the best of his ability. But while any believer can baptize, it is for the priests to complete the building up of the body in the eucharistic sacrifice.

PO 5 | Therefore the eucharistic celebration is the centre of the assembly of the faithful over which the priest presides.

PO 6 | However, no Christian community is built up which does not grow from and hinge on the celebration of the most holy Eucharist. From this all education for community spirit must begin. This eucharistic celebration, to be full and sincere, ought to lead on the one hand to the various works of charity and mutual help, and on the other hand to missionary activity and the various forms of Christian witness.

This 'eucharistic' first principle of the building-up of the

Church as community also contains within itself a hierarchical aspect. The uniting of the People of God is an integral part of the ministry and mission of those who have received from Christ the power to celebrate the Eucharist.

LG 26 | This Church of Christ is really present in all legitimately organized local groups of the faithful, which, in so far as they are united to their pastors, are also quite appropriately called Churches in the New Testament. For these are in fact, in their own localities, the new people called by God, in the power of the Holy Spirit and as the result of full conviction (cf. 1 Thess. 1 : 5). In them the faithful are gathered together through the preaching of the Gospel of Christ, and the mystery of the Lord's Supper is celebrated 'so that, by means of the flesh and blood of the Lord the whole brotherhood of the Body may be welded together'. In each altar community, under the sacred ministry of the bishop, a manifest symbol is to be seen of that charity and 'unity of the mystical body, without which there can be no salvation.' In these communities, though they may often be small and poor, or existing in the diaspora, Christ is present through whose power and influence the One, Holy, Catholic and Apostolic Church is constituted. For 'the sharing in the body and blood of Christ has no other effect than to accomplish our transformation into that which we receive'.

Moreover, every legitimate celebration of the Eucharist is regulated by the bishop, to whom is confided the duty of presenting to the divine majesty the cult of the Christian religion and of ordering it in accordance with the Lord's injunctions and the Church's regulations, as

> further defined for the diocese by his particular
> decision.

As this passage shows, the Church as a community centres around the Eucharist, whose uniting power joins with that of the Word of God which binds the faithful together. The community of the People of God is formed around these two laden tables both found in the Church from the very beginning: that of the Word and that of the Eucharist. The hierarchical aspect is seen both in the proclamation of the Word and in the celebration of the Lord's Supper.

LG 28
> The priests, prudent cooperators of the episcopal college and its support and mouthpiece, called to the service of the People of God, constitute, together with their bishop, a unique sacerdotal college (*presbyterium*) dedicated it is true to a variety of distinct duties. In each local assembly of the faithful they represent in a certain sense the bishop, with whom they are associated in all trust and generosity; in part they take upon themselves his duties and solicitude and in their daily toils discharge them.

LG 27
> As to the faithful, they should be closely attached to the bishop as the Church is to Jesus Christ, and as Jesus Christ is to the Father, so that all things may conspire towards harmonious unity, and bring forth abundant fruit unto the glory of God (cf. 2 Cor. 4:15).

And, as the Decree on the lay apostolate points out:

AA 10
> The parish offers an outstanding example of community apostolate, for it gathers into a unity all the human diversities that are found there and inserts them into the universality of the Church.

We may say that in this way the community shows its distinctive aspect on the scale of the local Church, which in turn constantly reveals the final and universal aspect of the Church as it was instituted by Christ.

LG 28 | Those who, under the authority of the bishop, sanctify and govern that portion of the Lord's flock assigned to them render the universal Church visible in their locality and contribute efficaciously towards building up the whole body of Christ (cf. Eph. 4:12).

The constitution of the Church established by Christ is such that the 'universal' and the 'local' dimensions interpenetrate each other. This has its own importance for the formation of consciousness and attitudes.

SC 42 | But as it is impossible for the bishop always and everywhere to preside over the whole flock in his church, he must of necessity establish groupings of the faithful; and, among these, parishes, set up locally under a pastor who takes the place of the bishop, are the most important, for in some way they represent the visible Church constituted throughout the world.

Therefore the liturgical life of the parish and its relation to the bishop must be fostered in the spirit and practice of the laity and clergy. Efforts must also be made to encourage a sense of community within the parish, above all in the common celebration of the Sunday Mass.

The hierarchical structure, as it were, flows down to all the communities of the People of God, including the smallest, and provides a framework for the construction based on the Word of God and the Eucharist. Hence the special character of the authority entrusted within the Church to the Pope, bishops and priests.

LG 21 | These pastors are servants of Christ and stewards of the mysteries of God (cf. 1 Cor. 4:1), to whom is entrusted the duty of affirming the Gospel of the grace of God (cf. Rom. 15:16; Acts 20:24), and of gloriously promulgating the Spirit and proclaiming justification (cf. 2 Cor. 3:8–9).

The Pastoral power is the keystone of every community and the condition of the interpenetration of its local and universal dimensions.

LG 23 | Individual bishops, in so far as they are set over particular Churches, exercise their pastoral office over the portion of the People of God assigned to them, not over other Churches nor the Church universal. But in so far as they are members of the episcopal college and legitimate successors of the apostles, by Christ's arrangement and decree, each is bound to have a care and solicitude for the whole Church which, though it be not exercised by any act of jurisdiction, does for all that redound in an eminent degree to the advantage of the universal Church. For all the bishops have the obligation of fostering and safeguarding the unity of the faith and of upholding the discipline which is common to the whole Church; of schooling the faithful in a love of the whole Mystical Body of Christ and, in a special way, of the poor, the suffering, and those who are undergoing persecution for the sake of justice (cf. Mt. 5:10); finally, of promoting all that type of active apostolate which is common to the whole Church, especially in order that the faith may increase and the light of truth may rise in its fullness on all men. Besides, it is an established fact of experience

> that, in ruling well their own Churches as portions of the universal Church, they contribute efficaciously to the welfare of the whole Mystical Body, which, from another point of view, is a corporate body of Churches.

After this general description of the community that is to be built up by all members of the Church, we may turn to more detailed considerations. The building up of the Church as the community of the People of God *ad intra* involves various spheres which, although different, pervade and condition one another, as we have observed previously. As regards the attitude that corresponds to the building up of the Church as a community, in the light of the Council's teaching we can and must consider both the Church as a whole and also each individual member of it. There is a clear analogy here, explained by the existence of both a hierarchical and a charismatic order. While each of these orders expresses a sharp individualization of vocations and activities in the Church, they both presuppose an orientation towards the community: both the hierarchical and also the charismatic gifts taken as a whole serve to build up the community of the People of God in the Church. Vatican II, while noting the various gifts of the Holy Spirit by means of which the Church is built up, points out that 'the primacy belongs to the grace of the Apostles to whose authority the Spirit himself subjects even those who are endowed with charisms (cf. 1 Cor. 14)' (LG 7).

We shall therefore try to follow the order corresponding to the divine constitution of the Church, and begin by analysing what is meant by the building up of the Church as a hierarchical community. By so doing we shall begin with the universal dimension and relate it to all the 'local' dimensions.

CD 2 | In this Church of Christ the Roman Pontiff, as the successor of Peter . . . has been granted by God supreme, full, immediate and universal

power in the care of souls. As pastor of all the
faithful his mission is to promote the common
good of the universal Church and the particular
good of all the churches. He is therefore endowed with the primacy of ordinary power over
all the churches.

The bishops also have been designated by the
Holy Spirit to take the place of the apostles as
pastors of souls and, together with the Supreme
Pontiff and subject to his authority, they are
commissioned to perpetuate the work of Christ,
the Eternal Pastor.

CD 3 | The bishops, sharing in the solicitude of all
the churches, exercise this their episcopal function, which they have received by virtue of their
episcopal consecration in communion with the
Supreme Pontiff and subject to his authority.
They exercise this function individually as
regards that portion of the Lord's flock which
has been entrusted to each one of them, each
bishop having responsibility for the particular
church assigned to him. On occasion a number
of bishops will cooperate to provide for the
common needs of their churches.

A few years after the Council, the extraordinary Synod of
Bishops in Rome (1969) studied the question of collegiality and
its application in the 'affective' and 'effective' sense. Here we
shall confine ourselves to the Council's teaching, which
indicates clearly enough the attitudes which correspond to the
need and duty to build up the Church as a community, this
duty 'is most incumbent on the college of those who collectively bear the chief responsibility for doing so. In the order of
bishops 'the apostolic college is perpetuated', and hence the
Council says, among other things: 'the sacred Synod decrees
that all bishops who are members of the episcopal college

[thus not merely ordinaries] have the right to take part in an ecumenical council' (CD 4). Finally Vatican II laid the basis for the episcopal Synod mentioned above as a new, permanent hierarchical institution of the Roman Church.

CD 5 | Bishops chosen from different parts of the world in a manner and according to a system determined or to be determined by the Roman Pontiff will render to the Supreme Pastor a more effective auxiliary service in a council which shall be known by the special name of Synod of Bishops. This council, as it will be representative of the whole Catholic episcopate, will bear testimony to the participation of all the bishops in hierarchical communion in the care of the universal Church.

CD 6 | They should be especially solicitous for those parts of the world in which the word of God has not yet been proclaimed or in which, especially on account of the scarcity of priests, the faithful are in danger of falling away from the obligations of the Christian life or even of losing the faith itself. Bishops should, therefore, do their utmost to ensure that the activities of evangelization and the apostolate are zealously supported and promoted by the faithful. It should, moreover, be their special care that suitable priests, as well as lay and religious auxiliaries, be trained for those missions and regions suffering from a lack of clergy . . .

Furthermore, bishops should bear in mind that in the expenditure of ecclesiastical resources they must take into account the needs not only of their own dioceses but of other individual churches, since they too form part of the one Church of Christ. Let it be their care also to give help according to their resources when other dioceses or regions are afflicted by disaster.

CD 7 | Above all, they should extend their brotherly care to those bishops who are harassed by calumny and hardship for the name of Christ, who are detained in prison or prevented from exercising their ministry. They should manifest an active fraternal interest in them so that their sufferings may be lessened and alleviated by the prayers and works of their brethren.

In its concern for the development of hierarchical activity in the Church, Vatican II expresses the wish that the departments of the Roman Curia, 'which have indeed rendered excellent service to the Roman Pontiff and to the pastors of the Church, should be reorganized and modernized, should be more in keeping with different regions and rites' (CD 9). This relates to the reform and the so-called internationalization of the Roman Curia. In addition the Council expresses full support for all traditional forms of 'local' collegiality and recommends the institution of national episcopal conferences, in order that 'synods and councils may flourish with renewed vigour, so that the growth of religion and the maintenance of discipline in the various churches may be more effectively provided for in accordance with the needs of the times' (CD 36).

It should perhaps be recalled here that Vatican II in a special Decree emphasized the need to preserve the spiritual heritage of the Eastern Churches, which it 'insists on viewing as the heritage of the whole Church of Christ' (OE 5): accordingly these Churches 'have the right and duty to govern themselves according to their own special disciplines' (OE 5), and 'can and ought always to preserve their own legitimate liturgical rites and ways of life' (OE 6). This also applies to their hierarchical constitution, in which the synodal principle is emphasized more than in the West.

Another area in which the Council laid stress on the need to build up the community of the Church is the *presbyterium*, the community of priests united around their bishop. Here we are directly in the sphere of local churches, but the Council expressly declares that:

> CD 22   For a diocese to fulfil its purpose it is necessary that the nature of the Church be clearly manifested in the People of God belonging to the diocese. Bishops myst be able to carry out their pastoral function effectively among their people, and finally the spiritual welfare of the People of God must be catered for as perfectly as possible.

Only on the basis of such a clear principle can the community be formed, or the totality of attitudes that constitute it on the part of bishops and priests. The latter should see in the bishop 'a true father and obey him with all respect. The bishop, on his side, should treat the priests, his helpers, as his sons and friends, just as Christ calls his disciples no longer servants but friends (cf. John 15:15)' (LG 28). This link between priest and bishop means that all priests in the Church are united with the episcopal college.

> LG 28   All priests, then, whether diocesan or religious, by reason of the sacrament of Orders and of the ministry correspond to and cooperate with the body of bishops and, according to their vocation and the grace that is given them, they serve the welfare of the whole Church.

Vatican II speaks separately of deacons, 'who receive the imposition of hands "not unto the priesthood, but unto the ministry" ', but who 'are dedicated to the People of God in conjunction with the bishop and his body of priests' (LG 29).

We may also quote a passage on ecclesiastical seminaries.

OT 5 | The bishop with his constant and affectionate interest should encourage those engaged in seminary work and show himself a true father in Christ to the students. Furthermore, all priests should regard the seminary as the very heart of the diocese and give it their willing support.

This too has its importance in a chapter concerned with building up the Church as a community.

The Council emphasizes in several places the paternal aspect of the bishop's mission towards all and especially towards his priests.

CD 16 | In exercising his office of father and pastor the bishop should be with his people as one who serves.

CD 16 | His priests, who assume a part of his duties and concerns, and who are ceaselessly devoted to their work, should be the objects of his particular affection. He should regard them as sons and friends. He should always be ready to listen to them and cultivate an atmosphere of easy familiarity with them, thus facilitating the pastoral work of the entire diocese.

The sacerdotal college (*presbyterium*) in every local church, forming 'one priestly body and one family of which the bishop is the father' (CD 28), is to to speak the basis of the construction of the community in the local church. As the quoted passages show, this is a community in both the 'affective' and the 'effective' senses. It should also include priests who are members of religious orders.

CD 34 | Religious priests, who have been raised to the priesthood to be prudent cooperators with the episcopal order, are able nowadays to give more help to bishops in view of the more pressing needs of souls. Thus they may be said in a certain sense to belong to the diocesan clergy inasmuch as they share in the care of souls and in the practice of apostolic works under the authority of the bishops. The other members, too, of religious institutes, both men and women, also belong in a special sense to the diocesan family.

Thus, under the bishop's direction, 'in view of their sacred ordination and of their common mission all priests are united together by bonds of intimate brotherhood, which manifests itself in a spontaneous and gladly given mutual help, whether spiritual or temporal, whether pastoral or personal, through the medium of reunions and community life, work and fraternal charity' (LG 28). This fraternal bond uniting the priests around their bishop is a kind of reflection of the collegial bond uniting all bishops around the successor of St Peter. In both cases we have to do with particular spheres of co-responsibility – that of priests or bishops – and consequently in both cases this co-responsibility is exercised with due regard to the responsibility of the head of the community in question.

PO 15

The priestly ministry, being the ministry of the Church itself, can only be fulfilled in the hierarchical union of the whole body of the Church. Hence pastoral charity urges priests to act within this communion and by obedience to dedicate their own will to the service of God and their fellow-Christians. They will accept and carry out in the spirit of faith the commands and suggestions of the Pope and of their bishop and other superiors. They will most gladly spend themselves and be spent in whatever office is

> entrusted to them, even the humbler and poorer. By acting in this way they preserve and strengthen the indispensable unity with their brothers in the ministry and especially with those whom the Lord has appointed the visible rulers of his Church. They also work towards the building up of the Body of Christ, which grows 'by what every joint supplieth' (cf. Eph. 4:11–16).

It appears from these words that the attitude which corresponds to the building up of the Church as a community is deeply rooted in the spirituality of the priest, built on living faith. This faith is expressed in a sincere and genuine bond of obedience, which the Council describes as follows.

PO 15 | This obedience, which leads to the more mature freedom of the sons of God, by its nature demands that priests in the exercise of their duties should be moved by charity prudently to seek new methods of advancing the good of the Church. At the same time it also demands that while putting forward their schemes with confidence and being insistent in making known the needs of the flock entrusted to them, they should always be prepared to submit to the judgement of those who exercise the chief function in ruling God's Church.

Obedience thus understood in no way suppresses initiative and creativity, but rather stimulates them; for it is precisely in this form that obedience is a virtue in the fullest sense and helps to build up the Church as a community. As the Decree says elsewhere:

PO 7 | Priests for their part should keep in mind the fullness of the sacrament of Order which bishops enjoy and should reverence in their persons the authority of Christ the supreme Pastor. They

should therefore be attached to their bishop with
sincere charity and obedience. This priestly
obedience, inspired through and through by the
spirit of cooperation, is based on that sharing
of the episcopal ministry which is conferred on
priests by the sacrament of Order and the
canonical mission.

The Decree then mentions another feature of obedience
from the viewpoint of building up community:

PO 7 | There is all the more need in our day for union
of priests with bishops because in this age of
ours apostolic enterprises must necessarily for
various reasons take on many different forms.
And not only that, but they must often overstep
the bounds of one parish or diocese. Hence no
priest is sufficiently equipped to carry out his own
mission alone and as it were single-handed.
He can only do so by joining forces with other
priests, under the leadership of those who are
rulers of the Church.

In these words the Council points out the need for a
'community' attitude on the part of priests, 'who are constituted in the order of priesthood by the sacrament of Order
and bound together by an intimate sacramental brotherhood'
(PO 8). The bond of obedience to the bishop or other superior
conditions the realization of the 'community' bond, which
at the same time requires an appropriate attitude on the
superior's part. Thus Vatican II calls not only for the building
up of an affective community but also of an effective one.

PO 7 | Bishops are to regard their priests as brothers
and friends and are to take the greatest interest
they are capable of in their welfare both temporal and spiritual. For on their shoulders
particularly falls the burden of sanctifying their

priests: therefore they are to exercise the greatest care in the progressive formation of their diocesan body of priests. They should be glad to listen to their priests' views and even consult them and hold conference with them about matters that concern the needs of pastoral work and the good of the diocese. But for this to be reduced to practice a group or senate of priests should be set up in a way suited to present-day needs, and in a form and with rules to be determined by law. This group would represent the body of priests and by its advice could effectively help the bishop in the management of the diocese.

As regards the economic side of the life of the priestly community, the Council declares that:

PO 20 | The so-called system of benefices is to be abandoned or else reformed in such a way that the part that has to do with the benefice – that is, the right to the revenues attached to the endowment of the office – shall be regarded as secondary and the principal emphasis in law given to the ecclesiastical office itself. This should in future be understood as any office conferred in a permanent fashion and to be exercised for a spiritual purpose.

According to the Council's teaching, the building up of the Church as a community explicitly involves the hierarchical aspect which, through the priestly ministry, extends to the whole body of the faithful.

PO 6 | Priests exercise the function of Christ as Pastor and Head in proportion to their share of authority. In the name of the bishop they gather the family of God as a brotherhood

> endowed with the spirit of unity and lead it in
> Christ through the Spirit to God the Father. For
> the exercise of this ministry, as for the rest of the
> priests' functions, a spiritual power is given
> them, a power whose purpose is to build up.

The process of building up is not only one for the hierarchy
but depends to a very large degree on the 'community'
attitude of the laity. The Council, as we know, went very
fully into this aspect, and we shall try to trace here the main
lines of its teaching as regards the community of lay people in
the Church and the communion of clergy and laity.

LG 30 | The pastors, indeed, know well how much the
> laity contribute to the welfare of the whole
> Church. For they know that they themselves
> were not established by Christ to undertake
> alone the whole salvific mission of the Church
> to the world, but that it is their exalted office so
> to be shepherds of the faithful and also recognize
> the latter's contribution and charisms that
> everyone in his own way will, with one mind,
> cooperate in the common task.

This may be considered a classic text for our purpose. Vatican II, the Council of the People of God, brings out the multiplicity and differentiation of vocations within the Church and
points out the ways whereby they complement one another
in the context of the Church's mission.

AA 6 | The Church's mission is concerned with the
> salvation of men; and men win salvation
> through the grace of Christ and faith in him.
> The apostolate of the Church therefore, and of
> each of its members, aims primarily at an-
> nouncing to the world by word and action the
> message of Christ and communicating to it the

grace of Christ. The principal means of bringing this about is the ministry of the word and of the sacraments. Committed in a special way to the clergy, it leaves room however for a highly important part for the laity, the part namely of 'helping on the cause of truth' (3 Jn. 8). It is in this sphere most of all that the lay apostolate and the pastoral ministry complete each other.

This clearly expresses the interrelation and coordination of tasks which can be achieved by a mature attitude on the part of pastoral clergy and lay people, whose activities thus serve in diverse ways to build up the Church as a community.

LG 33 | The laity, however, are given this special vocation: to make the Church present and fruitful in those places and circumstances where it is only through them that she can become the salt of the earth. Thus, every lay person, through those gifts given to him, is at once the witness and the living instrument of the mission of the Church itself 'according to the measure of Christ's bestowal' (Eph. 4:7) . . .

All the laity, then, have the exalted duty of working for the ever greater spread of the divine plan of salvation to all men, of every epoch and all over the earth. Therefore may the way be clear for them to share diligently in the salvific work of the Church according to their ability and the needs of the times.

The 'community' attitude on the part of lay people and members of the hierarchy and religious orders thus derives from the community of tasks and functions in accordance with the salvific work of the Church. The differentiation of tasks presupposes a community of purpose which they all share and serve.

AA 10 | Participators in the function of Christ, priest, prophet and king, the laity have an active part of their own in the life and action of the Church. Their action within the Church communities is so necessary that without it the apostolate of the pastors will frequently be unable to achieve its full effect.

GS 43 | The laity are called to participate actively in the whole life of the Church; not only are they to animate the world with the spirit of Christianity, but they are to be witnesses to Christ in all circumstances and at the very heart of the community of mankind.

Thus the Council, having analysed in detail the problem of the Church in the world, clearly formulates the principle of complementarity which should be the basis of the upbuilding of the Church as a community in our day.

GS 43 | For guidance and spiritual strength let them turn to the clergy; but let them realize that their pastors will not always be so expert as to have a ready answer to every problem (even every grave problem) that arises; this is not the role of the clergy: it is rather up to the laymen to shoulder their responsibilities under the guidance of Christian wisdom and with eager attention to the teaching authority of the Church.

It would be hard to express with greater frankness, clarity and precision the rights and duties of the laity within the Church's mission. If one may so put it, the Council here utters a warning against 'clericalism', which may consist not only of the clergy encroaching on aspects of the Church's activity that are beyond their competence, but also in the laity shirking their responsibilities and throwing them on to the clergy. According to Vatican II, one of the chief principles of the apostolate of the Church is that the laity should shoulder all the tasks that belong to their vocation in the Church and in the world. This does not by any means imply disrupting the community, but rather strengthening it. The Council mentions this in several places.

LG 37 | Like all Christians, the laity should promptly accept in Christian obedience what is decided by the pastors who, as teachers and rulers of the Church, represent Christ. In this they will follow Christ's example who, by his obedience unto death, opened the blessed way of the liberty of the sons of God to all men. Nor should they fail to commend to God in their prayers those who have been placed over them, who indeed keep watch as having to render an account of our souls, that they may do this with joy and not with grief (cf. Heb. 13:17).

The correlation between the attitudes of the hierarchy and the laity, corresponding to the building-up of the Church as a community, rests on a solid foundation. Basing itself on this, the Council teaches how mutual relations should be constituted between pastors and laity within actual church communities and in other spheres of activity.

PO 9 | Priests should, therefore, occupy their position of leadership as men who do not seek the things that are their own but the things that are Jesus Christ's. They should unite their efforts with those of the lay faithful and conduct themselves among them after the example of the Master, who came amongst men 'not to be served but to serve, and to give his life as a ransom for many' (Mt. 20:28). Priests are to be sincere in their appreciation and promotion of lay people's dignity and of the special role the laity have to play in the Church's mission. They should also have an unfailing respect for the just liberty which belongs to everybody in civil society. They should be willing to listen to lay people, give brotherly consideration to their wishes, and recognize their experience and competence in the different fields of human activity. In this way they will be able to recognize along with them the signs of the times.

While 'trying the spirits if they be of God', they must discover with faith, recognize with joy, and foster with diligence the many and varied charismatic gifts of the laity, whether these be of a humble or more exalted kind. Among the other gifts of God which are found abundantly among the faithful, special attention ought to be devoted to those graces by which a considerable number of people are attracted to greater heights of the spiritual life. Priests should also be confident in giving lay people charge of duties in the service of the Church, giving them freedom and opportunity for activity and even inviting them, when opportunity occurs, to take the initiative in undertaking projects of their own.

As will be seen, the Decree on the Life and Ministry of Priests, which goes into much detail concerning the priestly mission in the Church, contains a penetrating study of the mutual relation between pastors and the laity in the community of the Church. Priests, 'by their vocation to ordination, are set apart in some way in the midst of the People of God, but this is not in order that they should be separated from that people or from any man, but that they should be completely consecrated to the task for which God chooses them' (PO 3). The priestly vocation is thus directed towards the laity.

PO 6 | It is the priests' part as instructors of the people in the faith to see to it either personally or through others that each member of the faithful shall be led in the Holy Spirit to the full development of his own vocation in accordance with the Gospel teaching, and to sincere and active charity and the liberty with which Christ has set us free.

The document goes on to say significantly that: 'Very little good will be achieved by ceremonies however beautiful, or societies however flourishing, if they are not directed towards educating people to reach Christian maturity' (PO 6). It is the essential task of pastors *vis à vis* their brethren 'to enable them to determine the solution to their problems and the will of God in the crises of life, great or small. Christians must also be trained so as to live not only for themselves. Rather, according to the demands of the new law of charity, every man as he has received grace ought to minister it one to another, and thus all should carry out their duties in a Christian way in the community of their fellow-men' (PO 6). We also read:

PO 6 | Although priests owe service to everybody, the poor and the weaker ones have been committed to their care in a special way. It was with these that the Lord himself associated, and the preaching of the Gospel to them is given as a sign of his messianic mission. Priests will look after young people with special diligence. This applies also to married couples and parents.

Clearly the priests' task of building the Body of Christ rests on genuine pastoral activity.

PO 6 | The pastor's task is not limited to individual care of the faithful. It extends by right also to the formation of a genuine Christian community.

The pastor is not only animated by love for souls, but guides the community and helps it to achieve its salvific mission.

> PO 6 | The ecclesial community exercises a truly motherly function in leading souls to Christ by its charity, its prayer, its example and its penitential works. For it constitutes an effective instrument for showing or smoothing the path towards Christ and his Church for those who have not yet found faith; while also encouraging, supporting and strengthening believers for their spiritual struggles.

Such is the meaning of the building-up of the community and its significance to the Church. Relations between priests and the laity are intended to serve this purpose, as the Council shows.

> PO 9 | The faithful for their part ought to realize that they have obligations to their priests. They should treat them with filial love as being their fathers and pastors. They should also share their priests' anxieties and help them as far as possible by prayer and active work so that they may be better able to overcome difficulties and carry out their duties with greater success.

It appears more and more clearly that the build-up of the Church as a community must be the fruit of mature attitudes and of their mutual correlation. Pastoral care is a form of authority, but a very specific one corresponding to the evangelical vision of man and the community. The Council attaches particular importance to discovering and developing the charisms of the laity, those abilities and gifts of the Spirit which give a genuinely Christian form to social and ecclesial life. This is of great value to the whole pastoral activity of priests under their bishops' guidance. In the Decree on the Pastoral Office of Bishops in the Church we read:

CD 16 | In exercising his ministry he should ensure that the faithful are duly involved in Church affairs; he should recognize their right and duty to play their part in building up the Mystical Body of Christ.

It is the proper task of the bishop as pastor and head of the local church to animate and unify the whole of pastoral care and the lay apostolate as twin forms of activity through which the Church's saving mission is carried out. Vatican II makes several recommendations to this end. For instance: 'In order to be able to provide for the welfare of the faithful as their individual circumstances demand, the bishop should try to keep himself informed of their needs in the social circumstances in which they live' (CD 16); social research, the Council adds, is also useful for this purpose. 'He should be solicitous for all men whatever their age, condition or nationality, whether they are natives, visitors or foreign immigrants' (ibid). In this way

CD 17 | the various forms of the apostolate should be encouraged. Close collaboration and the co-ordination of all the apostolic works under the direction of the bishop should be promoted in the diocese as a whole or in parts of it. Thus all the undertakings and organizations, whether their object be catechetical missionary, charitable, social, family, educational, or any other pastoral end, will act together in harmony, and the unity of the diocese will be more closely demonstrated.

The bishop, as head of the local church, and all his helpers should look to this.

CD 30 | In exercising the care of souls parish priests and their assistants should carry out their work of teaching, sanctifying and governing in such a way that the faithful and the parish communities may feel that they are truly members both of the diocese and of the universal Church. They should therefore collaborate both with other parish priests and with those priests who are exercising a pastoral function in the district (such as vicars forane and deans) or who are engaged in works of an extra-parochial nature, so that the pastoral work of the diocese may be rendered more effective by a spirit of unity.

CD 34 | The other members, too, of religious institutes, both men and women also belong in a special sense to the diocesan family and render valuable help to the sacred hierarchy, and in view of the growing needs of the apostolate they can and should constantly increase the aid they give.

CD 30 | The care of souls should always be inspired by a missionary spirit, so that it extends with due prudence to all those who live in the parish. And if the parish priest cannot make contact with certain groups of people he should call to his aid others, including laymen, to assist him in matters relating to the apostolate.

As regards the share of the laity in building up the Church as a community, the Council considers it from the point of view of the lay community itself and also of their relations with the hierarchy and pastors. Here the Decree on the lay apostolate draws not only on the lively tradition of the primitive Church but also on the rich experience of the Church in our own day. The first, fundamental Christian community of lay Christians is marriage and the family. In various places the Council points out the importance of this fundamental community for the building-up of the Church.

LG 35 | Where the Christian religion pervades the whole structure of life with a continuous and ever more profound transformation, there is both the practice and an outstanding school of the lay apostolate. In it the married partners have their own proper vocation: they must be witnesses of faith and love of Christ to one another and to their children.

This school should produce mature witnesses to Christ, of whom *Lumen Gentium* goes on to say:

LG 35 | When there are no sacred ministers or when these are impeded under persecution, some lay people supply sacred functions to the best of their ability, or if, indeed, many of them expend all their energies in apostolic work, nevertheless the whole laity must cooperate in spreading and in building up the kingdom of Christ.

Although the lay apostolate stems from the spiritual maturity of every single Christian, it is none the less exercised in the community, which is its goal and which it helps to construct.

AA 16 | The apostolate to be exercised by the individual – which flows abundantly from a truly Christian life (cf. Jn. 4:11) – is the starting point and condition of all types of lay apostolate, including the organized apostolate; nothing can replace it.

The individual apostolate is everywhere and always in place; in certain circumstances it is the only one appropriate, the only one possible. Every lay person, whatever his condition, is called to it, is obliged to it, even if he has not the opportunity or possibility of collaborating in associations.

In the same document we also read:

AA 18 | The faithful are called as individuals to exercise an apostolate in the various conditions of their life. They must, however, remember that man is social by nature and that it has been God's pleasure to assemble those who believe in Christ and make of them the People of God (cf. 1 Pet. 2:5–10), a single body (cf. 1 Cor. 12:12). The group apostolate is in happy harmony therefore with a fundamental need in the faithful, a need that is both human and Christian. At the same time it offers a sign of the communion and unity of the Church in Christ, who said: 'Where two or three are gathered together in my name, I am there in the midst of them' (Mt. 18:20).

AA 18 | For that reason Christians will exercise their apostolate in a spirit of concord. They will be apostles both in their families and in the parishes and dioceses, which already are themselves expressions of the community character of the apostolate; apostles too in the free associations they will have decided to form among themselves.

As regards lay associations, the Decree observes that

AA 19 | Associations are not ends in themselves; they are meant to be of service to the Church's mission to the world. Their apostolic value depends on their conformity with the Church's aims, as well as on the Christian witness and evangelical spirit of each of their members and of the association as a whole.

AA 20 | The immediate end of organizations of this class is the apostolic end of the Church; in other words: the evangelization and sanctification of

> men and the Christian formation of their
> conscience, so as to enable them to imbue with
> the Gospel spirit the various social groups and
> environments.

The apostolate of lay people, who tend naturally to build up
their own communities and organize them independently,
must be properly integrated into the Church community.

AA 24 | In the Church are to be found, in fact, very
> many apostolic enterprises owing their origin to
> the free choice of the laity and run at their own
> discretion. Such enterprises enable the Church,
> in certain circumstances, to fulfil her mission
> more effectively; not seldom, therefore, are they
> praised and commended by the hierarchy. But
> no enterprise must lay claim to the name
> 'Catholic' if it has not the approval of legitimate
> ecclesiastical authority.

This integration is not a purely external condition or
'legalization' of the laity's apostolic initiative in the Church:
as the Council declares, it is 'an essential element of the
Christian apostolate'.

AA 23 | The lay apostolate, individual or collective,
> must be set in its true place within the apostolate
> of the whole Church. Union with those whom
> the Holy Spirit has appointed to rule the Church
> of God (cf. Acts 20:28) is an essential element
> of the Christian apostolate. Not less necessary is
> collaboration among the different undertakings
> of the apostolate; it is the hierarchy's place to
> put proper system into this collaboration.

Thus, referring once again to the tradition of the primitive
Church in which 'the Spirit himself subjected to the apostles'
authority even those who were endowed with charisms (cf.

1 Cor. 12:1–11)' (LG 7), and also to the rich experience of the Church in modern times, Vatican II lays down the principles of the edification of the Church in which both the laity and the hierarchy have a part to play, each with their respective tasks and responsibilities. Moreover 'the laity can be called in different ways to more immediate cooperation in the apostolate of the hierarchy, like those men and women who helped the apostle Paul in the Gospel, labouring much in the Lord (cf. Phil. 4:3; Rom. 16:3 ff.' (LG 33). In our own time this vocation has dimensions appropriate to the present-day Church's mission to all mankind. 'On the national and international planes the field of the apostolate is vast, and it is there that the laity more than others are the channels of Christian wisdom' (AA 14). In every field 'the laity, cooperating in their own particular way with the hierarchy, contribute their experience and assume responsibility in the direction of these organizations, in the investigation of the conditions in which the Church's pastoral work is to be carried on, in the elaboration and execution of their plan of action' (AA 20). Again:

AA 24 | As for works and institutions of the temporal order, the duty of the ecclesiastical hierarchy is the teaching and authentic interpretation of the moral principles to be followed in this domain. It is also in its province to judge, after mature reflection and with the help of qualified persons, of the conformity of such works or institutions with moral principles, and to pronounce in their regard concerning what is required for the safeguard and promotion of the values of the supernatural order.

Elsewhere the Council emphasizes that every layman has the right and duty to exercise his own charisms in the Church and in the world 'in the freedom of the Holy Spirit who "breathes where he wills" (John 3:8), and at the same time in communion with his brothers in Christ, and with his pastors especially. It is for the pastors to pass judgement on the authenticity and good use of these gifts, not certainly with a view to quenching the Spirit but to testing everything and keeping what is good (cf. 1 Thess. 5:12, 19, 21)' (AA 3).

In the foregoing pages we have outlined the wide subject of the Council's magisterium concerning the building up of the Church as a community of the People of God, which presents itself as a unique synthesis of structures and attitudes. In accordance with the premises of our study as a whole, we draw attention chiefly to the question of attitudes. Without ignoring the importance of structures in forming attitudes, we concentrated on the effect of the latter in giving substance to the former. Vatican II, of course, not only endorsed various structures that had already been tried, but introduced various new ones. For example, it maintained the structure of Church provinces and the institution of episcopal conferences. Among the new community structures, attention should be drawn to the Synod of Bishops at the level of the universal Church, and the Councils of priests and pastors at the local level. The object of these structures, both old and new, is to strengthen and consolidate the Church community in its various dimensions. For them to bear adequate fruit, however, the new structures must be complemented by the community spirit, that is the totality of attitudes which will help to build up the community of the Church itself.

There are two supplementary aspects of this theme, which plays a vital part in the Council's teaching.

2. The specific character of the missionary community

The object of the present section is to call attention to one of the Council documents which seems especially rich in doctrinal and pastoral content. We have referred several times to the Decree *Ad Gentes*, which deals with the Church's missionary activity.

In our analysis of the attitudes which seem appropriate to the implementation of the Council's teaching we have emphasized that of mission and witness-bearing, stressing the fact that the Church is by its nature a missionary body and the People of God is *in statu missionis*; but we have not yet spoken of missions in the institutional sense, since the missionary character of the Church is itself an 'ecclesiological' truth rather than a 'missiological' one. We may add that this manner of stating the problem does not in any way detract from the significance of missions as institutions of the Church, but on the contrary enables us to look for that significance in the heart of the Church itself.

In the present section, however, we have in view the whole of our preceding study of the attitudes which, in their relation to pre- and post-Conciliar ecclesiastical structures, are indispensable to the building-up of the Church as a community of the People of God. In this study particular importance seems to attach to the specifically missionary aspect, i.e. the fact that some communities are formed in terms of the missionary activity of the Church and also in the area of missionary institutions and structures. It is this point that we wish to develop here, not only so as not to overlook one of the richest documents of Vatican II but also because the 'missionary situation' often presents itself, though naturally in a new form, in countries and societies in which Christianity has been implanted and the Church organized, often for many centuries past.

This, however, is not the only reason why we think it appropriate at the end of our study to draw attention to the 'missionary character' of the Church. Other relevant circumstances and reasons may appear as we proceed with our remarks. In general our conviction in the light of the Council's teaching is that while the situation of the Church in countries and societies where it has existed for a long time affords a proper model for the building-up of a missionary Church, this 'missionary quality' is also a kind of model for the Church as a whole, not least for countries and societies which have long ceased to be *pays de mission* and, like Poland for instance, possess an ecclesiastical organization that has lasted for a thousand years.

A glance at the nature of the 'missionary quality' enables us to situate the process of building up the Church as an original community in the context of the 'apostolic history' which began on the Day of Pentecost.

AGD 4 | Throughout the ages the Holy Spirit makes the entire Church 'one in communion and ministry, and provides her with different hierarchical and charismatic gifts', giving life to ecclesiastical structures, being as it were their soul, and inspiring in the hearts of the faithful that same spirit of mission which impelled Christ himself. He even at times visibly anticipates apostolic action, just as in various ways he unceasingly accompanies and directs it.

AGD 6 | It is clear, therefore, that missionary activity flows immediately from the very nature of the Church. Missionary activity extends the saving faith of the Church, it expands and perfects its Catholic unity, it is sustained by its apostolicity, it activates the collegiate sense of its hierarchy, and bears witness to its sanctity which it both extends and promotes.

AGD 7 | So, although in ways known to himself God can lead those who, through no fault of their own, are ignorant of the Gospel to that faith the

Church, nevertheless, still has the obligation and also the sacred right to evangelize. And so, today as always, missionary activity retains its full force and necessity.

The Church's missionary activity is based on deep-seated theological premises, on an understanding of the very essence of the Church, and on its universality and catholicity, corresponding to the eternal design that all should be saved by God's action and redeemed through Christ. In the light of this truth of faith, 'The Church, which has been sent by Christ to reveal and communicate the love of God to all men and to all peoples, is aware that for her a tremendous missionary work still remains to be done.'

AGD 10 There are two billion people – and their number is increasing day by day – who have never, or barely, heard the Gospel message; they constitute large and distinct groups united by enduring cultural ties, ancient religious traditions, and strong social relationships. Of these, some belong to one or other of the great religions, others have no knowledge of God, while others expressly deny the existence of God and sometimes even attack it. If the Church is to be in a position to offer all men the mystery of salvation and the life brought by God, then it must implant itself among all these groups in the same way that Christ by his incarnation committed himself to the particular social and cultural circumstances of the men among who he lived.

For this reason,

AGD 5 The mission of the Church is carried out by means of that activity through which, in obedience to Christ's command and moved by the grace and love of the Holy Spirit, the Church makes itself fully present to all men and peoples in order to lead them to the faith, freedom and peace of Christ by the example of its life and teaching, by the sacraments and other means of grace. Its aim is to open up for all men a free and sure path to full participation in the mystery of Christ.

AGD 6 | The special end of this missionary activity is the evangelization and the implanting of the Church among peoples or groups in which it has not yet taken root.

In speaking of the missionary quality of the building-up of the Church as a community, we must first have in mind the community in its universal form. The 'missionary quality' belongs to the profoundest nature of the building-up of the Church in every dimension.

AGD 36 | As members of the living Christ, incorporated into him and made like him by baptism, confirmation and the Eucharist, all the faithful have an obligation to collaborate in the expansion and spread of his Body, so that they might bring it to fullness as soon as possible (cf. Eph. 4:13).

So all the children of the Church should have a lively consciousness of their own responsibility for the world, they should foster within themselves a truly Catholic spirit, they should spend themselves in the work of the Gospel. However, let everyone be aware that the primary and most important contribution he can make to the spread of the faith is to lead a profound Christian life.

The document, harking back to the Conciliar doctrine on ecumenism, adds that 'This witness of their life will achieve its effect more easily if it is borne in union with other Christian bodies, according to the norms of the Decree on Ecumenism, 12' (AGD 36).

As we have already seen, particular tasks fall on the episcopal collegium.

AGD 38 | All bishops, as members of the body of bishops which succeeds the college of the apostles, are consecrated not for one diocese alone, but for the salvation of the whole world. The command of Christ to preach the Gospel to every creature (Mk. 16:15) applies primarily and immediately to them – with Peter, and subject to Peter. From this arises that communion and cooperation of the churches which is so necessary today for the work of evangelization. Because of this communion, each church cares for all the others, they make known their needs to each other, they share their possessions, because the spread of the Body of Christ is the responsibility of the whole college of bishops.

By arousing, fostering and directing missionary work in his own diocese, with which he is one, the bishop makes present and, as it were, visible the missionary spirit and zeal of the people of God, so that the whole diocese becomes missionary . . . It likewise pertains to episcopal conferences to found and promote agencies which will fraternally receive those who immigrate from missionary territories for reasons of work or study, and which will aid them by suitable pastoral attention. By means of these immigrants people who are distant become, in a sense, neighbours, while a wonderful opportunity is offered to communities which have long been Christian to speak with nations which have not yet heard the Gospel, and of showing them the true face of Christ by their own acts of kindness and assistance.

Thus the missionary quality is indispensable to the building-up of the Body of Christ, both on the scale of the universal Church and at the local level. The whole Church, and all the churches that compose it, are well aware of the tasks imposed on them by God's design of salvation and the redeeming work of Christ, and by performing their missionary work they also help to build themselves up as a community.

The Council document also enables us to see how the community of the Church is formed in missionary territory, where the missionary aspect finds its proper fulfilment and typical expression. The Decree *Ad Gentes* deals in particular with the building-up of the community of the separate mission churches. Clearly this is the task of the missionaries themselves, of whom Vatican II speaks as follows:

AGD 15 | Therefore, missionaries, the fellow workers of God (cf. 1 Cor. 3:9), should raise up communities of the faithful, so that walking worthy of the calling to which they have been called (cf. Eph. 4:1) they might carry out the priestly, prophetic and royal offices entrusted to them by God. In this way the Christian community will become a sign of God's presence in the world. Through the eucharistic sacrifice it goes continually to the Father with Christ, carefully nourished with the word of God it bears witness to Christ, it walks in charity and is enlivened by an apostolic spirit.

From the start the Christian community should be so organized that it is able to provide for its own needs as far as possible.

AGD 1 | The Church is not truly established and does not fully live, nor is a perfect sign of Christ, unless deeply rooted in the people.

This last point seems particularly important as regards the missionary quality of the Church.

AGD 21 | The Church is not truly established and does not fully live, nor is a perfect sign of Christ, unless there is a genuine laity existing and working alongside the hierarchy. For the Gospel cannot become deeply rooted in the mentality, life and work of a people without the active presence of lay people.

It is a matter of forming the same type of community as the laity and hierarchy together constitute in each particular church, and at the same time creating a kind of vanguard of Catholicity, of the universality of the People of God. The missionary character of the universal Church and that of individual churches seem to express themselves in this endeavour and in a sense to be identified with it.

AGD 21 | The lay faithful belong fully both to the people of God and civil society. They belong to the nation into which they were born, they begin to share in its cultural riches by their education, they are linked to its life by many social ties, they contribute to its progress by personal effort in their professions, they feel its problems to be their own and they try to solve them. They belong also to Christ because by faith and baptism they have been reborn in the Church, so that by newness of life and work they might belong to Christ, in order that all things might be subjected to God in Christ and that God might be all in all.

The Decree points out that Christians in missionary

communities become new men and women and must

AGD 21 | give expression to this newness of life in their own society and culture and in a manner that is in keeping with the traditions of their own land. They must be familiar with this culture, they must purify and guard it, they must develop it in accordance with present-day conditions, they must perfect it in Christ so that the faith of Christ and the life of the Church will not be something foreign to the society in which they live, but will begin to transform and permeate it. They should be linked with their fellow countrymen by ties of sincere charity so that their manner of life reveals the new bond of unity and universal solidarity which derives from the mystery of Christ.

The whole process of building up the Church community in missionary lands is concentrated on bringing human beings to the mystery of Christ; and apart from incorporating them into the community of the Church, this is of great importance to the life they continue to lead among their fellow-countrymen. In this way the missionary community has an 'open' character, and for that very reason it must concentrate on imparting a mature Christian attitude to all its members, especially converts who are not long past the catechumen stage.

AGD 14 | The catechumenate ... is not a mere exposition of dogmatic truths and norms of morality, but a period of formation in the whole Christian life, an apprenticeship of sufficient duration, during which the disciples will be joined to Christ their teacher.

AGD 13 | Under the movement of divine grace the new convert sets out on a spiritual journey by means of which, while already sharing through faith in the mystery of the death and resurrection, he passes from the old man to the new man who has been made perfect in Christ (cf. Col. 3:5–10; Eph. 4:20–24). This transition, which involves a progressive change of outlook and morals, should be manifested in its social implications and effected gradually during the period of catechumenate. Since the Lord in whom he believes is a sign of contradiction (cf. Lk. 2:34; Mt. 10:34–9) the convert often has to suffer misunderstanding and separation, but he also experiences those joys which are generously granted by God.

These words not only describe the climate of inner conversion but also that of the missionary community: conversion must be 'manifested in its social implications', both within the community and outside it. In the churches themselves, 'the life of the People of God ought to mature in all those spheres of Christian life which are to be renewed in accordance with the norms of this Council' (AGD 19). For this purpose

AGD 20   the bishop should be, above all, a preacher of the faith who brings new disciples to Christ. To fulfil this noble task as he ought he must be fully acquainted with conditions among his flock and also with those notions about God which are current among his countrymen. He must take special account of those changes which have been brought about through urbanization, migration and religious indifferentism.

The laity for their part

AGD 12   ought to interest themselves, and collaborate with others, in the right ordering of social and economic affairs . . . In this work the faithful, after due consideration, should be eager to

> collaborate in projects initiated by private, public, state, or international bodies, or by other Christian or even non-Christian communities.

In this way the construction of the missionary community must have a particular dynamism which is the main element in its missionary character.

AGD 22

> The young churches, which are rooted in Christ and built on the foundations of the apostles, take over all the riches of the nations which have been given to Christ as an inheritance (cf. Ps. 2 : 8). They borrow from the customs, traditions, wisdom, teaching, arts and sciences of their people everything which could be used to praise the glory of the Creator, manifest the grace of the saviour, or contribute to the right ordering of Christian life.

Moreover

AGD 22

> To achieve this, it is necessary that in each of the great socio-cultural regions, as they are called, theological investigation should be encouraged and the facts and words revealed by God, contained in sacred Scripture, and explained by the Fathers and Magisterium of the Church, submitted to a new examination in the light of the tradition of the universal Church. In this way it will be more clearly understood by what means the faith can be explained in terms of the philosophy and wisdom of the people . . . Thus a way will be opened for a more profound adaptation in the whole sphere of Christian life. This manner of acting will avoid every appearance of syncretism and false exclusiveness; the Christian life will be adapted to the mentality and character of each culture, and local traditions together

with the special qualities of each national
family, illumined by the light of the Gospel,
will be taken up into a Catholic unity.

The model of the 'economy of the Incarnation' seems to
define most profoundly the meaning of that dynamism which
penetrates the whole process of building up the Church as a
community in accordance with the missionary spirit. We will
end this brief outline here: it does not, of course, exhaust the
richness of the theme, but draws attention to an area of
increasing importance to the formation of the attitudes of a
modern Christian, especially from the 'community' point of
view.

AGD 1 | In the present state of things which gives rise to a
new situation for mankind, the Church, the salt
of the earth and the light of the world (cf. Mt.
5:13–4), is even more urgently called upon to
save and renew every creature, so that all things
might be restored in Christ, and so that in him
men might form one family and one people of
God.

3. *The community of the Church and religious freedom*

The following supplementary remarks on the formation of
attitudes proper to the building-up of the Church community
are suggested by the Council's teaching on religious freedom.
The Declaration on this subject emphasizes not only the
rights of the individual but also those of communities: this
I would say constitutes the external but necessary condition
of the whole process of building up the Church as a community
and of the attitudes proper to that process. The problem is of
importance with regard to the formation of those attitudes

themselves: also Christians must be fully conscious of their own rights in this area, the more so as these rights also determine their duties *vis à vis* the Church community.

DH 4 | The freedom or immunity from coercion in religious matters which is the right of individuals must also be accorded to men when they act in community. Religious communities are a requirement of the nature of man and of religion itself.

The Declaration points out in the first place that 'the human person has a right to religious freedom' (DH 2), and it bases this statement on primarily rational principles, before proceeding in the second part of the document to expand on it from a theological standpoint analyzing religious freedom in the light of Revelation.

DH 2 | Freedom of this kind means that all men should be immune from coercion on the part of individuals, social groups and every human power so that, within due limits, nobody is forced to act against his convictions in religious matters in private or in public, alone or in associations with others.

DH 3 | Consequently to deny man the free exercise of religion in society, when the just requirements of public order are observed, is to do an injustice to the human person and to the very order established by God for men.

As the Council teaches, this fundamental right of the human person also belongs to religious communities, the right to form which is 'rooted in the social nature of man and in the very nature of religion' (DH 4). 'The right to religious freedom has its foundation not in the subjective attitude of the individual but in his very nature' (DH 2). Thus:

DH 3 | The civil authority, the purpose of which is the care of the common good in the temporal order, must recognize and look with favour on the religious life of the citizens. But if it presumes to control or restrict religious activity it must be said to have exceeded the limits of its power.

As regards the rights and duties of public authorities, the 'free practice of religion in society' is one of the primary requirements springing from the general principle that 'freedom in human society is concerned chiefly with man's spiritual values' (DH 1).

On this basis the Declaration, in a concise but forceful manner, describes the nature of religious freedom in relation to communities formed by people who unite in order to profess and practise their religion.

DH 4 | Therefore, provided the just requirements of public order are not violated, these groups have a right to immunity so that they may organize themselves according to their own principles. They must be allowed to honour the supreme Godhead with public worship, help their members to practise their religion and strengthen them with religious instruction, and promote institutions in which members may work together to organize their own lives according to their religious principles.

DH 4 | Also included in the right to religious freedom is the right of religious groups not to be prevented from freely demonstrating the special value of their teaching for the organization of society and the inspiration of all human activity. Finally, rooted in the social nature of man and in the very nature of religion is the right of men,

> prompted by their own religious sense, freely to
> hold meetings or establish educational, cultural,
> charitable and social organizations.

Clearly we are concerned here with every aspect of public
life which affects the building-up of the community and
encourages it to develop a sense of its own mission. All we said
so far about the building-up of the Church as a community
presupposes this freedom. To deny it is to violate the moral
order, since religious freedom is essential to the general
welfare.

DH 6 | The common good of society consists in the sum
total of those conditions of social life which
enable men to achieve a fuller measure of
perfection with greater ease. It consists especially
in safeguarding the rights and duties of the
human person. For this reason the protection of
the right to religious freedom is the common
responsibility of individual citizens, social
groups, civil authorities, the Church and other
religious communities. Each of these has its
own special responsibility in the matter according to its particular duty to promote the common
good.

As regards the civil power, it must

DH 6 | see to it that the equality of the citizens before
the law, which is itself an element of the common
good of society, is never violated either openly or
covertly for religious reasons and that there is no
discrimination among citizens.

From this it follows that it is wrong for a
public authority to compel its citizens by force
or fear or any other means to profess or repudiate
any religion or to prevent anyone from joining or

leaving a religious body. There is even more serious transgression of God's will and of the sacred rights of the individual person and the family of nations when force is applied to wipe out or repress religion either throughout the whole world or in a single region or in a particular community.

The Council particularly stresses the rights of parents and families in this respect.

DH 5 | Every family, in that it is a society with its own basic rights, has the right freely to organize its own religious life in the home under the control of their parents. These have the right to decide in accordance with their own religious beliefs the form of religious upbringing which is to be given to their children. The civil authority must therefore recognize the right of parents to choose with genuine freedom schools or other means of education. Parents should not be subjected directly or indirectly to unjust burdens because of this freedom of choice. Furthermore, the rights of parents are violated if their children are compelled to attend classes which are not in agreement with the religious beliefs of the parents or if there is but a single compulsory system of education from which all religious instruction is excluded.

In connection with its teaching as regards the right to profess one's religion either in public or in private, the Council observes that 'religious freedom has already been declared a civil right in most constitutions and has been given solemn recognition in international documents' (DH 15).

As regards the Church, its attitude towards religious freedom is based above all on the very nature of faith.

DH 10 | It is therefore fully in accordance with the nature of faith that in religious matters every form of coercion by men should be excluded. Consequently the principle of religious liberty contributes in no small way to the development of a situation in which men can without hindrance be invited to the Christian faith, embrace it of their own free will and give it practical expression in every sphere of their lives.

This corresponds to the Creator's design and the mode of action of Christ and his apostles.

DH 12 | The Church, therefore, faithful to the truth of the Gospel, is following in the path of Christ and the apostles when she recognizes the principle that religious liberty is in keeping with the dignity of man and divine revelation and gives it her support. Throughout the ages she has preserved and handed on the doctrine which she has received from her Master and the apostles. Although in the life of the people of God in its pilgrimage through the vicissitudes of human history there has at times appeared a form of behaviour which was hardly in keeping with the spirit of the Gospel and was even opposed to it, it has always remained the teaching of the Church that no one is to be coerced into believing.

Vatican II recalls this doctrine, reaffirms and proclaims it, not only in the Declaration on Religious Liberty but in other documents such as that on the Missions.

AGD 13 | The Church strictly forbids that anyone should be forced to accept the faith, or be induced or enticed by unworthy devices; as it likewise strongly defends the right that no one should be frightened away from the faith by unjust persecutions.

It adds that: 'In accordance with the very ancient practice of the Church, the motives for conversion should be examined and, if necessary, purified' (AGD 13). This is an essential point in the document on Missions. Thus the Council's position 'leaves intact the traditional Catholic teaching on the moral duty of individuals and societies towards the true religion and the one Church of Christ' (DH 1). Earlier it says: 'We believe that this one true religion continues to exist in the Catholic and Apostolic Church, to which the Lord Jesus entrusted the task of spreading it among all men' (DH 1).

The conviction of the legitimacy of the principle of religious freedom, based on the very nature of faith, is linked in the Christian's mind with his profound conviction concerning its truth. This is basic to the attitude of every follower of Christ, as regards his private outlook and the building-up of the Church community. The consciousness that 'this one true religion continues to exist in the Catholic and Apostolic Church' is of basic importance for the building-up of the Church as a community.

DH 14   The disciple has a grave obligation to Christ, his Master, to grow daily in his knowledge of the truth he has received from him, to be faithful in announcing it and vigourous in defending it without having recourse to methods which are contrary to the spirit of the Gospel. At the same time the love of Christ urges him to treat with love, prudence and patience those who are in error or ignorance with regard to the faith. He must take into account his duties towards Christ, the life-giving Word whom he must proclaim, the rights of the human person and the measure of grace which God has given to each

> man through Christ in calling him freely to
> accept and profess the faith.

The follower and disciple of Christ derives from his faith
a consciousness of his own mission and also a feeling of deep
respect for every man's conscience, since 'It is through his
conscience that man sees and recognizes the demands of the
divine law. He is bound to follow this conscience faithfully in
all his activity so that he may come to God, who is his last
end. Therefore he must not be forced to act contrary to this
conscience. Nor must he be prevented from acting according
to his conscience, especially in religious matters' (DH 3).
Applying this conviction sincerely in social life and in his
dealings with all men, the Christian not only regards it as
compatible with the apostolic attitude but sees it as an
essential factor in building up the community of the Church.
He is well aware that 'the leaven of the Gospel has long been at
work in the minds of men and has contributed greatly to a
wider recognition by them in the course of time of their
dignity as persons. It has contributed too to the growth of the
conviction that in religious matters the human person should
be kept free from all manner of coercion in civil society'
(DH 12). This same 'leaven of the Gospel' is the basis of the
authentic development of the Church and the essential
condition of the building-up of the Church community.

This community, whether on a world-wide scale or locally,
needs religious freedom in order to carry out its proper
mission.

> DH 13 | As the spiritual authority appointed by Christ the
> Lord with the duty, imposed by divine com-
> mand, of going into the whole world and
> preaching the Gospel to every creature, the
> Church claims freedom for herself in human
> society and before every public authority. The
> Church also claims freedom for herself as a

> society of men with the right to live in civil society in accordance with the demands of the Christian faith.

In the Decree on the Pastoral Office of Bishops in the Church we read:

CD 19 | In the exercise of their apostolic function, which is directed towards the salvation of souls, bishops enjoy as of right full and perfect freedom and independence from all civil authority. It is, therefore, unlawful to obstruct them directly or indirectly in the exercise of their ecclesiastical office or to prevent them from communicating freely with the Apostolic See and other ecclesiastical authorities or with their subjects.

Gaudium et Spes also discusses relations between Church and State:

GS 76 | It is of supreme importance, especially in a pluralistic society, to work out a proper vision of the relationship between the political community and the Church . . .

The political community and the Church are autonomous and independent of each other in their own fields. Nevertheless, both are devoted to the personal vocation of man, though under different titles. This service will redound the more effectively to the welfare of all in so far as both institutions practise better cooperation according to the local and prevailing situation. For man's horizons are not bounded only by the temporal order; living on the level of human history he preserves the integrity of his eternal destiny. The Church, for its part, being founded in the love of the Redeemer, contributes towards the spread of justice among nations, and within the borders of the nations themselves the Church respects and encourages the political freedom and responsibility of the citizen.

All this is important not only for a right relationship between the Church and the political community or the State, but also for the formation of the attitude of every Christian who takes part in building up the Church community and who is at the same time a son of his own nation and a citizen of the State. For:

GS 76 | There are close links between the things of earth and those things in man's condition which transcend the world, and the Church utilizes temporal realities as often as its mission requires it. But it never places its hopes in any privileges accorded to it by civil authority; indeed, it will give up the exercise of certain legitimate rights whenever it becomes clear that their use will compromise the sincerity of its witness, or whenever new circumstances call for a revised approach. But at all times and in all places the Church should have true freedom to preach the faith, to proclaim its teaching about society, to carry out its task among men without hindrance, and to pass moral judgements even in matters relating to politics, whenever the fundamental rights of man or the salvation of souls requires it. The means, the only means, it may use are those which are in accord with the Gospel and the welfare of all men according to the diversity of times and circumstances.

Every Christian who takes an active part in the Church's life and mission is aware of this, and he is also aware that 'With loyalty to the Gospel in the fulfilment of its mission in the world, the Church, whose duty it is to foster and elevate all that is true, all that is good, and all that is beautiful in the human community, consolidates peace among men for the glory of God' (GS 76). This awareness enables him to take a full share in the building-up of the Church.

Conclusion

The present study was undertaken for the purpose of repaying a debt to the Vatican Council. However, the way to repay that debt is to put the Council's precepts into practice. We have done our best to indicate how this can be done, more particularly in Poland and in that Church to which the writer is linked by the closest ties of his vocation. This is how the work was conceived from the beginning. It was defined as a 'working study' to emphasize that it was meant to be part of the great post-Conciliar work of the Church seeking to realize itself in the spirit of Vatican II.

Having reached the end of our task, however, we must clarify an essential point without which it would be incomplete.

The concept of the implementation of the Council, embodied in our sub-title, may have led the reader to expect a series of detailed explanations of the manner in which the Council's teaching is or should be put into practice in our Church. This might have comprised an account of practical methods, organizations or modes of action for the purpose of carrying out the plan traced by the Council. Such expectations from what is called a 'working' document are quite understandable and in line with contemporary ways of thinking. However, they do not correspond to the essential nature of Vatican II as a pastoral Council, nor to the way in which it ought to be implemented.

Certainly it would be possible to assemble information on the way in which the Council's teaching is already being put into practice, or a series of thoughts on how this could or should be done. But any ideas on such implementation must be preceded by a more basic study. The first thing to do is to understand what is meant by implementation, in other words to ascertain precisely what it is we are to implement. Therefore we have tried in the present study not so much to consider 'how', but rather 'what' it is we have to implement, which is the more important question.

Consequently we have tried from the beginning to clarify what is meant by a 'pastoral' Council, and we reached the conclusion that the answer lay in the premises, the observance of which had to be traced in the work of the Council itself. The Council, we recall, began by putting to itself the question: *Ecclesia, quid dicis de te ipsa?* Church, what do you say of yourself?

This question about the Church's idea of itself pointed the way to a whole series of tasks and labours carried out by the Council and is reflected in every one of the Council's constitutions, decrees and declarations. At the same time it implied a series of questions on the part of the Church, which is a Church of living beings: what does it mean to be a believer, to be a Christian, to be in the Church and also in the modern world? In replying to its own essential question about the Church's idea of itself, the Council tried at the same time to reply to the implicit questions about faith and the whole Christian life. In so doing it displayed itself as a pastoral Council.

In our implementation of the Council we must follow the same road. Every consideration of ways and means must be based on a clear understanding of this, and that is the chief purpose of the present study. The Council outlined the type of faith which corresponds to the life of the modern Christian, and the implementation of the Council consists first and foremost in enriching that faith. What is needed is 'the witness of a living and mature faith, one so well formed that it can see difficulties clearly and overcome them . . . This faith should show its fruitfulness by penetrating the whole life, even the wordly activities, of those who believe' (GS 21).

AA 4 | Only the light of faith and meditation on the Word of God can enable us to find everywhere and always the God 'in whom we live and exist' (Acts 17:28); only thus can we seek his will in everything, see Christ in all men, acquaintance or stranger, make sound judgements on the true meaning and value of temporal realities both in themselves and in relation to man's end.

Those with such a faith live in the hope of the revelation of the sons of God, keeping in mind the cross and resurrection of the Lord.

In this study we have concentrated on analysing the teaching of Vatican II from the point of view of the formation of the consciousness and attitudes of Christians at the present day. This seems to be the primary theme in the implementation of the Council. This is the process of 'initiation' whereby the Conciliar consciousness of the Church is to be shared by one and all, and it therefore stands in the forefront of our study. We may appear to have provided mainly a framework of selected texts, and indeed our work partly consists of this: as we said in the Introduction, it is intended to supply a vademecum to the Council's work. But the essential thing is the criterion on the basis of which we made our selection, and the purpose it is intended to serve.

In Poland the Church's endeavour to implement the Council began at the same time as the celebration of the thousandth anniversary of Polish Christianity. The Council finished its labours in December 1965, and the millenary celebrations began on New Year's Day, 1966. Recalling in this way the dawn of Christianity in our country and tracing its development through so many generations, we became particularly sensitive to the call to enrich our faith, which is at the root of the Council's whole pastoral orientation. Thus we see in the Council's teaching a fundamental opportunity to direct the rich experience of our Christian past towards a Christian future.

A profound sense of the greatness of that gift of faith in the soul of every man and in the life of society inspires the need to dedicate and entrust our faith in a special way to the Mother of Christ and of the Church. This humble and trusting devotion must be the soil in which the Conciliar enrichment of faith may gradually root itself and bear fruit. On the part of mankind this will require much study and reflection, many attempts and much activity. In the last resort, however, the enrichment of faith will always be a gift from above, although it will also be an expression of man's personal response to God's revelation of himself – a mature expression, adapted to the reality of our times.

It is our keen desire to implement the Council in this way and to do so with all proper speed. We must not be hasty and superficial, nor fail tardily to recognize 'signs of the times'. We must keep before our eyes what is most essential: our guiding idea is the enrichment of faith in line with the Council's teaching. This enrichment in the reality of the Church is a full initiation, it is the maturity of consciousness and attitudes on the part of every member of the People of God. Christ himself spoke plainly of the leaven leavening all the dough (cf. Matt. 13:33).

The author prays that this study may be in line with that process and help to further it. In this way he hopes to repay, at least in part, his debt to the Second Vatican Council.

List of Council documents

Latin title and abbreviation	English title
Apostolicam actuositatem (AA)	Decree on the Apostolate of the Laity
Ad gentes divinitus (AGD)	Decree on the Church's Missionary Activity
Christus Dominus (CD)	Decree on the Pastoral Office of Bishops in the Church
Dignitatis humanae (DH)	Declaration on Religious Liberty
Dei verbum (DV)	Dogmatic Constitution on Divine Revelation
Gravissimum educationis (GE)	Declaration on Christian Education
Gaudium et spes (GS)	Pastoral Constitution on the Church in the Modern World
Inter mirifica (IM)	Decree on the Means of Social Communication
Lumen gentium (LG)	Dogmatic Constitution on the Church
Nostra aetate (NA)	Declaration on the Church's Relations with Non-Christian Religions
Orientalium ecclesiarum (OE)	Decree on the Catholic Oriental Churches

Optatam totius (OT)	Decree on the Training of Priests
Perfectae caritatis (PC)	Decree on the Renewal of Religious Life
Presbyterorum ordinis (PO)	Decree on the Life and Ministry of Priests
Sacrosanctum concilium (SC)	Constitution on the Sacred Liturgy
Unitatis redintegratio (UR)	Decree on Ecumenism

Index